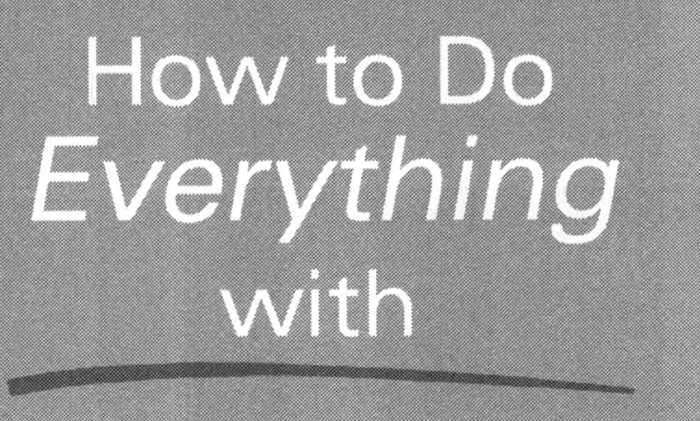

How to Do Everything with Musicmatch

Rick Broida
Denny Atkin

McGraw-Hill/Osborne

New York Chicago San Francisco Lisbon
London Madrid Mexico City Milan New Delhi
San Juan Seoul Singapore Sydney Toronto

The McGraw-Hill Companies

McGraw-Hill/Osborne
2100 Powell Street, 10th Floor
Emeryville, California 94608
U.S.A.

To arrange bulk purchase discounts for sales promotions, premiums, or fund-raisers, please contact **McGraw-Hill**/Osborne at the above address. For information on translations or book distributors outside the U.S.A., please see the International Contact Information page on the next page.

How to Do Everything with Musicmatch®

1234567890 CUS CUS 01987654

ISBN 0-07-225708-3

Publisher	Brandon A. Nordin
Vice President & Associate Publisher	Scott Rogers
Senior Acquisitions Editor	Jane Brownlow
Project Editor	Lisa Wolters-Broder
Acquisitions Coordinator	Agatha Kim
Technical Editor	Eliot Van Buskirk
Copy Editor	Mike McGee
Proofreader	Linda Medoff
Indexer	Rebecca Plunkett
Composition	International Typesetting & Composition, Melinda Lytle
Illustrators	International Typesetting & Composition, Melinda Lytle

This book was composed with Corel VENTURA™ Publisher.

INTERNATIONAL CONTACT INFORMATION

AUSTRALIA
McGraw-Hill Book Company
Australia Pty. Ltd.
TEL +61-2-9900-1800
FAX +61-2-9878-8881
http://www.mcgraw-hill.com.au
books-it_sydney@mcgraw-hill.com

CANADA
McGraw-Hill Ryerson Ltd.
TEL +905-430-5000
FAX +905-430-5020
http://www.mcgraw-hill.ca

GREECE, MIDDLE EAST, & AFRICA (Excluding South Africa)
McGraw-Hill Hellas
TEL +30-210-6560-990
TEL +30-210-6560-993
TEL +30-210-6560-994
FAX +30-210-6545-525

MEXICO (Also serving Latin America)
McGraw-Hill Interamericana Editores
S.A. de C.V.
TEL +525-1500-5108
FAX +525-117-1589
http://www.mcgraw-hill.com.mx
carlos_ruiz@mcgraw-hill.com

SINGAPORE (Serving Asia)
McGraw-Hill Book Company
TEL +65-6863-1580
FAX +65-6862-3354
http://www.mcgraw-hill.com.sg
mghasia@mcgraw-hill.com

SOUTH AFRICA
McGraw-Hill South Africa
TEL +27-11-622-7512
FAX +27-11-622-9045
robyn_swanepoel@mcgraw-hill.com

SPAIN
McGraw-Hill/
Interamericana de España, S.A.U.
TEL +34-91-180-3000
FAX +34-91-372-8513
http://www.mcgraw-hill.es
professional@mcgraw-hill.es

UNITED KINGDOM, NORTHERN, EASTERN, & CENTRAL EUROPE
McGraw-Hill Education Europe
TEL +44-1-628-502500
FAX +44-1-628-770224
http://www.mcgraw-hill.co.uk
emea_queries@mcgraw-hill.com

ALL OTHER INQUIRIES Contact:
McGraw-Hill/Osborne
TEL +1-510-420-7700
FAX +1-510-420-7703
http://www.osborne.com
omg_international@mcgraw-hill.com

Dedication

To Sarah and Ethan, who have some of the best dance moves
this side of Sesame Street.
—Rick

To Carter, who showed me that the best thing about music is watching
how much fun a two-year-old has dancing to it.
—Denny

About the Authors

Rick Broida has written about computers and technology for over 15 years. A regular contributor to CNET, ZDNet, and *Computer Shopper,* he specializes in mobile technology. In 1997, recognizing the Palm PDA's unparalleled popularity and the need for a printed resource covering the platform, Rick founded *Handheld Computing* (formerly *Tap Magazine*). He has authored over a dozen books, including *How to Do Everything with Your GPS* and *How to Do Everything with Your Palm Handheld.* He writes the Tech Savvy column for Michigan's *Observer & Eccentric* newspapers, and lives in Michigan with his wife and two children.

Denny Atkin has been writing about technology topics since the days when you could buy Commodore 64s at your local department store. He's worked for a number of pioneering technology magazines, including *Compute!, OMNI,* and *Computer Gaming World,* and has contributed technology articles to magazines ranging from *Entertainment Weekly* to *Wired.* He's written a number of books related to computer games and handheld computers. He lives in Washington state with his wife, son, and keyboard-warming cat.

About the Technical Reviewer

Eliot Van Buskirk has been a journalist with CNET covering music-related technology since the first MP3 player came out in 1998. His "MP3 Insider" column is the longest-running single-writer column at CNET, the largest online tech publication in the world. He's also a home recording enthusiast and has made music with a number of groups, including the New York City Opera, Solarium, and Planet Vegas, among others. His column received the 2004 Maggie award for Best Regularly Featured Online Column.

Contents

Acknowledgments ix
Introduction xi

PART I **Get Started**

CHAPTER 1 **Welcome to Musicmatch** **3**
Welcome to Musicmatch 4
An Introduction to Digital Audio 5
What Is MP3? 5
Okay, Then What's WMA? 6
What's the Big Deal About Compressing Music? 6
Where Do MP3 and WMA Files Come From? 7
An Introduction to Musicmatch 8
What Can You Do with Musicmatch? 9
Different Versions of Musicmatch 11

CHAPTER 2 **Get Your Computer Ready** **19**
Is Your PC Ready? 20
Upgrades to Consider 21
Our Favorite Portable Players 27
Setting and Adjusting Volume Settings in Windows 38
Where to Find It 41

CHAPTER 3 **Your First Steps with Musicmatch** **43**
Downloading and Installing 44
Downloading Musicmatch 45
Installing the Program 47
Launching and Configuring Musicmatch 49
Starting Musicmatch for the First Time 50
A Brief Tour of the Musicmatch Screen 51
Changing Musicmatch's Look 52
Playing CDs 54
Adding Your Existing Digital Music Library to Musicmatch 56

PART II Build and Manage a Music Library

CHAPTER 4 **Rip Songs from CDs** **61**
Ripping a CD 63
Understanding Bit Rates 66
Suggested Bit Rate Settings 68
Choosing an Encoding Format 68
Storing and Naming Your Music 73
Where to Put It 73
What to Call It 75
CD Lookup, and Manual Track Info Entry 77
Advanced Options 79

CHAPTER 5 **Rescue Albums and Cassettes** **83**
Making the Connection 85
Sound Card Inputs 85
Record Players and Other Audio Sources 89
Cabling It All Together 90
Recording Audio with Musicmatch 95
Recording LPs and 45s 96
Recording Cassettes 102
Post-Production: Fixing Your Recordings 103
Editing Your Music 105
Cleaning Up Noisy Audio 108
Giving Your Music the Gift of ID3 110
Where to Find It 115

CHAPTER 6 **Buying Music from Musicmatch Downloads** **117**
Signing Up for Musicmatch Downloads 119
Our Own Purchases 122
Finding Album and Artist Information 123
Buying and Downloading Your First Song 129
Understanding Musicmatch's Digital Rights Management 133
What You Can Do with Musicmatch Downloads WMA Tunes 134
What You Can't Do with Musicmatch Downloads WMA Tunes 134
Moving Your Music to a New Computer 135

CHAPTER 7 **Download Songs from Other Online Services** **139**
Downloading Music from Other Online Services 141
How Download Services Deliver Songs 142
Free Music from Download.com 145
The Format Workaround 146
One-Stop Shopping for Music 147
Live-Concert Downloads 148

File-Sharing Services 149
A Brief History of the MP3 Controversy 149
Our Favorite Songs from the '80s 152
How to Not Break the Law 155
File-Swapping Ethics 155
And in the End... 159
Fixing Filenames and ID3 Tags in Songs You've Downloaded 159
What's the Difference Between a Filename and an ID3 Tag? 160
Editing ID3 Tags 160
Fixing Filenames 163
Brilliant Reasons to Manually Edit Your ID3 Tags 163
Recording NPR and Other Internet Radio Shows 165
Understanding Internet Radio 165
Getting Started with Replay Radio 167
Work the Internet to Find Songs You've Heard and Liked 173
Where to Find It 174

PART III **Play That Funky Music**

CHAPTER 8 **Playing Your Music 177**
Listening 101 178
Organization, of Sorts 182
AutoDJ: The Element of Surprise 186
Music for Moods 187
Those Shiny Silver Discs: Playing CDs 188
Internet Radio, the Free Variety 189
Internet Radio, the Pay-to-Play Variety 191
How to Play 192
Enhancing Your Listening Experience 196
The Small Player View 196
Control Shortcuts 197
Where to Find It 199

CHAPTER 9 **All About Playlists 201**
Top Five Things You Should Know about Playlists 203
Playlist Basics Revisited 204
Editing Playlists 207
Exporting Playlist Songs 210
Playlists... of Doom! 211
Sharing the Playlist Joy 212

CHAPTER 10 **From PC to CD: Burn, Baby, Burn!** **215**
Burning Your First CD: A Quick-Start Guide 216
Why Burn CDs? 218
The Two Kinds of CDs You Can Burn 219
Our Ultimate Mix Tapes 220
What about WMA CDs? 221
The Right Equipment: Hardware and Media 223
All about Burners 223
Choosing the Right Blank Media 224
Burning CDs with Musicmatch 226
Modifying Burn Options 227
And, Finally, Burning a CD 235
When to Use SmartSplit 236
DRM Limitations for Burning Downloaded Songs 237
Making Labels 238
Printing CD Labels 241
Printing Jewel-Case Inserts 244
Where to Find It 246

CHAPTER 11 **Working with Portable Players** **247**
Choosing a Portable Player 249
The Different Kinds of Portable Players 249
Our Favorite Players 251
Configuring Musicmatch to Work with Your Player 252
Copying Songs to Your Portable Player 254
A Note to iPod Users 254
Hey, Why Won't My Songs Play on My Portable Player? 255
Case Study: The Dell DJ (or Any Other Hard-Drive Player) 256

CHAPTER 12 **Playing Your Music** **267**
Tweaking Your Tunes with the Equalizer 269
Getting Psychedelic with Visualizations 272
Choosing a Visualization 272
Customizing Visualizations 274
Watching a Slideshow while the Music Plays 278
Volume Leveling: Your Ears Will Thank You 280
Enhancing Your Audio 283
Songs of Two Misspent Youths 285
Converting Files Between Formats 286
Keeping Musicmatch Up-to-Date 287
Finding Help Online 288

Acknowledgments

This book would have been impossible without the help of Osborne's crackerjack team of editors, led by the tenacious Agatha Kim, who, despite our very best efforts, wouldn't let us get away with turning in chapters late. We're equally grateful to Jane Brownlow, Lisa Wolters-Broder, Mike McGee, and especially tech editor Eliot Van Buskirk.

Thanks also to Joni Berkley, Jason Klein, and Jennifer Roberts of Musicmatch, who came through with the information we needed when we needed it.

We'd particularly like to thank the folks who contributed to the book's Voices From the Community sections: Joni Berkley, Seth Forman, Dave Johnson, Chris Leckness, Sheldon Leemon, Doug Luzader, Tom Pettigrew, John Steup, and James Stewart.

Finally, endless thanks to our families for their support during the always-grueling book writing process. We couldn't do it without you.

Introduction

Musicmatch Jukebox has grown from a simple music cataloging application to a full-blown music toolbox, online music store, radio network, and more. The name "Jukebox" is an understatement in the extreme; the classic Wurlitzer that The Fonz used to kick was a few records short of the 600,000+ tunes that Musicmatch offers instant access to.

This book gives you the A to Z on Musicmatch, from organizing your existing music collection to ripping your old tapes and CDs to digital music files. You'll learn how to buy songs online, listen to Internet radio stations, and get instant access to hundreds of thousands of tunes. We'll show you how to make your tunes sound better, send your favorite playlists to friends, and much, much more.

In most chapters you'll also find real-world stories from Musicmatch users or industry professionals that illustrate some of the program's most amazing, amusing, and useful applications.

Each chapter contains special elements to help you get the most from the book:

- **How to...** These special boxes explain, in a nutshell, how to accomplish key tasks. Read them to discover key points covered in each chapter.
- **Did you know?** These are interesting facts and/or background information related to the subject at hand.
- **Notes** These provide extra information that's often very important to gain understanding of a particular topic.
- **Tips** These tell you how to do something smarter or faster.
- **Sidebars** These contain additional information about certain subjects that warrant special coverage.

We hope you find this book enjoyable, entertaining, and, most of all, helpful. If you have questions or comments, please feel free to steer them our way at *rickbroidal@excite.com* or *denny@datkin.net*. Be sure to include "Musicmatch book" in the subject line so we don't accidentally overlook it. Thanks, and enjoy the book!

Part I

Get Started

Chapter 1

Welcome to Musicmatch

How to…

- Find and create digital music
- Differentiate between MP3 and WMA
- Take advantage of Musicmatch's capabilities
- Distinguish between Jukebox Basic and Jukebox Plus
- Upgrade to Jukebox Plus

"Without music to decorate it, time is just a bunch of boring production deadlines or dates by which bills must be paid."—Frank Zappa, musician

"Music is well said to be the speech of angels."—Thomas Carlyle, essayist

"This one goes to eleven."—Spinal Tap, rock band

With so many great words already written on the subject of music, we don't feel compelled to reinvent the wheel. You like music. We like music. That's why we're all here (in this book, not on this planet—that's a totally different discussion). Call it art, call it entertainment, call it something to pass the time in elevators—music is magic.

Just as magical is the technology that enables us to listen to music on our computers and portable players. With just one software application, you can convert your albums, cassettes, and CDs into a digital music library. You can purchase music right from the Internet, downloading it directly to your PC for near-instantaneous listening. You can organize your music in ways you never thought possible (and if you think arranging your CDs in alphabetical order is a big deal, you're in for a pleasant surprise). You can listen to Internet radio stations, sample new music, get recommendations based on your musical preferences, and so on. All that (and more) from just one software application.

Welcome to Musicmatch

And welcome to digital audio, which is part and parcel with the subject of this book. In this chapter, we're going to give you a bit of the history behind digital audio so you can understand how and why it's used today, then crack the shrink-wrap (figuratively speaking, of course) on Musicmatch itself—what it is, what it does, and why you need a whole book to use it.

An Introduction to Digital Audio

The evolution of recorded music goes something like this. In 1877, at his Menlo Park laboratory, Thomas Edison invented the phonograph. Then, for a long while, nothing happened. For nearly a century, the phonograph remained the preferred means for listening to music. But in the last three decades of the 20th century, the music industry experienced a technological revolution that produced the 8-track tape, the audiocassette, the compact disc, and, finally, digital audio.

In 1997, Edison's invention came full circle (no pun intended) when a man named Tomislav Uzelac unveiled Amp—a computer program designed to play so-called MP3 files (more on those in a minute). There was no media required—no wax record, no thin spool of magnetic tape, no shiny silver disc. Music had become digital, electronic, computerized. Liberated.

When we refer to digital audio, then, we're referring to music that's in a digital format such as MP3—the best-known and most widely used means for digitally recording and playing music without being tied to physical media such as CDs. But there are other formats, such as WMA, that play a key role in today's digital audio scene—and in Musicmatch. Let's look at these formats: what they mean, how they're used, and where they came from.

What Is MP3?

First things first: the "M" in MP3 doesn't stand for music. The "P" doesn't stand for power or platinum or anything cool like that. And the "3" has nothing to do with triangles or Three Dog Night. MP3 is a simple, albeit catchy, abbreviation for a kind of compression technology, one that has become universally popular for sharing, downloading, and transporting songs. (Think of someone zapping a 45-rpm record and turning it into zeroes and ones.)

If you're really interested in the technical description, MP3 stands for MPEG audio layer 3. And just what the heck is MPEG? It stands for Motion Picture Experts Group, a consortium of companies and organizations that develops compression, decompression, and processing standards for audio and video. So, all spelled out, those innocuous three characters become Moving Picture Experts Group audio layer 3.

Whew—glad that's out of the way. That's just about the most complicated aspect of MP3, and it's not even important that you remember it. Here's a more real-world explanation: an MP3 file is a song, usually taken from a CD, that's converted into an electronic format and compressed to become very small. It can then be played on a PC, a portable Walkman-like player, or any number of other devices.

NOTE *By "electronic," we generally mean in a digital format, without any kind of media (record, 8-track tape, CD, and so on) involved. This should not be confused with "electronic music," the kind that Denny likes to jam to on his Casio keyboard.*

Today, the MP3 file is the de facto standard for sharing music, and it's rapidly gaining ground on the CD player as the preferred means for listening to music. In fact, many of the latest car stereos, DVD players, and portable music players support MP3 technology in one manner or another.

Okay, Then What's WMA?

MP3 is not the first compression standard for music files, nor will it be the last. It is, however, the most popular, despite increasing competition from a Microsoft-backed alternative: *Windows Media Audio.* WMA technology is similar to MP3, but with a couple notable advantages. First, according to Microsoft (and most people who've tested their claim), it delivers CD-quality sound at a much lower *bit rate* than MP3 (64 Kbps vs. 128 Kbps—more on that in Chapter 4). Theoretically, that means a computer or portable player could store twice as much music in the same space, assuming it supported the WMA format. What's more, WMA includes a digital rights management (DRM) system, which helps deter piracy enough that record labels feel safe selling their music over the Internet.

So, it is precisely because of DRM that WMA has started to catch on in a big way. You've probably heard of music-download services like, iTunes, Napster, and WalMart (and let's not forget Musicmatch—see Chapter 6). Many of these services sell their songs in the WMA format, which enables them to impose certain restrictions on how you can use the songs. Only one service we know of sells songs in the MP3 format (eMusic, which has a pretty limited selection but is still worth checking out), as MP3s can easily be traded online—and the music industry doesn't like that one bit (as you may have heard).

Musicmatch supports both MP3 and WMA files (as well as a few other formats, which we'll discuss in later chapters), which you can mix and match on your PC with little trouble. We'll return to this discussion of file formats as needed—for now, we just wanted you to understand the basics.

What's the Big Deal About Compressing Music?

Remember trash compactors? They were popular in homes built in the '70s. Basically, you'd toss your garbage into a drawer, and the compactor would smash it all down into a little cube. Efficient, practical, and kinda cool. (That they aren't still in use today is a disappointment to environment-conscious Rick.)

When you copy a song from a CD to your computer using the "traditional" file format (which is called *WAV*), the resulting file is usually upwards of 40–50 megabytes (MB) in size. Figure ten songs to an album, and now you're talking about nearly 500MB of hard drive space for *Abbey Road* alone. Even if you have a 60-gigabyte (GB) hard drive, it doesn't take a math genius to see how impractical it is to store music electronically.

By compressing a "raw" song file into an MP3 or WMA file, it becomes, on average, ten times smaller, with little discernible loss in sound quality. Now the B-52s' "Love Shack" is 5MB instead of 59MB. Suddenly you can store a *lot* more music on your computer. And you can carry songs in a portable player. This, friends, is the big deal about compression. Oh, and, of course, the fact that the smaller files are much easier to transfer across the Internet. That's kind of a big deal, too.

The degree to which a song file is compressed is expressed as bit rate*—the lower the bit rate, the smaller the file. You'll learn more about this important topic in Chapter 4.*

Where Do MP3 and WMA Files Come From?

Okay, so just where do these super-compressed, book-worthy music files come from? Most commonly, MP3 and WMA files originate on ordinary audio CDs (though an increasing number come directly from record companies via Internet download services—but they probably still started on CD). As you'll learn in Chapter 4, you can perform a process called "ripping" that extracts songs from your CDs and turns them into compressed digital audio files. It's also possible to convert songs from old libraries of albums and cassettes (see Chapter 5).

The Internet is another major source for MP3 and WMA files. The former tend to come from file-sharing services like KaZaa and Morpheus, which have gained notoriety owing to the legal and ethical issues of trading music with strangers. However, it's now possible to get music legally from the Internet (most of it in WMA format), thanks to online music stores like the one built into Musicmatch (see Chapter 7).

To answer the big question, then, MP3 and WMA files can come from your own music collection or from online sources.

An Introduction to Musicmatch

Musicmatch is the name of the company that makes Musicmatch Jukebox, the program that's the main focus of this book. We tend to use the two interchangeably, but usually when we refer to Musicmatch we're talking about Musicmatch Jukebox (see Figure 1-1). Musicmatch (the company) is also the entity behind Musicmatch Downloads, the service that sells songs you can download directly to your PC. Whew—got all that? To keep things simple, let's just say that unless we note otherwise, Musicmatch = Musicmatch Jukebox. We abbreviate it because if we tacked on "Jukebox" every time we referred to Musicmatch, the book would be a good 50 pages longer—and we're trying to conserve trees. We're authors who care, dammit.

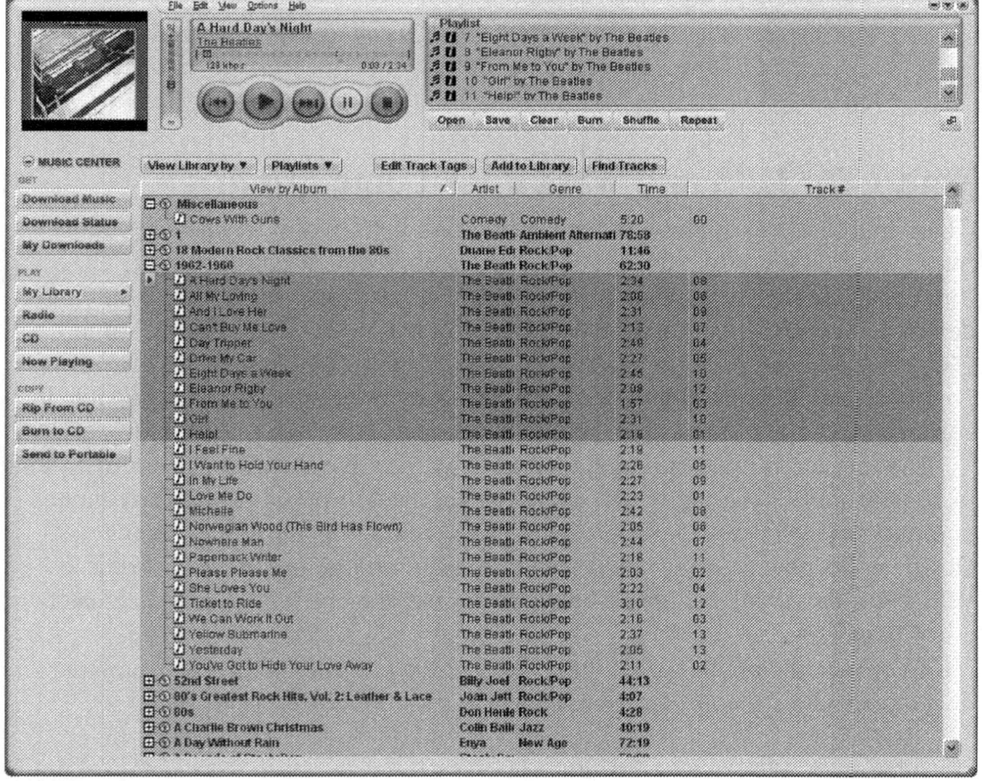

FIGURE 1-1 This is Musicmatch Jukebox, the program that's the focus of this book. We usually call it Musicmatch for short.

So, what is Musicmatch, what can you do with it, and why did we devote a whole book to it? Those are some mighty good questions you're asking. Clearly you're smarter than the average reader. You're our kind of people. Let's have lunch.

Put simply, Musicmatch is music management software, a program that enables you to build, organize, manage, and listen to your digital audio collection. Remember that old milk crate you used to store your record albums in? Musicmatch is nothing like that. We just have fond memories of our record albums is all.

The reason you need a book about it is that Musicmatch, while among the most powerful programs of its kind, can be a bit daunting—especially if you're new to digital audio. It's not immediately evident, for instance, how you play a song stored on your hard drive—even though you can see it *right there* in your song library. Much as we love Musicmatch (and think you'll come to love it as well), it's a somewhat confusing piece of software. Have no fear—Rick and Denny are here.

What Can You Do with Musicmatch?

Now that you have a general idea as to Musicmatch's capabilities, let's get into specifics. With Musicmatch you can

- **Listen to music** Musicmatch is, by name, a jukebox, so it stands to reason you'd be able to listen to music with it. You don't need quarters or the Fonz to start this jukebox jumping, though—just an audio CD, some MP3 or WMA files, or an Internet connection.

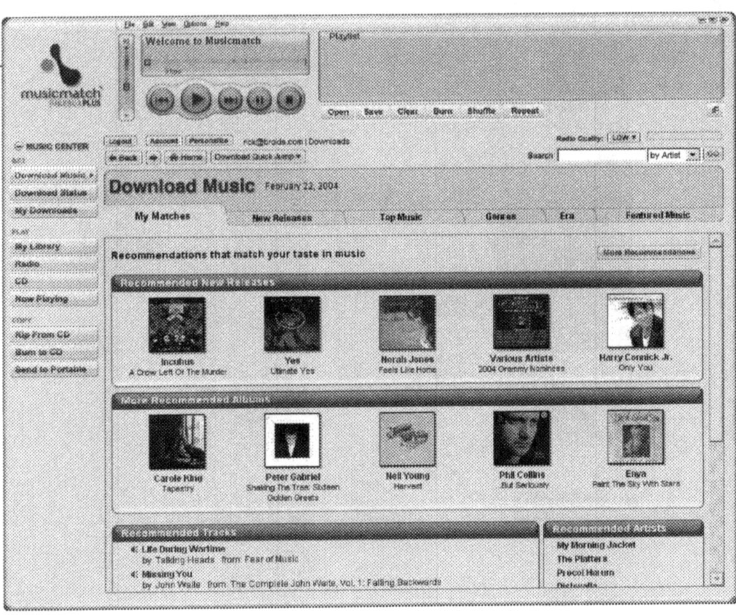

- **Rip CDs** *Ripping* is the process of copying songs from your audio CDs to your PC, converting them to a digital format (such as MP3 or WMA) in the process. See Chapter 4 for details.
- **Rip albums and cassettes** If you have an old library of albums and cassettes you want to make digital, Musicmatch can handle it. Although this process isn't technically the same as ripping, it's functionally similar—so let's let it rip, so to speak.
- **Create CDs** Remember those mix tapes you used to make? You can do the same thing with blank CDs, filling them with the digital songs stored on your hard drive. We call this *burning* a CD, and it's explained in Chapter 10.
- **Organize your music** Thanks to a nifty invention known as *playlists,* you can organize your music collection into any number of mini-collections. The idea here is that you wouldn't necessarily want, say, your Mozart to mix with your Marley. Get the scoop on playlists in Chapter 9.
- **Discover new music** You've heard of satellite radio? Musicmatch gives you Internet radio, meaning you can listen to a huge selection of stations "broadcasting" an endless variety of music. More on this way-cool option in Chapter 8.

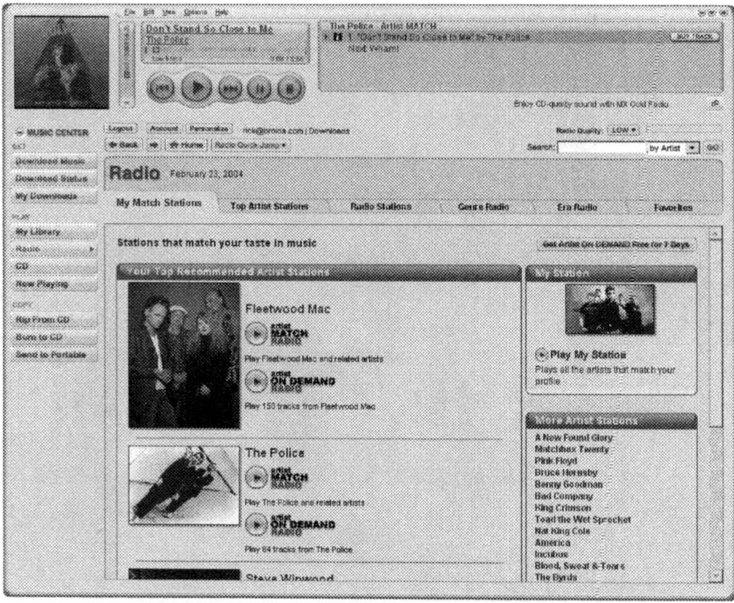

- **Buy music** Don't get us wrong—we have very fond memories of spending hours browsing the aisles at our local music emporium. But that's the old-fashioned way to buy music. Nowadays, we click, sample, and download—no trip to the mall required. Chapter 6 is the place to learn about buying music from Musicmatch.

TIP *As of press time, Musicmatch was selling songs for 99 cents each—a good price, but you can do better. At Wal-Mart (yes, Wal-Mart—www.walmart.com), for instance, tracks sell for 88 cents each. And at BuyMusic (www.buy.com), they're cheaper still: just 79 cents each. You can listen to these tunes in Musicmatch just as readily as you can if you'd purchased them with it. Find out more in Chapter 6.*

- **Take your entire music collection anywhere** Imagine all 200 of your CDs stored in a player no larger than a deck of cards. It's possible. Musicmatch supports a wide variety of portable digital-audio players. See Chapter 11 for details.

All this is just the tip of the iceberg. In the pages to come, we'll teach you everything you need to know about these and other cool features, at the same time venturing into sticky areas like legal versus illegal music downloads. First, let's take a look at the different versions of Musicmatch and why you might want one over another.

Different Versions of Musicmatch

As of press time, there were two versions of Musicmatch:

- Musicmatch Jukebox Basic 8.2
- Musicmatch Jukebox Plus 8.2

By the time you read this, however, Musicmatch Jukebox 9.0 should be available (again in both Basic and Plus versions). Let's start by looking at the differences between Basic and Plus, then delve into what's new in 9.0 and how it affects you (and this book).

Musicmatch Jukebox Basic

Musicmatch Jukebox Basic is a free program. That's right—for the total price of nothing at all, you can download yourself a pretty capable music manager, one that lets you listen to tunes, rip and burn CDs, and more. If you're not sure yet whether

Musicmatch is the right program for you, you should definitely download the Basic version and take it for a spin.

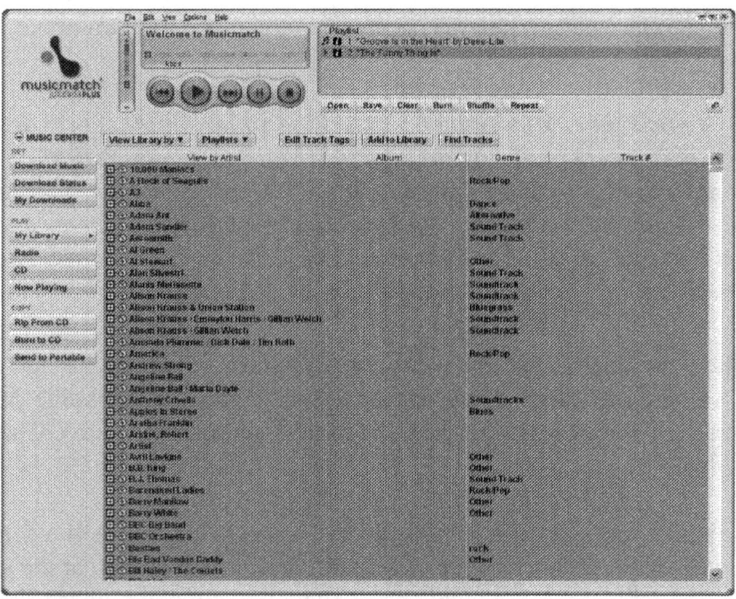

Of course, you may already have it. Many new computers come preloaded with Musicmatch Jukebox Basic, and we've also seen it bundled with various portable players (most notably the Dell DJ, a large-capacity player similar to Apple's iPod). A few players even come with Jukebox Plus, which, as you'll learn in the next section, is a $20 value.

While Jukebox Basic is undeniably powerful and more than sufficient for many users, there are reasons you might want to consider upgrading to Jukebox Plus. Let's find out what those reasons are.

Musicmatch Jukebox Plus

Musicmatch Jukebox Plus not only has more features than Jukebox Basic, it has certain features that are faster as well. For the one-time cost of $19.99, Jukebox Plus nets you these upgrades and extras:

- **Super Tagging** If you download a lot of music from the Internet (using file-sharing services like KaZaa and Morpheus), you'll appreciate this feature. Jukebox can automatically fix the ID3 tag (which contains song, artist, album, and other information) for a song or group of songs. By doing so, you'll have a much easier time organizing them.

- **Faster CD ripping** Jukebox Basic is limited to "5x" speed when ripping songs from your CDs, meaning if a CD contains 60 minutes' worth of music, it could take upwards of 15 minutes to rip it. Multiply that by several dozen (or hundred) CDs and you're looking at a pretty major investment of time to rip your collection. Jukebox Plus can rip songs at up to 40x (depending on the speed of your CD-ROM drive). If you have a big CD collection you're planning to convert to digital audio, this feature alone can be worth the price of upgrading. Same goes for burning CDs.

NOTE *Our esteemed tech editor would like us to point out that many CD-ROM drives can't rip much faster than 5x, despite specs that indicate otherwise. Our experience bears this out; we've seen rip speeds of only around 8x on supposedly high-speed drives. So, this isn't necessarily a compelling reason to upgrade.*

- **Album and cassette recording** Jukebox Plus can record digital audio files from any line-in source, be it a turntable, cassette player, or even an old reel-to-reel deck.
- **CD label printing** When you buy music from Musicmatch Downloads, you may want to burn it to a CD so you can pop it in your car stereo or another player. Jukebox Plus enables you to print CD labels and jewel-case covers and inserts, complete with album art and custom text and graphics.

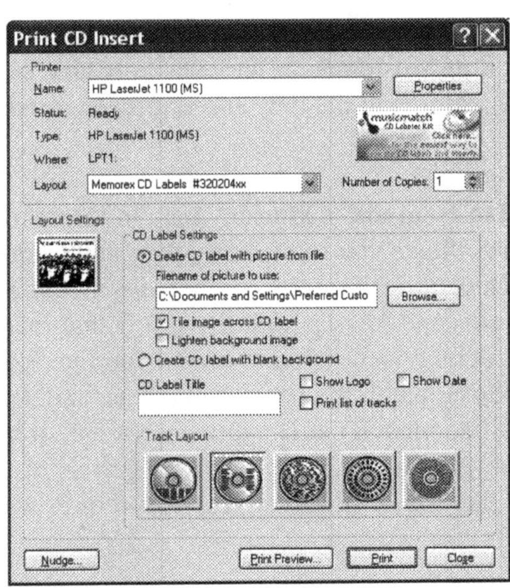

- **Tech support** You don't need tech support—you've got this book! Much as we wish that were true, we can't address every possible problem in these pages. (Grammar alert! We don't mean that the pages themselves have problems—we're talking about Musicmatch problems, of course. It seemed easier to explain that than to rewrite that sentence to be grammatically accurate. Sometimes the English language just ain't all it's cracked up to be. Now, where were we?) By upgrading to Jukebox Plus, you can get in touch with Musicmatch's technical support department (though only via e-mail). With Musicmatch Basic you're pretty much on your own. See Chapter 12 for troubleshooting and where-to-find-help information.

TIP *For an additional $39.99, you can purchase a "lifetime key" for Musicmatch Jukebox Plus, meaning you're entitled to all future versions of the software—no extra charge. Our advice: don't do it. Let's say you buy Jukebox Plus 9.0 for $19.99, then version 10 comes out a year later. That'll cost you another $19.99. Only by the time you get to version 11 (another $19.99) will you break even on the lifetime key. And by then, who knows what the digital music scene will look like? Much as we think Jukebox Plus is worth buying, we don't think the lifetime key is a particularly good deal.*

What's New in Musicmatch 9.0

At press time, Musicmatch 9.0 was still in the beta stage. Alas, we weren't able to get the software for hands-on coverage. However, after careful rummaging through the Dumpsters out back of Musicmatch, Inc., we were able to dig up some dirt on the new and improved features in the new and improved version of the software. Here's an overview:

- **Musicmatch On Demand** Musicmatch On Demand is a breakthrough new service that allows you to instantly play any of the 600,000 tracks in the Musicmatch catalog. The service includes an extensive database of artist relationships and track popularity levels that make it easy for you to discover music. Once you've found tracks you like, you can easily save them to your Musicmatch library and playlists, and access them remotely from any PC. Musicmatch On Demand tracks are streamed in CD quality over the Internet, and as long as you are logged in, you can organize and play them just like music files that you ripped or downloaded.

- **A new user interface** Musicmatch has spent the last year focused on usability testing and ease of use. The Musicmatch Jukebox 9.0 library, playlist manager, burner, recorder, and right-click menus are all redesigned and easier to use. Version 9.0 also includes a new full-screen view, a better download-tracks status indicator, and an improved installation process.
- **Faster library** The music library in Musicmatch Jukebox 9.0 sorts and changes folder views significantly faster than previous versions. Users with large libraries will see the biggest improvements. Other library improvements include new right-click features and an improved "view by album art" track information display.
- **Burner enhancements** A simplified user interface makes it easier to create CDs.
- **Recorder** A simplified user interface (including a Copy From CD button) makes it easier to record tracks from music CDs.
- **Playlist window** The new Playlist button provides easier access to your saved playlists and the AutoDJ. The new Send To button provides an easy method to burn tracks to a CD, transfer tracks to a portable device, or e-mail a track listing to a friend. The new Play Last Playlist option provides an easy method to switch play between file, CD, and radio.
- **Portable Device Manager** A simplified user interface makes it easier to transfer music to your portable player.
- **Explicit Lyrics Filter (Musicmatch Radio)** Accessible from within Jukebox, this new feature allows users to filter out explicit lyrics and includes password protection for parental control.
- **Personalization** Accessible from the new Tools button available from within any of the music services (On Demand, Music Store, Radio, and so on), users can now better set up and manage artists associated with their unique profile. Users who have an account can log into their account from multiple PCs and retain their profile.

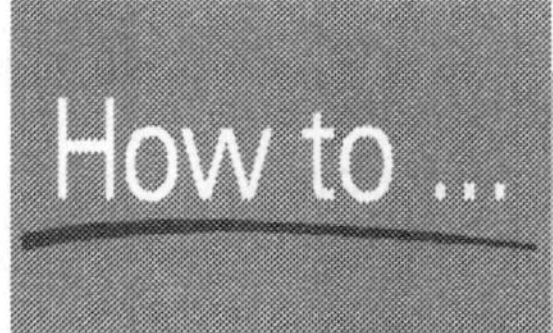

Upgrade to Jukebox Plus

Let's say your computer or digital audio player came with Jukebox Basic (or you downloaded that version to give it a try) and you're ready to take the plunge on Jukebox Plus. Here's how:

1. Start Musicmatch.
2. Click Help | Purchase Upgrade, then choose the desired method: Internet, mail, or phone.

Obviously, the Internet is the easiest method—it takes you to the Musicmatch web site, where you type in your credit card number and immediately receive the code necessary to "unlock" Jukebox Basic (effectively adding the features and enhancements that turn it into Plus). If you'd rather not send your credit card into cyberspace, you can call Musicmatch's toll-free number (800-347-2566) and get the code that way. Don't have a credit card? The mail option lets you print a form that you can send in along with a check. This option will not, however, bring you forward in time from the 19th century, where you're obviously living.

Voices from the Community

It's All About CDs, Baby

John Steup is Vice President and Manager of All Things at CD Baby (**www.cdbaby.com**), an online music store that sells music the old-fashioned way: on CDs. And not just any CDs, either, but music from independent artists whose albums you usually won't find elsewhere. The site is a treasure trove of alternatives to the Britney Spears and OutKasts of the world. In fact, before we even asked John to share his words of wisdom in this book, Rick discovered a couple of really great bands at the site (In the Buff and Tallulah—check 'em out!). Anyway, here's our Q&A with one of the heads, er, babies at CD Baby.

Q: Tell us a little about CD Baby and how it's different from other music stores (online or otherwise).

A: CD Baby was one of the first online stores that featured only independent artists and has become the biggest seller of indies online. The difference (and what has kept us growing while others have fallen by the dot-com wayside) is that we have never lost sight of our customers or our artists and have never taken on investors, so our bottom line has never had to be about money; it is getting the music out there.

Q: Do you think Musicmatch Downloads (and other music-download services) threaten the very existence of the CD?

A: Not at all. We welcome the whole concept of selling downloads online and actually act as an agent to help our artists get their music into all of the online "pay for download" sites. We find that CD sales have actually gotten better over the years even as the concept of paying for "instant music" has been coalescing.

Q: You're stranded on a desert island. What five CDs will keep you happy until you're rescued?

A: Only five?!

Number 1 on my CD player is Lucie Idlout—*E5-770: My Mother's Name.* Amazing.

Number 2 would be Robbie Robertson—*Contact from the Underworld of Redboy.*

Number 3 is How to Build a Rocketship—*Thank You Easter Bunny.*

Number 4 is Patti Smith—*Horses.*

Number 5 is Pink Floyd—*Animals.*

Q: How has the Internet changed the way people shop for and buy music?

A: I feel that it has made it immensely easy for people from all over the world to get new music. CD Baby has artists from all over the planet and ships out 1,000 CDs a day to all parts of the world. It's amazing to see a guy from Ohio sell a CD to someone in Japan. As far as "instant" sales, the downloadable sales market is just underway. I think it's a great model but it may be too early to tell what directions it will take.

Chapter 2

Get Your Computer Ready

How to...

- Meet Musicmatch's system requirements
- Upgrade your computer's memory
- Add a second hard drive
- Replace your CD-ROM drive
- Upgrade to USB 2.0
- Choose new speakers
- Connect your PC to your stereo
- Determine if you need a new sound card
- Set and adjust volume levels in Windows

"I'll play it first and tell you what it is later."—Miles Davis, musician

Musicmatch doesn't run on all computers, but it runs on most of them. For instance, the software is compatible only with Windows-based systems—sorry, Mac users. Within those Windows systems are certain requirements that must be met for Musicmatch to work. Let's take a look at those requirements, look at ways to bring your computer "up to code" if it's not already there, and discuss upgrades you may want to consider to improve the Musicmatch experience.

Is Your PC Ready?

Let us preface this by saying that if you have a relatively new computer—one made in 2002 or later—you should have absolutely no trouble running Musicmatch Jukebox (either Basic or Plus). Nevertheless, here are the system requirements for Musicmatch 8.2. (They're likely to be very similar for version 9.0.) Keep in mind that these are the bare minimums required to run the software—in many cases, you'll want far more horsepower.

- **300MHz Pentium processor or faster (1GHz recommended)** The faster the processor in your computer, the better. We're currently running the software on a 2.8GHz Pentium 4 system, and it's still pretty slow to load. We shudder to think what it would be like on a 300MHz machine.

- **128MB of RAM** The more RAM your computer has, the less it has to access the hard drive—and hard drives are much, much slower than RAM.
- **150MB hard drive space** Although Musicmatch itself is only a 100MB program (that's an approximate figure), it requires a chunk of free space in order to function. In fact, you should have at least 500MB available if you plan to take advantage of Musicmatch Downloads or the software's Internet radio features—and even more for CD ripping, which we'll get to later. As with RAM, more is always better.
- **A sound card and speakers** We hope this goes without saying, but your computer must have a sound card (it's been a *long* time since we've seen one that didn't) and at least two speakers. Otherwise, where's the music going to come from? The floppy drive? Be serious.
- **USB** If you're planning to copy songs from your PC to a portable player like the Creative MuVo or Apple iPod (the Windows version), you'll need a Universal Serial Bus (USB) port. Most computers made in the 21st century have at least one of them; if yours doesn't, it's a simple matter to add one (see the next section, "Upgrades to Consider," for details).
- **Windows 98 SE, Windows Me, Windows 2000, or Windows XP** If you're still using a computer with Windows 98, it's high time to consider an upgrade—not just of the operating system, but of the computer itself. More on that in the next section.
- **An Internet connection** You need one not only to download Musicmatch itself (though, admittedly, you can buy it in stores—see Chapter 3), but also to purchase and download music and listen to Internet radio, among other things.
- **Internet Explorer 5.0 or later** This shouldn't be a problem for most users, as Windows already comes with Internet Explorer preloaded. Don't worry if you use another web browser, such as Netscape or Opera—Musicmatch just borrows certain bits of Internet Explorer behind the scenes. To use Musicmatch Downloads or Internet radio, you need Internet Explorer 6.0 (or later) with Service Pack 1 installed. Again, for most users this won't be an issue.

Upgrades to Consider

If your computer is more than a few years old or it's an inexpensive, low-end model (machines purchased at Wal-Mart come to mind), you may want to upgrade certain components to improve the Musicmatch experience (and, for that matter, enjoy your computer a little more). Let's take a look at a few key upgrades and how they'll affect Musicmatch.

- **More RAM** Adding memory to your computer is often the most inexpensive and effective upgrade. Rick recently added 128MB to his parents' machine, bringing the total memory to 256MB, and the difference was remarkable. Before the upgrade, the machine took upwards of five minutes to boot—afterwards, about 90 seconds. And the memory module cost all of $30. The key thing to remember when adding RAM is to buy the right kind for your computer. Check with the manufacturer to find the exact specs, or try a site like Crucial.com (see Figure 2-1), which has an online memory-configurator that can determine (and sell you) the right kind of RAM for thousands of different PCs. If you have Windows XP, we highly recommend at least 512MB of RAM. Earlier versions of Windows can get by with 256MB.

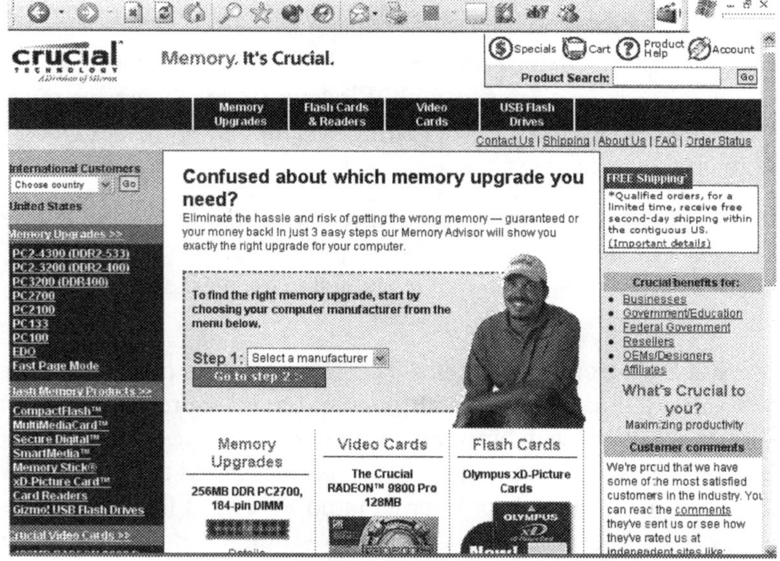

FIGURE 2-1 At web sites like Crucial.com, you can find exactly the right memory upgrade for your computer.

- **A bigger hard drive** If you have a particularly large music collection—several hundred CDs (and/or albums and cassettes) plus a countless number of downloads—you may find yourself running low on hard drive space. Fortunately, it's easy and relatively inexpensive to add a second hard drive to most computers. At press time, you could buy an 80GB internal drive for under $100 (often even less—check your Sunday paper for the CompUSA/BestBuy/Circuit City special of the week). However, if you have a notebook or don't feel like monkeying around inside your PC, you can buy an external drive—one that connects via a standard USB port—for just a few dollars more. There's something to be said for storing your music collection on an external hard drive—it's like a portable jukebox that moves easily from one computer to another.

- **A faster CD drive** In order to "rip" songs from your CDs (as discussed in Chapter 4), you'll need a CD-ROM drive. In order to "burn" CDs from your digital music collection (as discussed in Chapter 10), you'll need a CD-RW drive. The faster your drive, the faster you'll be able to accomplish both tasks—and if you do them a lot, you can save a considerable amount of time by installing a newer, faster drive. Without getting overly technical about different kinds of drives, drive speeds, and so on, we recommend investing in a DVD burner. Yes, DVD. You've probably been thinking about one anyway, and the drives have gotten so inexpensive (under $100 for internal models), there's little sense buying anything else. A DVD burner allows you to burn not only DVDs (which has little to do with Musicmatch but is great for home movies and data storage), but also acts as a CD-RW drive, so that you can burn audio CDs. Plus, most of them are faster at CD ripping and burning than the plain-jane CD-RW drives of yesteryear.

- **A broadband Internet connection** There are only three certainties in life: death, taxes, and that once you try broadband, you'll never go back to dial-up. A dial-up connection, like the kind you traditionally get with America Online, is okay—but a broadband (that is, high-speed) connection is vastly preferable. Ultimately, you want to be able to download Musicmatch updates, purchase songs from Musicmatch Downloads, and listen to Internet radio. You can do all that with dial-up, but it's better with broadband. (By "better" we generally mean "faster," but in the case of Internet radio, a faster connection also means better sound quality—like the difference between a CD and AM radio.) If you start buying music from Musicmatch (or another online service), you'll find you can download entire albums in a matter of minutes with a broadband connection. With dial-up, however, it can take several minutes to download just one song. An album might take half an hour or longer. Sure, we know you're the patient sort, but trust us when we say a broadband Internet connection is one upgrade you'll never regret.
- **Better speakers** The speakers that come bundled with most computers are—how to put this tactfully?—god-awful. They're usually the cheapest, weakest models the manufacturers can come by, for the simple reason that computer buyers rarely look at speakers (processors and DVD burners get all the attention). If you plan to use Musicmatch to actually listen to music while you're sitting at your PC, a new set of speakers can be a worthwhile investment. See the "Speaker Upgrades" section later in this chapter for buying advice.
- **USB 2.0 ports** As mentioned in the previous section, you need USB if you want to connect a portable audio player like the Rio Cali or Dell DJ. We recommend upgrading to USB 2.0 ports if your computer doesn't already have them. See the upcoming section, "USB Upgrades," for details.

USB Upgrades

Musicmatch supports USB 2.0—a newer, faster implementation of USB. That means if your computer has USB 2.0 ports, it can transfer songs to portable players (assuming they, too, support this faster version of USB—not all of them do) much faster than if it has only USB 1.1 ports. How much faster? USB 2.0 can move data at up to 480 megabits per second (Mbps), while USB 1.1 plods along at just 12 Mbps. Let's say you have 5 gigabytes' worth of songs you want to copy to a Dell DJ. With USB 1.1, the process could take over an hour; with USB 2.0, under five minutes. Pretty big difference, no?

How to ... Build Your Own External Hard Drive

In recent months, Rick has become a big fan of external hard drives. Thanks to USB 2.0 (see the "USB Upgrades" section), an external drive can transfer data almost as speedily as an internal one, meaning it's just as practical. Plus, you can easily move the drive from one computer to another—helpful if you want to transport, say, a large collection of audio files. It's a terrific way to add storage space to a desktop or notebook computer.

Rick is also really, really cheap. On any given weekend you'll find him perusing the CompUSA and Best Buy ads and exclaiming to his wife, "Look at this! An 80-gigabyte hard drive for only $75!" His wife would say, "That's nice, dear," and go back to reading ads for unimportant items like food and clothes.

Of course, that $75 drive is an internal model, and Rick doesn't have time to go monkeying around inside his computer—which is already full anyway. But with a $25 hard-drive enclosure, he can turn that internal hard drive into an external one—and save a good $50 or so over a prebuilt external drive. That's exactly what he did:

You can find these hard-drive enclosures at any number of online stores—one of our favorites is Newegg (www.newegg.com). Rick also found a wide selection on eBay. Wherever you buy, make sure the enclosure has the following specs:

- **USB 2.0 interface** (some also have FireWire, which is just as good—as long as you make sure your computer has a FireWire port)

- **3.5-inch drive bay** (you'll see many with 2.5-inch bays, which aren't large enough for standard internal hard drives)
- **Power supply and cables**

All it takes to install the drive in the enclosure is a screwdriver and about 10 minutes. Make sure to follow the instructions provided with the enclosure—you may have to change a jumper setting on the hard drive so your computer can recognize it.

With a little careful shopping, you can build your own external hard drive for $100 or less—and add tons of extra storage space to your PC. For most users, adding a second drive is much more practical than trying to replace the primary drive with a larger one.

NOTE *A little caveat here: USB 2.0 is undeniably faster than USB 1.1, but based on our real-world observations, neither port moves data as quickly as the specs would have you believe. That said, if your computer has no USB 2.0 ports, it's time to upgrade. Read on for details.*

How can you tell what kind of USB ports your computer has? Unfortunately, a sight check won't do it—all USB ports look identical. Try consulting the invoice or packing slip that came with the computer; it may specify the port speed. You can also try contacting the manufacturer. Most computers built in 2003 and later have USB 2.0, but there may be exceptions. Finally, there's always the real-world test: if it takes a few minutes, rather than a few seconds, to copy a handful of songs to your player, your computer has USB 1.1. (See Chapter 11 for information on copying songs to portable players.)

Thankfully, it's a relatively easy matter to upgrade most computers—even notebooks—with USB 2.0 ports. For desktops, try the Belkin (www.belkin.com) Hi-Speed USB 2.0 5-Port PCI Card (see Figure 2-2), which plugs into one of your machine's open PCI slots. It's available direct from Belkin for $44.99. If you own a notebook, consider Belkin's USB 2.0 Notebook Card, which plugs into almost any PC Card slot and provides two USB 2.0 ports. It's $64.99.

Speaker Upgrades

It's time to start thinking of your computer as more than just a storage facility for your programs and data. It also has the potential to serve as a truly incredible

FIGURE 2-2 Belkin's USB card is very easy to install and adds four external USB 2.0 ports to any desktop computer.

Our Favorite Portable Players

Part of the joy of using Musicmatch is using it to copy your songs and playlists to a portable audio player for on-the-go listening (see Chapter 11). So, while we're on the subject of USB—the interface used to connect portable players to your PC—we thought we'd take this opportunity to recommend a few of our favorite models.

Rick: Although high-capacity hard-drive players like the Apple iPod and Dell DJ are all the rage these days, I'm still a fan of small, lightweight flash players like the Rio Cali. Although they store far less music, it's usually more than enough for half an hour of jogging or time on the elliptical machine. Plus, there are no internal moving parts, so you don't have to worry about damaging a hard drive with sharp impact (as you have to with a hard drive–based player). That's what I like about flash players—they're ideal for exercise. In addition to playing MP3 and WMA tunes, the Cali includes an FM radio and a stopwatch. It also comes with an armband and hip holster so you don't have to hold it while working out. It even has an expansion slot, just in case its 256MB of memory aren't enough for you. Not bad for a $150 player. On the hard-drive side, I like the Dell DJ—and not just because I'm the co-author of *How to Do Everything with Your Dell DJ*. It's because it has much better battery life than the trendy Apple iPod, costs significantly less, and supports the increasingly popular WMA format (which the iPod does not).

Denny: My flash-based MP3 players are collecting dust in my file cabinet along with my Iomega Zip drive and dial-up modem. I'm a confirmed convert to hard drive–based players, which let me carry dozens of albums—enough music to fit any mood. With a flash player, I have to stop and load up new music every time I leave my PC. My absolute favorite is the iPod—or the tiny, lightweight iPod Mini for exercise use. If you rip all your own music, it's my top recommendation. Sure, the iPod commands a price premium, but for your extra money you get style, quality construction, smaller size, and less heft than the Dell DJ, and the best interface ever to grace a portable music player. However, if you use the Musicmatch Downloads service—or just about any other online music store besides iTunes—you'll need WMA support, which the iPod doesn't offer. In that case, I'd suggest the Creative Nomad MuVo^2, a compact, featherweight 4GB player that rivals the iPod Mini in the size and weight departments. Its battery life rivals that of the Dell DJ, and it supports both MP3 and WMA formats.

jukebox. Musicmatch is half the equation; a good set of speakers is the other half. If you're the kind of person who's very choosy when it comes to speakers for your stereo, you should put the same thought into speakers for your PC. After all, speakers can make or break your setup's sound quality more than any other factor.

For starters, we highly recommend getting a three-piece or five-piece speaker system (see Figure 2-3). The key element in both is a subwoofer—essentially a big speaker designed solely to produce bass. We're not talking about the annoying, head-rattling bass that emanates from many a teenager's car stereo—just subtle lows that compliment the highs produced by the other speakers (which are known as satellites). Many computers come with just two speakers; adding a subwoofer to the mix is the difference between night and day.

NOTE *In case you're thinking about digging out those old speakers that used to be connected to your stereo, forget it. Not only do they have the wrong kind of connectors (wires instead of stereo plugs), they're non-powered speakers, and computers require powered speakers. Now, that said, it is possible to use your stereo and its speakers for listening to music stored on your PC. In fact, it's highly desirable. See "The PC-to-Stereo Connection" section later in this chapter to find out how to do it.*

FIGURE 2-3 The Altec Lansing 2100 (left) and Logitech Z-680 are great replacements for bundled speakers.

Here's a little speaker terminology to help you understand the basics:

- **Satellites** The main speakers, usually numbering anywhere from two to six.
- **Subwoofer** A large, floor-standing speaker that produces only bass.
- **Remote** Many PC speaker systems now come with wired volume-control remotes instead of controls mounted directly on one of the satellites.
- **2.1** A three-piece speaker system: two satellites and one subwoofer.
- **4.1** A five-piece speaker system: four satellites and one subwoofer. Also known as a surround-sound system.
- **5.1** A six-piece speaker system: five satellites (one of them a "center channel" used expressly for DVD movie dialogue) and a subwoofer.

The leading manufacturers of PC speaker systems include Altec Lansing, Creative, Klipsch, and Logitech, though you can also find some interesting choices from Harman Kardon and JBL. Let's take a look at various speaker options, broken down by category.

TIP *If you like to listen to music through headphones and your PC doesn't have an easily accessible headphone jack, look for speakers that do. The Logitech Z-3, for instance, includes a headphone jack on its wired remote.*

Budget Speakers Don't want to spend a fortune on speakers? Although you can easily pay upwards of $400 for a high-end set, you can also pay as little as $50 for a five-speaker surround-sound bundle. The Creative SBS 4.1 450, for instance, includes four satellites and a subwoofer, but sells direct from Creative for just $49.99.

Of course, a speaker system in that price range may not sound much better than what came bundled with your PC. There's an argument to be made for buying a good 2.1 system instead of a low-end 4.1 system. That said, you need to spend closer to $100 if you want halfway decent speakers. Whether you go 2.1, 4.1, or even 5.1 is up to you.

Mainstream Speakers If you're willing to spend as much as $200, you can buy some truly excellent speakers. Consider, for instance, the Logitech Z-2200, a 200-watt 2.1 system with the coveted THX certification. That means professional audio specialists at the eponymous company (created by George Lucas for a little movie called *Star Wars*) have certified the quality of the speakers. Translation: they rock. The Z-2200 has a list price of $149.99.

TIP *Shop online and save big! At sites like Buy.com and Newegg.com, we found the Z-2200 selling for around $110. Check price-comparison sites like PriceGrabber.com and you may find even better deals.*

For another $50, Logitech offers an even more powerful package: the Z-560. This 4.1 system is also THX-certified and cranks out a whopping 400 watts—perfect for bugging the neighbors. If we had $200 to spend, these are the speakers we'd likely spend it on.

High-End Speakers Really want to listen in style? For about $400, you can enjoy award-winning speaker systems like the Klipsch ProMedia Ultra 5.1 (see Figure 2-4) and Logitech Z-680. Admittedly, these almost qualify as overkill for music alone—they were also designed with games and movies in mind. But if you use your computer for that stuff, you won't regret investing in high-end speakers. Just be prepared for a rather massive snake's nest of wires under your desk!

Cool Speakers Superficial guy that he is, Rick would rather have speakers that look good than sound good. Sure, it's possible to have both—but most computer speakers look pretty blah. That's why Rick is partial to the Harman Kardon SoundSticks II, a three-piece system that would look right at home on the bridge of the Enterprise (not that Picard and Co. ever jammed much). Take a look:

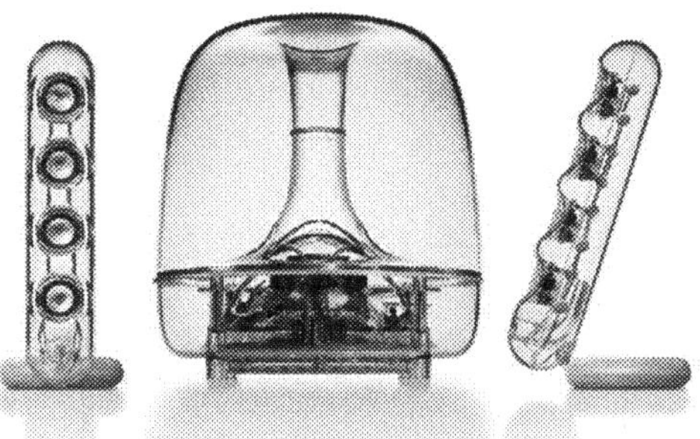

Needless to say, these see-through babies are mighty sweet-looking. At $199 list, they're also on the expensive side—but they sound better than their novelty design would suggest. Another nifty non-blah option is the JBL Creature II, a three-piece system priced at $99.

They not only look cool, they *are* cool: volume is controlled just by *touching* one of the satellites!

FIGURE 2-4 They don't come any better (or pricier) than the Klipsch ProMedia Ultra 5.1. Send a set to your favorite authors today!

The PC-to-Stereo Connection

Suppose you own a really sweet stereo, one with equally sweet speakers. Instead of spending money on new speakers for your PC or settling for the wimpy ones that came with it, wouldn't it be great if you could pipe music from your PC to that really sweet stereo? That way you could enjoy the best of both worlds: your entire digital music collection (plus Internet radio to boot—see Chapter 8) and your fancy roof-raising speakers.

TIP *And let's not forget games and movies. If you like to play games or watch DVDs on your PC, nothing beats having "big" audio to go with them. So now you have three times the motivation to connect your stereo. Obviously it needs to be in the same room as your PC, preferably in close proximity.*

There are two main ways to go about this: wired and wireless. The wired approach is fairly obvious: connect your PC's sound card to an available set of RCA line-in jacks at the back of your stereo. All that's required is the right cable—visit your local Radio Shack to find it.

TIP *In Chapter 5, you'll learn about connecting a turntable to your sound card's line-in jack for recording purposes. You can use the very same stereo-to-RCA cable to pipe audio from the sound card to your stereo. Just plug it into the speaker jack instead of the line-in jack. One cable, two uses. Whee!*

However, if you're serious about sound quality, you may want to bypass the sound card altogether, as it can produce (or reproduce) the hums and buzzes generated by the computer itself. It's possible to connect your PC to your stereo by way of an "external sound card," a box that plugs into a USB port. The $49 Xitel HiFi-Link is one such product—it's designed expressly for linking PCs to stereos. It has RCA jacks and comes with 30 feet of stereo-to-RCA cable, so it's a complete out-of-box solution.

Of course, the problem with any wired solution is that your stereo must be in relatively close proximity to your PC. If it's more than, say, 30 feet away or it's in a different room, you'll probably want to investigate a wireless solution. This requires a little more setup time and technical savvy, but the results are well worth it. What could be cooler than wirelessly beaming your music collection and Internet radio to your stereo? Nothing, that's what. Nothing!

NOTE *There is one fairly important factor to consider regarding wireless PC-to-stereo connections: Most of them take Musicmatch out of the loop. In other words, they often rely on their own software for organizing and playing music. Most of them won't stream Musicmatch Radio (though some support web browser–based Internet radio) or songs purchased via Musicmatch Downloads. In other words, in some ways you limit yourself by going from wired to wireless. Caveat emptor.*

We could fill a separate book covering these so-called *digital audio receivers,* which have proliferated like crazy in recent months. Most are designed to take advantage of 802.11*x* (also known as Wi-Fi) wireless networks, which some computer users already have installed in their homes. If you're one of them, it's a pretty simple matter to install a digital audio receiver (DAR) and start enjoying your music. We've got a few DAR summaries lined up for you just a few paragraphs away.

Okay, but what if you *don't* already have a Wi-Fi network installed in your house? Isn't there some kind of lower-tech wireless technology you can use to get the same results? In fact, there is: X10's Lola kit, which combines a 2.4GHz RF transmitter that connects to your PC with a receiver that connects to your stereo and TV. (Yes, TV—you use an onscreen menu to choose tracks, control volume, and so on.) The company claims Lola works at distances of up to 100 feet and can transmit through walls. The kit also includes a wireless remote so you can skip through tracks, pause playback, mute the audio, and do other nifty things. At $49.99, it's a pretty small investment, so it might be just the thing if you don't want to mess around with Wi-Fi.

That said, we think Wi-Fi is the greatest thing since sliced bread, and not just for DARs. Rick, for instance, has a Wi-Fi network in his home, which enables him to enjoy high-speed Internet access on any Wi-Fi-equipped notebook or PDA—in any room of the house. And, of course, it paves the way for adding a DAR to his stereo.

TIP *If you're a Wi-Fi novice and want to learn more about the technology and setting up your own network (it's inexpensive and painless, trust us), visit Cnet.com and check out their Wi-Fi section. It includes product reviews and a buyer's guide that shows you everything you need.*

So, on to the DARs themselves. Let's take a look at a few of the most noteworthy products and what they have to offer:

- **Cd3o c300** This digital audio receiver, which can stream MP3 and WMA files (but not Internet radio, darn it), was one of the first of its kind. And what remains unique about it is its Voice-Guide system, which announces information (song title, artist, and so on) over your stereo. And using the included wireless remote, you can spell out the first few letters of an artist or album to navigate directly to it, without having to flip through an endless number of tracks. That's an innovative alternative to display-based navigation, be it on the remote or your TV. At press time, the c300 was selling for $199; the c200, which lacks an extended-range antenna and digital outputs (but is otherwise identical), was $149.

- **Slim Devices Squeezebox Wireless** One of the top-rated DARs currently available, the Squeezebox supports virtually all digital music formats (MP3, WMA, Ogg Vorbis, and others) and Internet radio. The box that connects to your stereo has digital outputs (ideal if your stereo has digital inputs)

and an LED display that shows song title, elapsed play time, and so on. One caveat: the Squeezebox doesn't play protected music files, like the kind you'd purchase from Musicmatch Downloads (see Chapter 6). Another caveat: at $279, the Squeezebox is one of the priciest DARs around.

- **Creative Sound Blaster Wireless Music** Another highly rated device, the Sound Blaster Wireless Music includes digital outputs and a wireless remote. The latter sports a backlit screen used to navigate your music collection and see information on the song that's playing. However, it doesn't play Internet radio or protected music files, and it relies on Creative's own music manager instead of Musicmatch.

Sound Card Upgrades

With all this talk about speakers, you may be wondering if your sound card has the right stuff to realize their full potential. Or, you may be wondering, "What's a sound card?" We've got answers to these and other audio-hardware questions.

For starters, a sound card is a device inside your computer that produces, well, sound. Specifically, it's the hardware that enables Musicmatch (and other programs) to send music to your speakers. Without a sound card, the best your computer can do is produce a few beeps.

"Sound card" is something of a misnomer these days, as more and more computers now have audio hardware built right onto the motherboard instead of an actual card residing in an expansion slot. While this built-in (or "onboard") hardware is more than adequate for most users, it's not always ideal for surround-sound speaker systems. That's because most onboard audio hardware provides just one jack for connecting speakers, and most surround-speaker systems require at least two jacks—one for the front speakers, another for the rear. If you get a 5.1 system, you'll need a third jack for the center-channel speaker.

NOTE *Most surround-sound speakers come with an adapter that enables all the speakers to plug into a single jack. You won't get true surround sound, but you will get sound from all the speakers.*

If your computer has only one speaker jack and you want true surround sound, you may want to consider a sound card upgrade. All you have to do is install the new card into an open PCI slot (see your system manual for details) and it should automatically override any onboard audio hardware. We recommend the Creative Sound Blaster Audigy LS, a basic but high-quality sound card with 5.1-channel outputs for surround-sound speakers. It sells for about $70.

TIP *If you want the most pristine sound quality of all (or you own a notebook, which doesn't have room for internal upgrades), consider investing in an external "sound card." These devices, which connect to your PC via USB, avoid all computer noise, such as the sound of the hard drive spinning, while at the same time giving you easily accessible ports for connecting speakers, headphones, and other audio peripherals. One of the most popular external PC-audio products is the Creative USB Sound Blaster Audigy 2 NX, which, at $99.99 list, is only a few dollars more than the aforementioned internal Sound Blaster card.*

If you'd like to read some sound-card reviews and learn more about their capabilities, check out the CNET feature, "Which Sound Blaster Is Right for You?" You can find it here: reviews.cnet.com/4520-3022_7-5133933.html.

Setting and Adjusting Volume Settings in Windows

Upgrades aren't the only part of getting your computer ready for Musicmatch. There's also the all-important matter of volume settings. When you play music on a stereo, all you have to do to adjust the volume is turn a knob. On a computer, there's a little more to it.

Specifically, Windows, Musicmatch, and your speakers each have their own volume controls, and it takes a little fine-tuning to get them to play nice. Here's what we recommend:

1. In Windows' System Tray (the area with the little icons in the lower-right corner of the screen), find the Volume icon (represented by a picture of a speaker) and double-click it.

NOTE *If you don't see this icon, go into Windows' Control Panel, choose Sounds and Audio Devices, and check the box marked Place Volume Icon In The Taskbar.*

2. The Master Volume dialog box will appear. Drag the Master Volume slider to its halfway point, then do the same with the Wave slider. Click the X to close the volume controls.

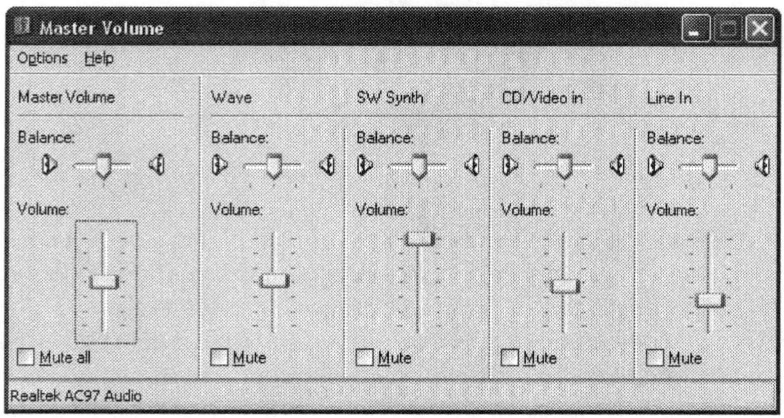

3. Now, when you're listening to music and want to change the volume, use the controls on your speakers—not the ones in Windows or Musicmatch. In most cases, the amplifier in your speakers does a better job with volume than the one in your sound card.

This is just a suggestion to help manage volume consistently. If you're constantly making changes to both Windows' settings and your speakers' volume, you may find you can't get Musicmatch to play as softly as you'd like, or music unexpectedly blares out when you first start playing it.

TIP *If your computer's keyboard has volume-control buttons of its own, you may want to handle this setup in reverse. In other words, set your speakers' volume at the halfway point, then use the keyboard controls to raise and lower volume—often more convenient than reaching for speaker controls.*

In case you're wondering, when you use Musicmatch's own volume-control slider, it raises and lowers Windows' Wave and CD volume settings. If you fiddle with the Master Volume dialog box (as described previously), you'll see that these settings are independent of Master Volume. Yes, this gets confusing. That's why we recommend using your speakers to adjust the volume and leaving Windows' settings alone.

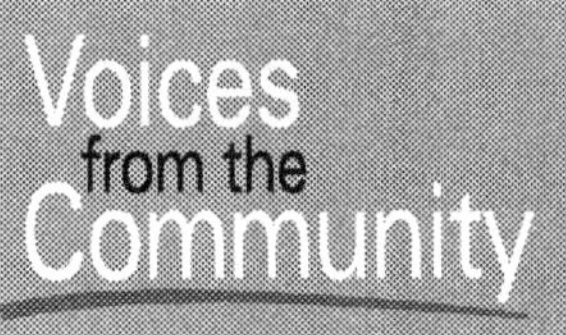

A Few Words with a Musicmatch Bigwig

Ever wondered what goes on "behind the scenes" at Musicmatch? We did, too, so we went around banging on doors (virtually speaking, of course) until we found someone willing to share all of Musicmatch's deep, dark secrets. Okay, so she didn't really share any secrets to speak of, and we didn't get into anything really deep, like religion or philosophy. But it's still a darn interesting Q&A! So without further adieu, we give you Musicmatch's Joni Berkley, Senior Manager of Desktop Products.

Q: Tell us about your job. Sounds really cool.

A: In a nutshell, I'm responsible for the product definition of the Musicmatch Jukebox software. Or, as I like to say, I get to figure out all the cool new bells and whistles that go into the Jukebox.

Q: What's your single favorite Musicmatch feature?

A: Personally, I love SuperTagging. I recently finished ripping all of my CDs and SuperTagging does an awesome job of automatically adding all the artist and album info—and cover art—to all my tracks. I also love waking up to my favorite music with the Alarm Clock feature.

Q: If you could pass along one killer tip to Musicmatch users, what would it be?

A: The coolest tip would be that you can view your music library by album art. That's a great hidden gem. It's just like browsing through your record or CD collection. Slideshow is another really fun feature that came out in version 8.0. It lets you enjoy your favorite pictures with a personal soundtrack.

Q: What do you think the digital music landscape will look like in five years? Will iPods still be around? Will every home be wired (make that wireless) for Internet radio? Give us your vision of the future.

A: At some point in the not-so-distant future, everyone will have access to a celestial jukebox. The celestial jukebox will be a combination of music you either ripped from CDs purchased in the old-school days or purchased from a store like the Musicmatch Download Store, Internet radio, and on-demand streaming music services. But the beauty of it will be that consumers won't have to even think about it. Musicmatch will take that huge universe of music and create the perfect mix of music based on his/her individual taste. And, sure, iPods will still be around... hey, paperweights never go out of style, do they? :-)

Q: You're stranded on a desert island. What five albums would you want to have with you to help pass the time?

A: Okay, I'm going to age myself with this one. In no particular order, I would pick

Substance—New Order
Boy—U2
Boys Don't Cry—The Cure
Led Zeppelin I
Songs in the Key of Life—Stevie Wonder

Where to Find It

Web Site	Address	What's There
Altec Lansing	www.alteclansing.com	Altec Lansing 2100 and other speaker systems
Belkin	www.belkin.com	USB 2.0 upgrade cards
Creative	www.creative.com	Creative SBS 4.1 450 and other speaker systems; Sound Blaster Audigy LS and other sound cards
Crucial	www.crucial.com	Memory upgrades
Dell	www.dell.com	The Dell DJ portable player
Harman Kardon	www.harmankardon.com	SoundSticks II speakers
JBL	www.jbl.com	Creature II speakers
Klipsch	www.klipsch.com	ProMedia Ultra 5.1 and other speaker systems
Logitech	www.logitech.com	Logitech Z-3, Z-2200, Z-560, Z-680, and other speaker systems
Rio	www.rioaudio.com	Rio Cali and other portable players
X10	www.x10.com	MP3 Anywhere
Xitel	www.xitel.com	HiFi-Link

Chapter 3

Your First Steps with Musicmatch

How to...

- Download and install the software
- Launch and configure Musicmatch
- Navigate the Musicmatch interface
- Change the program's look using skins
- Play CDs
- Search your hard drive for music

"Get this party started right now." —Pink, singer

"Get ready to wiggle!" —The Wiggles, a kids' rock band

The big tease has ended. You've read all about Musicmatch's capabilities, and your PC's audio has been tuned to an acoustically astonishing level. Just like one of Rick's stories, the prologue has been fascinating, but you're ready to get to the point already! So without further ado, let's download Musicmatch, install it, and put it to work.

NOTE *If you're merrily skipping around this book, ignoring the handy numbers we went to all the trouble of putting at the bottom of every single page—in order, even—be sure you read Chapter 2 before proceeding further. It has important tips on making sure your computer is properly set up for Musicmatch that you should read now to avoid potential headaches later.*

Downloading and Installing

You won't need to make a trip to the software store to acquire Musicmatch, nor will you need to stalk your mailman every day hoping he's got your Musicmatch package. Assuming you have an Internet connection, a quick visit to the Musicmatch web site will have you installing the program minutes from now.

TIP *Musicmatch Jukebox Deluxe is available on CD at many retailers, such as CompUSA and Best Buy. But unless you don't have an Internet connection, or you don't have a credit card, go for the downloadable version instead. Musicmatch is updated frequently, and buying it online ensures you'll have the latest version. Also, when this book was written, the boxed version of Musicmatch Jukebox Plus cost $29.99—a full $10 more than the download. You can try the program for free, then pay via web, phone, or snail mail if you decide to upgrade to the Plus version. See Chapter 1 for details on payment options.*

Downloading Musicmatch

To get started, open your favorite web browser and go to www.musicmatch.com. On the front page, you should see a button that reads Get It Now. Click this to go to the download page.

NOTE *If you've spent much time browsing the Web, you know that sites are often updated and changed. The download page design may change, but Musicmatch is sure to keep the download easy to find.*

On the next page, you should see options to download Jukebox Basic and to buy Jukebox Plus. (See Chapter 1 for details on the differences between the two versions' capabilities.) The downloads are actually the same for both versions. Choosing Plus first takes you to a page where you can purchase the necessary registration code to upgrade to Jukebox Plus, then it takes you to the download page.

A bit confusingly, even if you choose the Basic version, the download page mentions Musicmatch Jukebox Plus and "updating" your program, as seen in Figure 3-1. Choose your language from the drop-down menu and then click Download Now.

Assuming you're using Internet Explorer, the File Download window should appear, offering Open, Save, and Cancel choices. If you'd like to keep a local copy of the installer on your hard drive for later use, choose Save. Otherwise, click Open to download and install the program.

NOTE *If you choose to save the file to disk first, pay special attention to the filename displayed in the download window, as it's not something nice and self-explanatory like Musicmatch.exe. The most recent version as this book went to press had the not-so-obvious name DLM_2100004_ENU.exe.*

FIGURE 3-1 The Musicmatch download screen. Choose your language, and then click Download Now.

Note that this file isn't the full Musicmatch program, which weighs in at nearly 20MB. Rather, it's a 700K installer application. When you run it, it connects to Musicmatch's servers and downloads the rest of the program. If you have an earlier version of Musicmatch installed on your system, the installer will update that to the latest release.

TIP *In some situations you might want to download the entire program, rather than just the installer. For instance, you may wish to install the program on multiple computers in a household, or on a computer without an Internet connection. If this is the case, cancel the installer download when it begins and click Directly Download The Installation File on the Download Confirmation screen. This will download the entire 18MB program in a single setup file.*

Installing the Program

Once you've completed downloading the program, launch the installer. (This will happen automatically if you chose Open in the previous step.) The Musicmatch Setup Wizard will appear, taking you step-by-step through the installation process. After the Welcome screen and license agreement, you'll see the User Registration page. Be sure to uncheck the Send Me Music-Related News And Special Offers button if you don't want periodic e-mails touting new artists and Musicmatch services.

The next screen asks whether you give Musicmatch permission to monitor which songs you play the most. This data will be used by Musicmatch to suggest new music, offer free downloads, and tailor the Musicmatch online services' musical offerings to your tastes. If this sounds appealing, click Yes. Click No if you don't like the idea of Musicmatch monitoring your listening habits. Keep in mind, though, that the company assures that it never sells or shares your listening data, and they don't care if you're like Rick and you make it a nightly habit to sit and listen to ABBA's "Fernando" on repeat for hours at a time. Really, they don't.

The installation wizard's next step offers Express and Custom installs. Choose Custom, as it will let you configure some basic settings now, saving you some further setup after you start the program. (Also, the Express Install will set Musicmatch as the default player for audio files and CDs, which you may or may not want to do.) Now click Next, and you'll be offered a chance to change the destination folder. You'll typically want to leave this as is, unless you want to install the program to a drive other than C:.

The next screen offers you a chance to choose your music folder. This is where files you rip from your own CDs, as well as files you download from the Musicmatch store, will be saved. This defaults to My Documents\My Music. You may want to change this, especially if you have a second hard drive that you use for music and other media storage.

Next you'll be asked whether to set your Online Music Service Cache feature to Active. Choosing Yes will help keep your music from cutting out should your Internet connection bog down briefly while listening to one of Musicmatch's radio stations, which happens more often if you're running other bandwidth-intensive programs at the same time. The program will use slightly more memory with the cache active.

The installer will now ask which program folder on your Start menu you want to place the Musicmatch icons in. After you make your choice, you'll be asked where you want shortcuts to Musicmatch placed. Desktop places an icon on your

Windows desktop, Quick Launch Toolbar places a small icon on your system toolbar next to the Start button, and Taskbar Notification Area places an icon in the system tray next to the clock. The first two options just create icons; the last option actually runs a small program that sits in your system tray, so you may want to disable that choice if your system has 256MB or less memory.

The next screen, pictured in Figure 3-2, lets you choose which music formats you want Musicmatch to play automatically—that is, if you double-click one of these file types or drop in a music CD. Typically, you'll leave all of the options checked. On slower systems, you may want to use a smaller, less feature-packed player such as Winamp 2 for playing back single MP3 tunes you double-click. If you have such a player installed, you may want to leave the MP3 option unchecked so that double-clicking a file will launch the other player. You'll still be able to use Musicmatch's more advanced features to manage and play back your MP3 tunes by launching Musicmatch directly instead of double-clicking an MP3 file.

With all your choices made, clicking Next will copy Musicmatch to your hard drive. Congratulations, you are now ready to rock. (So to speak.)

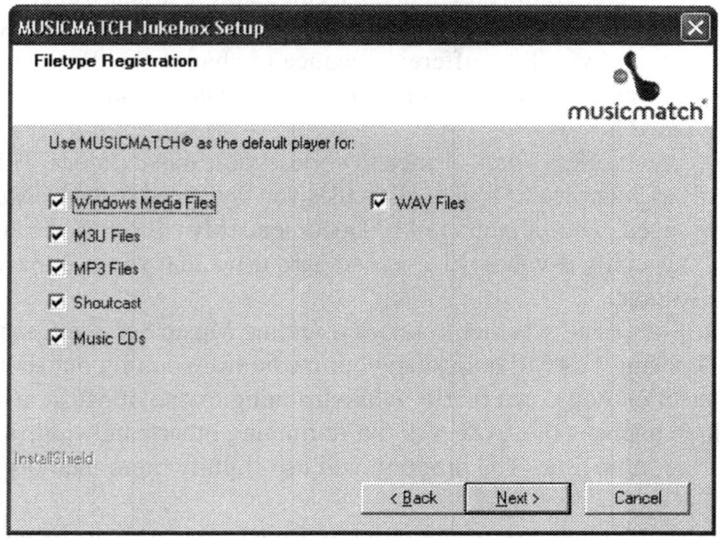

FIGURE 3-2 Select which files types should automatically load in Musicmatch when you double-click them.

Voices from the Community

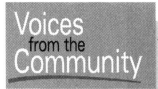

Why Digital Music Rocks

3

Chris Leckness is the founder and operator of several popular "fan" sites, including Dell DJ Site (www.delldjsite.com) and iPAQ HQ (www.ipaqhq.com). He's also a Musicmatch user and a big fan of digital music. Let's find out why...

Do you remember the '80s? You'd go down to the music store and buy the new tape for that one song you heard on the radio. You get home all excited, rip the plastic off, and pop it in the old player. First thing you do is fast-forward to the song you like. After you listen to it four or five times, you decide to investigate the rest of the tape—only to find that the song you liked is the only worthwhile one. Remember this? That was life without digital music.

I am an older member of the "new generation," which I like to call the Digital Generation. I was lucky enough to have a father who was a "computer geek" before it was considered cool. Because of my father, I am now a gadget freak in every sense.

Digital music players are no exception to my gadget addiction. Having owned several smaller players prior to the Dell DJ that I currently own and love, I grew fond of taking my favorite jams on the road everywhere I went. With the smaller players, the task of loading them up for a day trip was more of a hassle than it is today. Digital media software like Musicmatch makes it so much simpler.

What I love most about digital music today is the freedom. No, not the freedom that made Napster so popular a few years ago, but the freedom to choose the songs I like. Instead of paying $15 for a CD with two or three songs I want and a dozen more I don't, I can legally download 15 songs I actually like—and for the same price! Digital music rocks.

Launching and Configuring Musicmatch

Installing Musicmatch is the first step, but there's more to do before the fun really starts. It's like buying a new CD player. Getting everything hooked up and connected to the rest of the stereo gives you a sense of accomplishment (Rick was beaming with pride when he figured out the audio cables were color-coded all by himself), but until you learn the controls and actually drop in a CD, your new toy isn't that exciting. So let's get everything "wired up" so we can drop some music into our spiffy new player.

Starting Musicmatch for the First Time

To launch Musicmatch, left-click your PC's Start button, navigate to the Musicmatch program group, and then left-click the Musicmatch Jukebox icon. The program will start and you'll see a screen that looks very much like Figure 3-3. If you didn't purchase an upgrade to Musicmatch Jukebox Plus when you first downloaded the program and you'd like to do so now online, click either the Upgrade item in the pull-down menu or the Upgrade to Plus—Click Here line just below the menu. If you want to order the upgrade via phone or mail, pull down the Help menu, choose Purchase Upgrade, and then choose the method you'd like to use. (For more on these options, see Chapter 1.)

If you've purchased an upgrade and received your registration code, enter it by pulling down the Help menu, choosing Registration, and then choosing Enter Key from the submenu that pops up. A window will appear asking for your Upgrade Key. Enter this number; it will be shown in your web browser after you make your

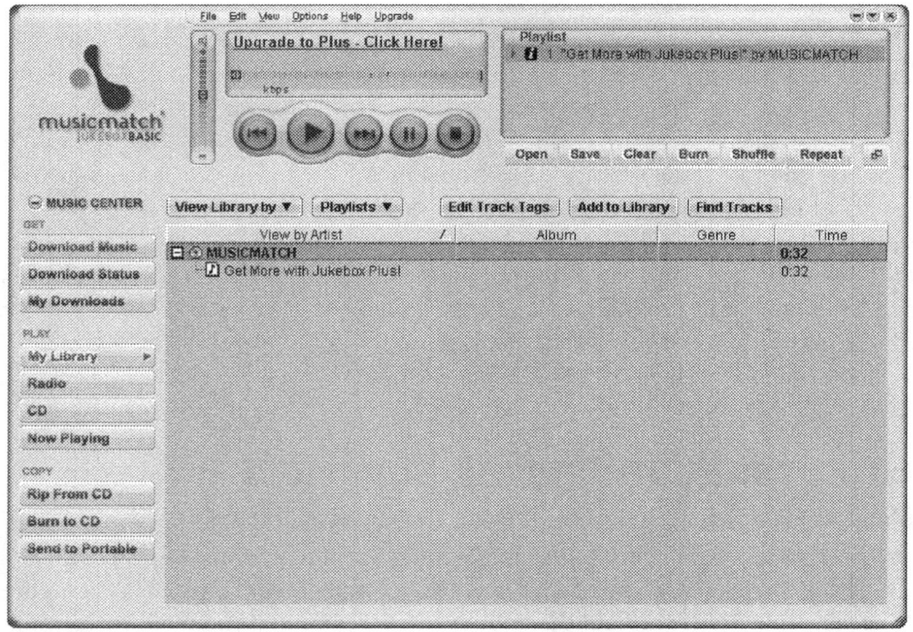

FIGURE 3-3 Musicmatch will look like this the first time you run it. You almost get the impression that the company would like you to buy the Plus version.

purchase, and will be sent in a confirmation e-mail as well. To avoid the possibility of mistyping the key and having to enter it again, highlight the key in your web browser or e-mail program, press CTRL-C (the shortcut for Copy), switch to Musicmatch by pressing ALT-TAB until the program appears, and then press CTRL-V (Paste). Click the OK button and Musicmatch will display a window offering you congratulations for successfully upgrading. And hey, isn't it worth $19.99 to get a sincere "congratulations?" That's a lot cheaper than, say, having a baby or earning your Master's degree.

A Brief Tour of the Musicmatch Screen

Musicmatch has a highly configurable interface. You can fill the screen with multiple modules, or shrink the entire program to a tiny control bar. Let's look at the default setup, as pictured in Figure 3-4.

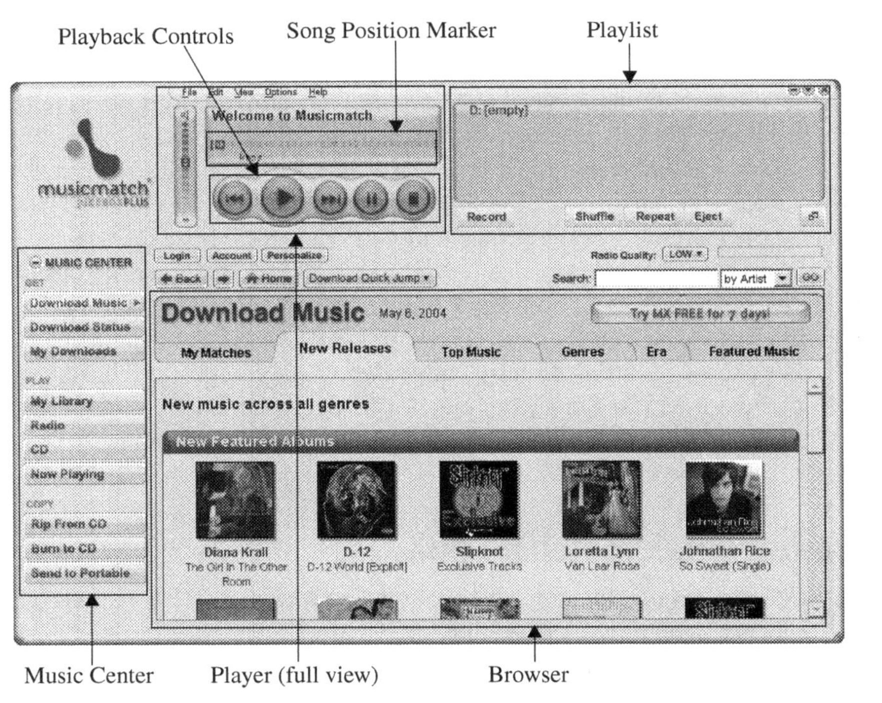

FIGURE 3-4 The components of Musicmatch's default view

In the top-left corner of the Musicmatch window, you'll see the Player, which is the hub of the program. It's always present, though you can shrink it to the size of a Windows title bar by selecting Small Player View from the View pull-down menu. The Player holds the pull-down menus, the Volume control slider, and the playback controls. Anyone who's ever used a stereo should find these controls obvious—from left to right, they're Previous Track, Play, Next Track, Pause, and Stop. We'll cover playback in more detail in Chapter 9.

TIP

Where are the fast forward and rewind controls? Musicmatch omits them, and uses a progress bar directly above the playback controls that lets you take advantage of digital audio's nimbleness and move anywhere in your song instantly. Just grab the position marker on the bar with the mouse pointer, hold down the left button, and drag it to the point in the song you'd like to hear.

To the right of the Player is the Playlist window. Here's where you can view and create the digital equivalent of the "mix cassette" by adding and arranging songs from a variety of sources—but this digital approach doesn't require you to baby-sit a pair of cassette players for 90 minutes. (Again, e-mailing a playlist to the cute girl down the hall to show off your wonderful taste in music isn't likely to have the same effect as making her a mix tape, but that's the price we pay for progress.) Head to Chapter 9 for the full skinny on playlists.

Head to the lower left of the screen and you'll see the Music Center, a vertical row of buttons that give instant access to Musicmatch's most powerful features. Click any of these functions, such as Download Music or My Library, and your choice will either appear in the browser window to their right or in a new window. There's also a row of buttons directly above the browser window; these change depending on your Music Center options. Rather than inundate you with a massive list of buttons and windows—now *there's* some thrilling reading—we'll cover them as we cover the various Musicmatch functions in future chapters.

Changing Musicmatch's Look

The earliest versions of Musicmatch had an interface only a programmer could love, with a dark design that looked like the cybernetic equivalent of a fake-wood-paneled 8-track deck. Today's Musicmatch ships with a sleek, silver-blue interface that's both attractive and functional. But hey, tastes differ—you may prefer something in a nice, basic black for listening to your Anthrax MP3 catalog, or perhaps something in a retro style when you're playing your favorite Sinatra CD. Or if you're listening to some mellow music on a starry night, you might choose a skin like the one in Figure 3-5.

Musicmatch offers about 35 skins on its site, which you can install from within the program. Choose Skins from the View pull-down menu, and then choose Download from the submenu that pops up. Musicmatch's built-in download browser will appear, showing you samples of the various free skins available. Find one you like, click the Download icon next to it, and Musicmatch will download and install the skin automatically.

To swap between skins you've installed, choose Skins from the View pull-down menu. On the submenu that appears, you'll see a list of currently available skins. If you know the name of the skin you'd like to switch to, just left-click it to install it. Otherwise, select Chooser from the menu to bring up a window displaying a list of installed skins. If you want to preview a skin, left-click its name and click the Apply button to activate it. Repeat this process till you find the skin you want to use, then click OK to confirm your selection and close the window.

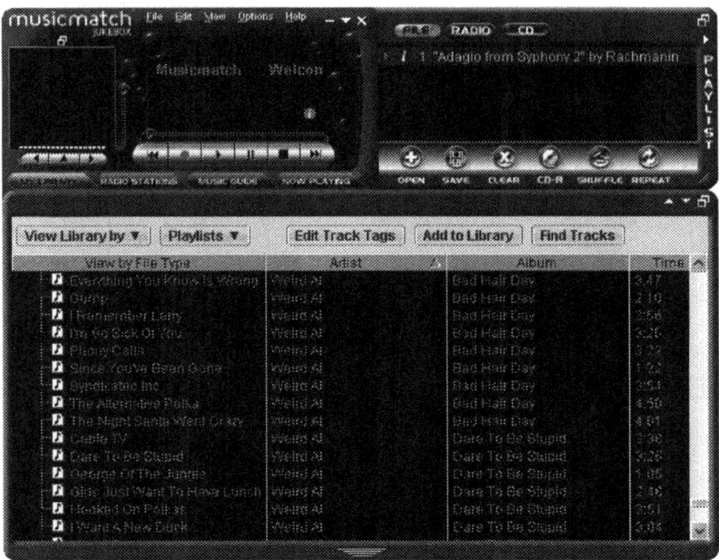

FIGURE 3-5 The dark blue Bloop! theme is just one of many free skins available from Musicmatch.

Customize Musicmatch's Windows

Musicmatch's interface can range in size and function from a tiny toolbar that just gives access to playback and volume controls to a full-screen display that shows the playlist, music library, CD recorder module, visualization window, and more, all at once.

The View menu is the key to customizing Musicmatch. Selecting any module from the menu opens it. Some windows coexist with others, such as the music recorder and library. Others replace existing windows—for instance, opening the Musicmatch Downloads store replaces the library window on the screen.

Most of these windows can be resized by grabbing a corner and holding down the left mouse button while dragging. Many windows can be detached from the main interface and moved around. Move them back next to the main Musicmatch window and you'll find it's "sticky." The window reattaches to the main window and moves along with it.

Go ahead and experiment. If you make a jumble of things, just select Auto Arrange Components from the View menu and Musicmatch will slide everything neatly back into place.

Fancy yourself an artist? Musicmatch offers a free PDF manual called the Skin Development Kit that contains thorough documentation on how to create your own skins. Just open the skin download browser, scroll to the bottom of the page, and click Create Your Own Skin to download the manual.

Playing CDs

Before we wrap up the configuration process, let's take a break and actually listen to some music! (Pause for applause….) We'll leave the creation of a digital music collection alone for the moment and start with a good old-fashioned CD. Musicmatch offers features beyond the typical CD player program. You can reorder songs, for instance, and the program displays the track artist and song titles for most commercial discs. And with just a couple clicks of the mouse, it can convert your CDs to digital MP3, MP3Pro, or WMV format—a feature we'll look at in Chapter 4.

If you put an audio CD in your computer while Musicmatch is running, the interface will automatically switch to CD mode. If you're connected to the Internet, it will also download the CD title and a track listing for the disc so you can view songs by name, not just track number.

If Musicmatch doesn't automatically shift into CD mode when you put a disc in your PC—it may not, for instance, if you're currently playing a digital music file—just click the CD button in the Music Center section on the left side of the screen to put the program in CD mode.

If you chose to leave Musicmatch as the default player for music CDs when you installed the program, you don't even need to launch the program to play CDs. When you put a music disc in your computer, Musicmatch should start up and begin playing automatically. (If Musicmatch isn't set up to automatically play CDs and you want it to do that, go to the program's Options menu and choose Settings, then click the General tab. Click the checkbox next to Music CDs and click OK.)

We covered the basic playback control buttons earlier in the chapter, but Musicmatch has a few additional tricks up its sleeve to improve your CD playback experience. You can double-click any file in the playlist to jump immediately to that song, for instance. Or click a song, hold down the left mouse button, and drag that song title up or down in the playlist to change the order in which Musicmatch plays the songs. And if there's a song on a CD that you don't particularly like, just click it and press the DELETE key on your keyboard to remove it from the playlist. Unfortunately, Musicmatch doesn't let you save CD playlists—once you remove the CD, your changes are lost.

If you double-click the song title or artist name in the Player window while listening to a CD, the browser window will display information on the current album or artist. You'll also get the opportunity to download additional tracks or albums by the artist, or to view related artists that might be of interest to you.

Below the playlist, you'll see four additional icons. From left to right, they are

- **Record** Press this to launch the CD recorder and rip the current CD into digital audio files. We'll cover how to do that in Chapter 4.
- **Shuffle** Play the current CD in random order.

- **Repeat** Repeat the current song. Handy when you have a toddler in the room who wants to hear "Baby Beluga" over and over and over again.
- **Detach** This icon splits the playlist window from the Player, allowing you to rearrange or resize either window independently.

Adding Your Existing Digital Music Library to Musicmatch

As the final step in setting up Musicmatch, you'll need to tell it where to look for digital music. Launch MusicMatch, and then choose Add New Tracks(s) To Music Library from the File menu. The window shown in Figure 3-6 will appear.

Using the folder window on the right, navigate to the folder on your hard disk where your music files are stored. (If you don't have any existing digital music files yet, you can skip ahead to the next chapter.) Before you add your files, check out the options in the lower-left corner of the window:

- **Also add tracks from subfolders** If you keep individual albums or music genres in their own folders, you'll want to be sure this option is selected.
- **Ignore system folders** If you're searching your entire hard drive for music, choosing this option will prevent Musicmatch from adding WAV audio files that it finds in your Windows directory.
- **Skip tracks smaller than (100) KB** Useful for eliminating very small audio files, such as system beeps or short voice interludes between songs that are recorded in separate files.

NOTE *Musicmatch can read songs in MP3, MP3Pro, WAV, and WMA formats only. If you have songs saved in other formats, such as Ogg Vorbis or iTunes AAC format, you'll need to convert them to a supported format or burn them to a CD to use them in Musicmatch. For more on digital audio formats, see Chapter 4.*

Once you've selected a folder, you'll see all the songs contained within it in the file window on the right side of the screen. If you want to add all the files in a folder, click the Select All button above the file window. If you only want to add specific songs, hold down the CTRL key while clicking each song you'd like to add

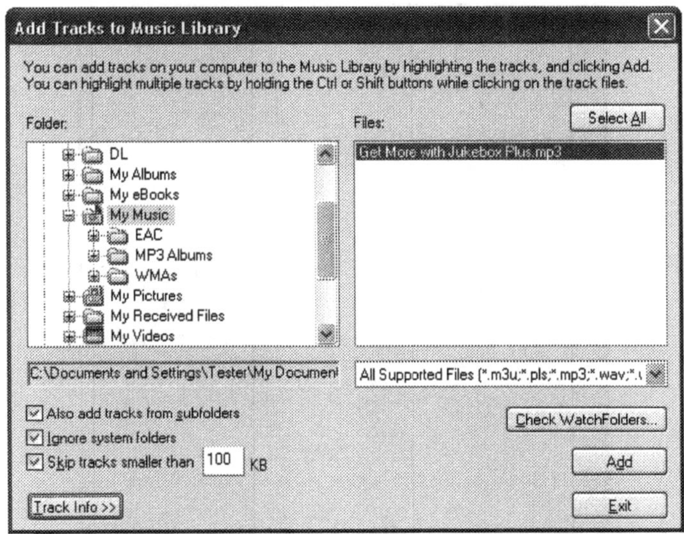

FIGURE 3-6 Pointing Musicmatch at a directory where music files are stored.

to the list. To add a sequence of songs, click the first file, hold down SHIFT, and click the last file in the sequence. Once your songs are selected, click the Add button to add the tunes to your music library.

Repeat this process for each directory that contains music files. If your music library is spread out among multiple directories or even drives, you may find it easier to manage if you move all the tunes to a central location, but Musicmatch can handle them just as well, even if they're scattered around your computer.

Musicmatch lets you save multiple music libraries. This can be handy if some of your music is on removable media or a network. We'll cover how to do this, and how to get the most out of music libraries, in Chapter 9.

Musicmatch adds new songs to your library when you purchase them from Musicmatch Downloads or use Musicmatch to rip them from CD. But if you copy them from another computer or download or rip them outside of Musicmatch, they must be added manually. To avoid this hassle, Musicmatch offers WatchFolders. You can designate directories on your computer that Musicmatch will watch for new files. If it finds supported music or playlist files, they'll be added to the library automatically.

FIGURE 3-7 Any songs added to directories marked as WatchFolders are automatically added to your music library.

To designate WatchFolders, choose WatchFolders from the File pull-down menu. The window shown in Figure 3-7 will appear. First, make sure that Enable WatchFolders is checked. Now click the Add button and navigate to the folder you want to watch using the directory browser that will pop up. Once you've selected a folder, click OK. You can repeat the process if you want to watch multiple folders.

WatchFolders will watch these directories for new files while Musicmatch is running. To have the program recognize new additions made when Musicmatch isn't loaded, select the Always Check WatchFolders At Startup checkbox. If your WatchFolders contain a lot of songs, this could increase the time it takes Musicmatch to start up dramatically. An alternative is to use the Check WatchFolders Now… button—found on this screen and on the Add New Tracks window—when you know you added new tunes to your library between Musicmatch sessions.

That's it! Musicmatch is installed, configured, and ready to play. If you're interested in learning how to transfer your CD, tape, and record collections to your digital music library or how to download music online, read on to the next section. If your library is already in order and you'd like to start playing some music, skip ahead to Chapter 9, then come back and check out the intervening chapters later.

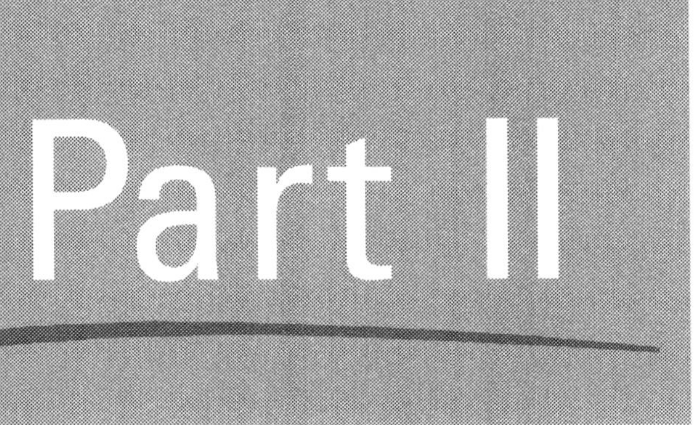

Build and Manage a Music Library

Chapter 4

Rip Songs from CDs

How to...

- Convert your CD library into digital audio
- Understand bit rates
- Choose between MP3, mp3PRO, and WMA formats
- Decide where to store your songs
- Customize song filenames
- Manually enter track information
- Adjust advanced recording options

"Let 'er rip, let it fly."—Dixie Chicks, band

"Art is making something out of nothing and selling it."—Frank Zappa, musician

To twist Frank Zappa's words around a bit, ripping is the process of making nothing out of something—that is, making a digital music file from a physical CD. When you rip a song, you create a copy of the digital data contained on the CD, and then store it on your computer's hard drive. Generally these files are compressed so that they take up less space—otherwise, you'd only be able to fit about six-and-a-half minutes of music on a 64MB MP3 player, instead of an hour or two. The downside of compression is that it's "lossy"—that is, it sacrifices some of the sound detail to make a smaller file. There are ways to minimize this loss; you'll learn about those in this chapter.

Notice we talk about "digital music" and not "MP3." That's because there's a bunch of different digital music formats out there. Musicmatch supports MP3, mp3PRO, WMA, and WAV formats. As you delve deeper into digital music, you'll also find files in AAC (used by iTunes), Ogg Vorbis, and a few other obscure formats.

NOTE *Though CDs are the easiest music sources to rip since the data is already in digital format, you can also rip music from old analog sources, such as cassettes and record albums. See Chapter 5 for the scoop.*

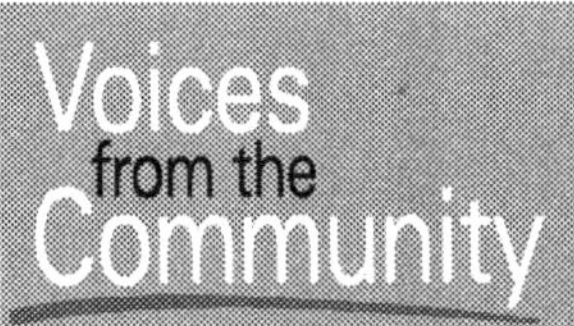

Forget the Radio—for New Music, the Internet Is Where It's At

Dave Johnson, co-author of How to Do Everything with MP3 and Digital Music, *has one regret in life: that he didn't grow up to be a rock star. (That probably explains his decision to wear black most days of the week.) Dave is a music lover in the truest sense of the word, and a few years back he used Musicmatch to convert his library of 400+ CDs to MP3 format. Here he discusses his penchant for new music and one possible future for its distribution.*

New music. To my ears, those are the two most exciting words on earth. I live for the promise of new songs from new artists and from my existing favorites. And though I go to live shows as frequently as I can, I've found that the Internet is now the easiest way to get access to new songs and discover new bands.

Case in point: throwingmusic.com. Perhaps my favorite artist of all time is Kristin Hersh, the genius behind the cult alternative band Throwing Muses. Kristin maintains a web site called throwingmusic.com, and publishes new music there on a monthly basis. If you are already a Muses fan, you can subscribe to her Works in Progress program for $15 and get a new MP3 every month of the year. Some songs are unreleased demos of older, classic material; other songs are new, in-development tracks for her next record. Either way, they're always delicious.

Some artists have talked about connecting more directly with their fans for a long time, but it's only in the last few years that any of it has started to become a reality. The success of Works in Progress suggests that eventually, most artists will bypass the big record companies and offer music directly to the fans. In the meantime, I've got Kristin and Works in Progress.

Ripping a CD

There's a lot to consider before you go ripping your entire CD collection: bit rates, formats, where to store your songs, whether to bother ripping your *William Shatner Sings* CDs.... You'll have to consider the consequences of the last one yourself, but we can help with the rest. Before we start talking tech though, let's get straight to the action and rip a CD using Musicmatch's default settings, which produce "CD quality" 128-Kbps digital audio files. (We'd argue that you need at least 192 Kbps to approximate CD quality; look for more on bit rates in a couple of pages.)

To rip an entire CD to MP3 format, do the following:

1. Launch Musicmatch.
2. Insert the CD you want to copy. The CD may start playing automatically. You can click the Stop button on the Player window if you'd like, but playback will stop automatically when you begin recording.
3. From the View pull-down menu, choose Recorder. The Recorder window will appear, as seen in Figure 4-1.
4. Click the Record button—it's the leftmost button, with a large red circle in it.
5. Musicmatch will begin encoding (that is, converting) your songs in MP3 format. If you're connected to the Internet and the CD is recognized by Musicmatch, a status window directly above the Record button will show you the name of the song being recorded. A progress bar indicates how much of the current song has been converted.
6. When Musicmatch finishes copying the disc, it will eject the CD. The resulting MP3 files are stored in the music folder you chose during the setup process in Chapter 3. By default, this is My Documents/My Music. The album and its songs will also be listed in your music library.

NOTE *If another program, such as Windows Media Player or WinAMP, launched when you inserted the CD, you should close that program before ripping. Then consider setting Musicmatch to the default player for CD audio by choosing Settings from the Options window, clicking the General tab, and checking the box labeled Music CDs.*

That's all there is to it! You've ripped a CD. Each song is stored in an individual file, encoded at 128,000 bits per second (or 128-Kbps), which Musicmatch calls CD quality. These files take up about one megabyte per minute of recording, so a 60-minute CD will take about 60MB of hard drive space.

TIP *If you don't want to rip all the songs from a CD, remove the checkmarks next to the songs you don't want to record. Musicmatch will rip only the checked songs.*

FIGURE 4-1 Musicmatch's Recorder, ready for action

Give the songs you've just ripped a listen, preferably on a good set of headphones. If you're feeling ambitious, you might even listen to the CD original first, then play the MP3. If you're happy with the quality of the music and the other default choices Musicmatch offers, you may be all set. But Musicmatch offers a wealth of options for customizing how it records music. You can tweak filenames, recording quality, recording format, and much more. So even if your "rip test" brought out the finest details of your *The Monkees Greatest Hits* disc, you may still want to read through the rest of this chapter.

(Disclaimer: Denny actually owns *The Monkees Greatest Hits,* so we're not making fun of anyone here. Really.)

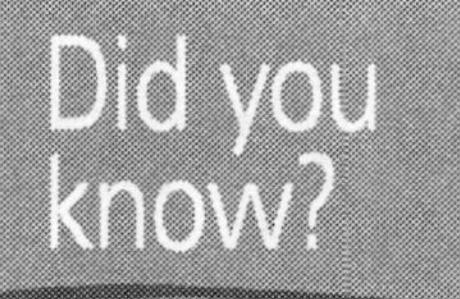

Why It's Called Ripping

Ripping actually refers to the process of copying digital data from a CD to the computer. Why call it "ripping" instead of "copying?" Well, probably because "ripping" sounds a whole heck of a lot cooler. The term originated on the Internet, though its exact origin has been lost to time.

Technically, ripping simply refers to the initial copying process, not the subsequent compression into a format like MP3 or WMV. However, common usage often redefines words, and this is one of those cases. Music fans typically use "ripping" to refer to the entire process of copying and converting songs from CD to compressed digital music files.

Understanding Bit Rates

Reading about digital music, you'll inevitably run into terms like "an MP3 song recorded at a bit rate of 128-Kbps." "Huh?" you ask, "what's a "kay-bips?" The "k" stands for kilo, or thousand, and the "bps" is shorthand for "bits per second." Essentially, the bit rate describes how many bits of data are used to describe each second of music when it's encoded (that is, converted or translated) to a compressed digital music file. The more bits you use—that is, the higher the bit rate—the truer the sound is to the original. Lowering the bit rate makes for smaller files, but also sacrifices some of the "detail" of the sound.

Choosing which bit rate to use to encode your music is a very personal decision that depends on a wide variety of factors. These include

- Your "ear" for music. Can you hear the difference between high and low bit rates? Some users are perfectly happy with 128-Kbps MP3 songs. Others with a more demanding ear are only happy with 192 Kbps or higher.
- Whether size matters. If you're using a 64MB MP3 player, you may want to sacrifice some music quality in order to get longer play. If you have a 20GB player, size may not be a factor at all. And if you have a computer with a 160GB hard drive, size *really* doesn't matter.

- The devices you'll be using. Some players, particularly older models and some personal digital assistants (PDAs), don't handle very high or very low bit rates, or variable bit rate files. (More on those in a moment.)
- The kind of music you listen to. Not to knock anyone's favorite artist, but if your library is packed with the works of Tenacious D, Spinal Tap, Ratt, and Black Flag, you can probably record your music at a lower bit rate without perceived loss of quality than someone listening to Bach, Brahms, Paganini, and Pink Floyd.
- Your music format of choice. Due to differences in how compression is handled, WMA and Mp3PRO can manage higher-quality music at lower bit rates than MP3. A 64-Kbps WMA or Mp3PRO file is similar in quality to a 128-Kbps MP3. See the "Choosing an Encoding Format" section later in this chapter to learn about these and other kinds of digital audio files.

There's another decision to make as well if you're planning to rip CDs using the MP3 or Mp3PRO format—CBR (Constant Bit Rate) versus VBR (Variable Bit Rate) encoding. CBR uses a single bit rate throughout the entire song. So if a passage is relatively silent or simple, it's represented by just as much data as a complex passage with multiple instruments and vocals. That means space is wasted on the simpler parts of the song, while more complex portions of the song may not have enough detail to be fully represented. VBR is an unquestionably superior way to record, as it produces a higher and more consistent quality level. VBR varies the bit rate depending on the complexity of the music. If the encoder encounters a segment with a single instrument or a quiet vocal, it will use a slow bit rate, which will still be plenty to capture all the musical details. As passages get more complex, the bit rate will speed up in order not to miss any musical detail.

NOTE *Windows Media Player version 9 added support for VBR encoding of WMA files, a first for that format. However, MusicMatch 8.2, the most current version as this was written, supports encoding WMA only in CBR format.*

You might wonder why there's even any question as to which to use, since VBR is obviously superior. But VBR has a few caveats. First, its files can be somewhat larger than CBR tunes, particularly with more complex music. You can predict how large a CBR MP3 file will be when encoded—not so with VBR. Also, because many MP3 players calculate elapsed/remaining time by counting how many bits of the file have been played so far, readouts that display how much time has elapsed or is left in a song are often inaccurate. And finally, a few portable players don't support VBR playback—though that limitation falls mostly on older models.

Musicmatch uses a somewhat unusual method of setting VBR quality. While some encoders let you set VBR quality by average (and sometimes maximum and minimum) bit rates, Musicmatch uses a "quality percentage" rating. A setting of 70 percent VBR provides quality similar to 192-Kbps CBR files, but with a smaller file size. It's a good compromise when space is somewhat of a concern, but you don't want to sacrifice music quality.

Generally, we suggest you stick with 128-Kbps CBR as a minimum for MP3, and 64 Kbps for mp3PRO and WMA. The exception is encoding spoken-word material such as audiobooks and radio shows, where you can dramatically lower the bit rate with little loss of quality.

To set the bit rate for CD ripping, click the Options button on the Recorder window to bring up the Settings window shown in Figure 4-2.

The following table shows suggested bit rates for a variety of playback devices. These are guidelines only, of course, and they favor quality over size. You may want to record the same song at a number of bit rates and see what the sweet spot is for your own ears. Rick is fine with 64-Kbps WMA songs, for instance, while Denny finds that WMAs recorded at less than 96 Kbps show a noticeable degradation over the CD versions. Of course, the fact that Denny did his listening tests by ripping Pink Floyd's *Animals,* while Rick dug out his *Karaoke: Hits of Britney Spears* for the comparison, might have a little something to do with it.

Suggested Bit Rate Settings

Usage	MP3	Mp3PRO	WMA
Music on a portable player with <256MB	128 Kbps	64 Kbps	64 Kbps
Music on a portable player with 256MB to 4GB	70% VBR	70% VBR	96 Kbps
Music on a portable player with >4GB	80% VBR	80% VBR	160 Kbps
Music on a desktop computer	100% VBR	100% VBR	192 Kbps
Spoken word (audiobooks, talk radio)	32 Kbps	32 Kbps	32 Kbps

Choosing an Encoding Format

Musicmatch can rip CDs in four formats: MP3, WMA, mp3PRO, and WAV. You can find out more about MP3 and WMA—the two most popular audio formats the program supports—in Chapter 1.

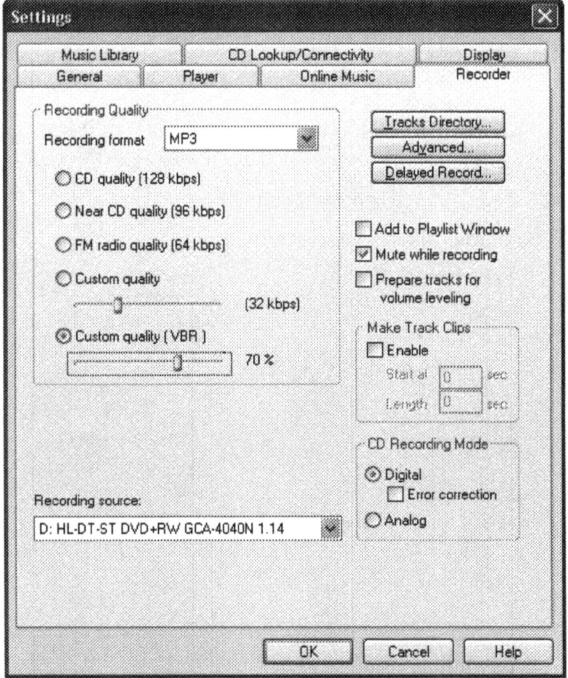

FIGURE 4-2 The recording Settings window is where you'll choose format, bit rate, and a variety of other options.

The audio format setting is in the same window as the bit rate adjustments. Click the Options button on the Recorder window to adjust the format settings; you'll see the screen in Figure 4-3.

Let's take a quick look at the formats:

- **MP3** MPEG audio layer 3 is by far the most popular, and most universal, format for digital audio files. The sound quality is excellent at higher bit rates, it supports VBR (variable bit rate) encoding to ensure consistent sound reproduction throughout a song, and just about any electronic device that handles digital music files supports MP3 playback. It currently has no digital rights management (a.k.a., copy protection) built in, so its use for commercial music downloads is extremely rare.

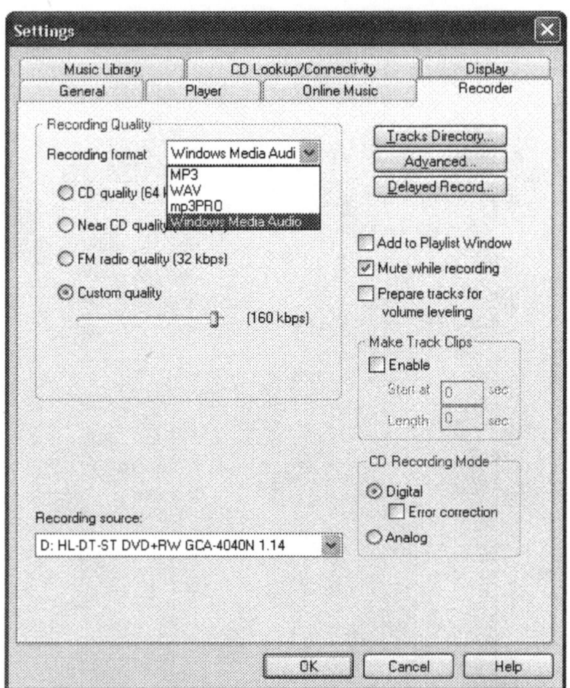

FIGURE 4-3 Choose your recording format from the drop-down menu.

- **WMA** Windows Media Audio is the strongest competitor to MP3. At lower bit rates, it offers similar sound quality in a file that's often half the size of an MP3. It supports digital rights management, making it the format of choice for the majority of commercial online music providers. Though the newest Windows Media release, version 9, adds support for VBR encoding, this feature wasn't yet supported in Musicmatch 8.2. Not long ago, few portable players supported WMA; today, you can find WMA support in a variety of hard disk–based, Flash-RAM, and CD-based digital music players, in addition to wireless home media center players.
- **mp3PRO** This format is based on the traditional MP3 file format, but it uses a technology called Spectral Band Replication (SBR) to better replicate high-frequency sounds in highly compressed music. This allows mp3Pro songs to provide similar quality as WMA files at lower bit rates, saving

space over traditional MP3 tunes. mp3Pro songs can actually play on devices that support only MP3—the SBR information is simply ignored. The quality suffers significantly without mp3Pro support, however. Relatively few players—at press time just a handful of offerings from RCA and Philips—support mp3Pro.

- **WAV** Short for WAVeform audio format, this is the Windows standard format for storing uncompressed audio. Because there's no compression, you can rip a song from CD to a WAV file and maintain 100 percent of its original quality. However, the files are huge; we're talking 30MB for a three-minute song. Though a few portable players support WAV format, the massive size of the files makes transferring and storing them on portables impractical.

So, how to choose a format to rip to? MP3 is the safest bet—as we said, you can play MP3 audio on just about any device that plays digital music. If you want to be able to play the songs you rip on a variety of devices, including portable music players, PDAs, cutting-edge DVD players, and so on, then MP3 is the way to go.

If you're a fan of consistency and you plan to purchase music online, then WMA may be the format of choice, as ripping in that format will help you avoid having a mix of MP3 and WMA tunes. WMA is used by the Musicmatch Downloads store, Napster 2.0, and a variety of other online music retailers. Keep in mind, however, that the WMA files you download from commercial services include digital rights management copy protection, and they can't be freely copied between systems or given to friends or family members. WMA files you create yourself using Musicmatch don't suffer from these restrictions, of course.

WMA is also a good choice if space is a consideration since you can rip files at lower bit rates than MP3 without sacrificing quality.

TIP *There's no reason you can't double-dip when it comes to ripping. That is, rip your songs once in MP3 format and again in WMA. You'll probably want to store them in different folders on your hard drive, but at least then you'll have the best of both worlds: MP3s for devices that don't support WMA, WMA for devices that do. Also, keep in mind that Musicmatch doesn't care if you mix and match. You can rip your songs as MP3s, purchase WMAs from Musicmatch and other services, and so on. The software is pretty much platform-agnostic. The only major format it can't play is AAC—the format of songs purchased from Apple's iTunes store.*

mp3PRO is an interesting format, but it has little to recommend it. Its sound quality and compression are similar to WMA, but it doesn't enjoy nearly as much support on portable players, so WMA is the better choice under most circumstances. You can play mp3PRO songs on players that only support standard MP3, but the audio quality is poor, so that's no real advantage. If you have an aversion to Microsoft products, or you own one of the few portable players that supports it, there might be reason to choose mp3PRO. Otherwise, go for WMA if maximum compression is a requirement.

NOTE *mp3PRO ripping support is included only with Musicmatch Jukebox Plus. It's not available as an option if you're using the Basic version.*

Other Formats You May Encounter

Musicmatch rips—and plays—only MP3, WMA, mp3PRO, and WAV files. However, you may find music online in a variety of other formats. You'll need to convert these to a supported format to play them in Musicmatch—this can often be accomplished by burning the files to CD and then ripping the CD in Musicmatch. These are the other formats you're likely to encounter:

- **AAC** Short for Advanced Audio Coding, this format is used by Apple's iTunes store. It ranks between MP3 and WMA in compression and quality.
- **ATRAC** An acronym for Adaptive TRansform Acoustic Coding, Sony's proprietary music format is used by its Connect music store. This format can only be played on PCs and Sony portable players. Also, it can only be stored on MagicGate Memory Stick cards, and Sony VAIO computers are the sole machines that can burn standard CDs from ATRAC songs. It's a viable choice, but just for all-Sony households.
- **OGG** Short for Ogg Vorbis, this open-source format was created as a response to licensing fees charged for distributing software that encodes in MP3 format. Quality and compression are similar to MP3. A few portable players from Neuros, iRiver, and even Rio support the format in addition to MP3.

Ripping to WAV format is mostly useful for creating your own mix CDs since there's no quality loss. You can rip songs from a variety of CDs, and then use Musicmatch to create a new playlist and burn them to a CD-R. (See Chapter 10 for the full scoop on just how to do this.) Because the files are so large, though, you'll probably want to delete them after creating your new CD.

Storing and Naming Your Music

The default location for storing ripped CDs is My Documents/My Music. That's fine when you have enough space on your C: drive to store all of your MP3 songs. In some cases, though, you may need more room. When Denny decided to rip the 150-plus CDs he and his wife had accumulated over the years, he set aside room on a second drive that he had added to his PC specifically to store audio and video files. Musicmatch not only lets you customize where you store your music files, but also how you name them.

Where to Put It

Setting where you'd like Musicmatch to store the songs you rip couldn't be easier. Left-click the Options button on the Recorder window to bring up the Recorder Settings window (shown earlier in this chapter in Figures 4-2 and 4-3). Click the Tracks Directory button to bring up the New Tracks Directory Options window, shown in Figure 4-4.

The current directory for ripped songs is shown at the top of the screen. To change the setting, click the ellipsis (...) button next to the directory name. A window will open allowing you to select the folder you want to use to store files, as seen in Figure 4-5.

NOTE *The selection window doesn't allow you to create a new folder. If the folder you want to use to store your music doesn't already exist, you'll need to create it using the Windows Explorer or My Computer New Folder command, then choose that folder from within Musicmatch.*

Click the folder you want to use, and then click OK to select it. You'll be returned to the New Tracks Directory Options window. Don't close it yet; we still have some customization to do.

Musicmatch lets you store songs in subfolders within the main music folder, organized by artist and album. In the section labeled Make Sub-Path Using, shown in Figure 4-4, you'll see two checkboxes labeled Artist and Album. Leaving both of

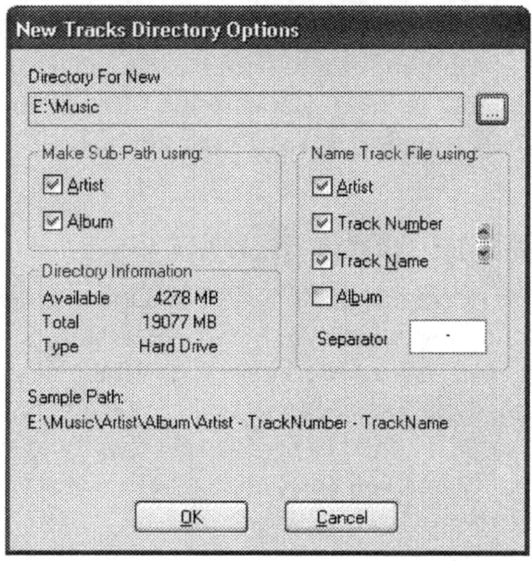

FIGURE 4-4 The New Tracks Directory Options window lets you choose where to store your songs, and how they should be named.

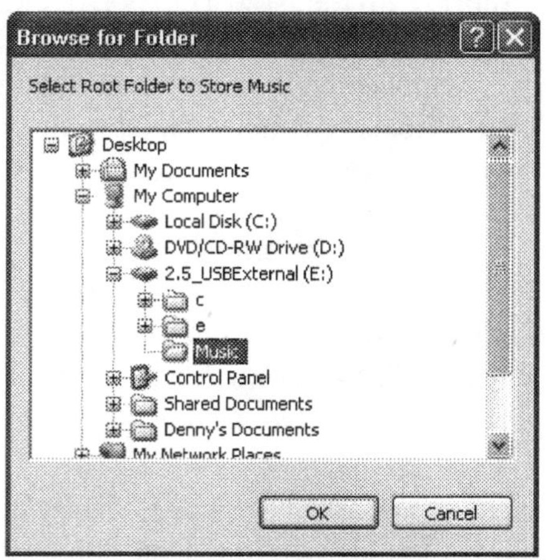

FIGURE 4-5 Choosing a folder to store ripped tunes in

these checked organizes your songs by artist, with individual albums stored in the artist's directory. For instance, if you were looking for the song "Radio Free Europe," you'd find it stored in the directory REM\Murmer in your music folder.

If you uncheck the Artist checkbox, Album folders will be created in the main music directory. Deselecting the Album checkbox will cause all songs by an artist to be placed in a single folder together, rather than sorted by album. Deselecting both checkboxes will cause all your ripped songs to be placed in the main music directory. That could be an organizational disaster if you rip your entire CD collection that way, but it could be useful if you're just ripping a couple of songs each from a variety of CDs. Rip them to the main directory, and then create a "Misc" directory for individual songs and move the files there manually.

What to Call It

Musicmatch lets you customize how the files are named. The program itself doesn't normally use filenames to organize tunes; instead, it uses the information contained within the files, in ID3 tags, if it's present. (See the sidebar "The Hidden Name: Introduction to ID3 Tags" for more information on ID3.) However, choosing an optimal file-naming scheme is important if you're planning to access the files outside of Musicmatch, using Windows or other music-playback programs.

To customize how Musicmatch names its files, click the Options button on the Recorder window, then click the Tracks Directory button to bring up the window shown in Figure 4-6. On the right side of the window, you'll see a section labeled Name Track File Using. This is where you can customize what information is used to name your files.

There are four choices in the section: Artist, Album, Track Name, and Track Number. You probably don't want to select all of them. This can result in the creation of really long filenames, such as Pink Floyd—Dark Side of the Moon—04—The Great Gig in the Sky. Not only are names this long cumbersome to view in Windows, but they can also be truncated when copied to CD-R discs or Macintosh computers. Note that Musicmatch doesn't typically use the filename to identify songs. Instead, it uses information stored in the file's ID3 Tag.

When choosing a naming scheme, keep in mind that Windows sorts files alphabetically, so if you want to view songs in the same order they're stored in on the album, you'll want to be sure that the track number is the first thing that's "different" in the filename so that it'll be used for sorting purposes. The most common schemes for naming files are "artist—track number—track name" (the one we use, and recommend) and "track number—track name," with album (and possibly artist) information stored in the folder name.

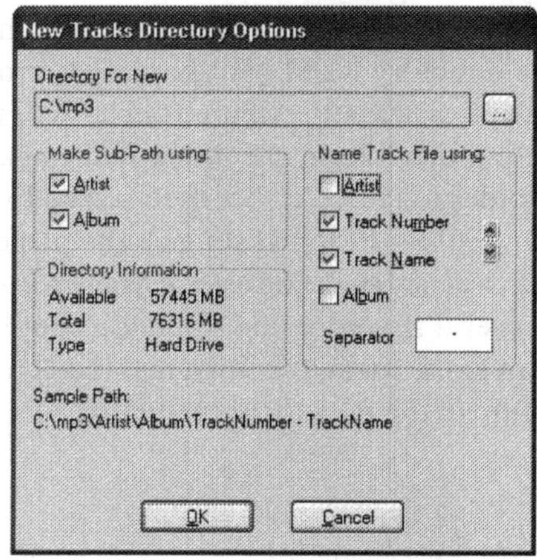

FIGURE 4-6 Customizing the filenames used for the music you rip

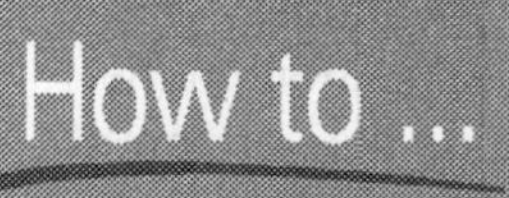

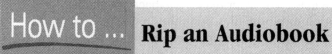

Rip an Audiobook

You can rip audiobook CDs as easily as you can music CDs. There are a few things to keep in mind though.

- If the audiobook is purely spoken-word, you can use a very low bit rate for recording. An audiobook typically sounds just fine at 32 Kbps, even though music at that bit rate would be a muddy mess. This is particularly important since audiobooks tend to run much longer than typical music albums.
- You may want to store your audiobook files in another directory, separate from your music rips. Similarly, you might want to create a separate Music Library just for them, so you don't get James Joyce mixed in with your James Brown next time you set Musicmatch to Shuffle play.

- When setting up filenames, be sure the track number is at the beginning or following the artist name so that the files will be played back in the proper order on players that default to playing back filenames alphabetically, such as CD-R–supporting players and certain portable audio players. It's not that big a deal if "When the Levee Breaks" gets played before "Black Dog," but if Poirot stumbles across the bloody knife before the murder is committed, you're in for a surreal listening experience.

To set the filename scheme, you click the checkboxes next to the elements you want to include, and then set the order of the elements. To move an element, click its name, then click the up and down arrows to the right of the name until the element is in the right spot in the sequence. Repeat this process for each element until you have the filename as you'd like it. You can preview how the filename will look at the bottom of the options window, where a sample path and filename is shown.

CD Lookup, and Manual Track Info Entry

When you rip a CD, Musicmatch accesses its Internet CD Lookup service to automatically gather the name of the CD, artists, tracks, and so on. This saves you the hassle of typing (and possibly mistyping) the name of every song. In those rare cases that a disc isn't included in the CD Lookup database—such as an extremely obscure indie band, or a custom mix CD—you can input the track information manually.

To enable the CD Lookup service, choose Settings from the Options pull-down menu, and then click the tab labeled CD Lookup/Connectivity. Now click the checkbox labeled Enable CD Lookup Service. If you have a broadband Internet connection—or if you don't mind Musicmatch triggering your dial-up ISP when you rip CDs, you're all set. If you use dial-up Internet and you don't want Musicmatch to force your computer to go online, click Enable Deferred CD Lookup Service. With this setting active, Musicmatch will go ahead and rip your CDs, and then next time you're connected to the Internet with Musicmatch loaded, the program will access the Lookup service and fill in the missing track information for the songs you ripped offline.

The setting Prompt To Submit CD Information When Not Found will cause Musicmatch to ask you if you want to send information about unknown CDs to its server for the use of others. If you're ripping some of the few commercial CDs that aren't in the CD Lookup database, this option makes sense to enable. If you're ripping a mix CD created by your girlfriend or any other CD that's not commonly available (such as that custom CD you created of yourself singing "Papa Don't Preach" at the state fair last year), you'll want to pass on the opportunity to submit the track list to Musicmatch, since the information won't be useful for anyone.

When you insert a CD that's not recognized by the CD Lookup service, the window shown in Figure 4-7 will appear. If it's a commercial CD that you think should be in the database, you can try typing the artist or album name and clicking the Search button. Sometimes a CD's layout doesn't exactly match the information in the CD Lookup database—it might be a record club CD, an import, or a custom copy with a slightly different track layout, for instance. If the album appears in the list, click its name and click the Select button. Otherwise, click the Not Found button so you can enter the information manually.

The Submit CD Information window will appear. Type the Artist and Album info in the appropriate spots, and then select the most appropriate genre from the pop-up menu. Now click each track name and enter the appropriate song name. When you finish, click the OK button to use this information. It'll be used both to generate filenames and to embed ID3 tag information in the songs.

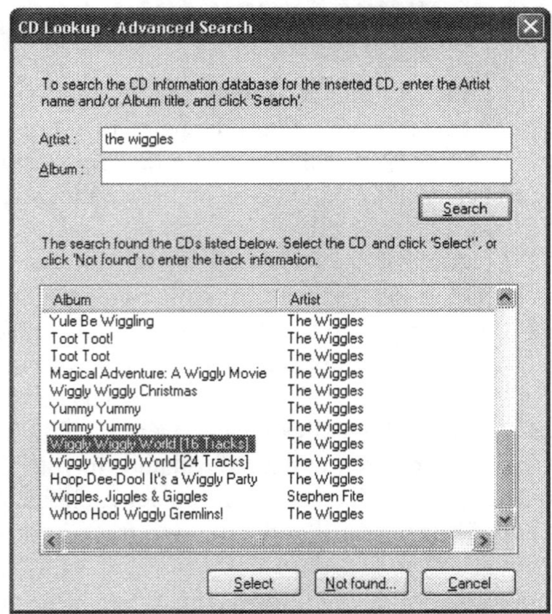

FIGURE 4-7 Selecting the proper album from a list of close matches in the CD Lookup database

The Hidden Name: Introduction to ID3 Tags

The filename isn't the only place where information about the song is stored. A number of tidbits are contained right in the song file itself, in a small chunk of data at the end of the song called an *ID3 tag*. (There was never an ID1 or ID2; the name is meant to represent "identification for MP3.") The ID3 tag stores the song title, artist, album, year, track number, genre, and a comment. If an ID3 tag is present, Musicmatch uses the ID3 information, not the filename, to gather information about your music files.

Musicmatch automatically embeds ID3 tag information in your MP3 songs, based on the information it downloads about your CD when you rip it, or the information you manually enter for CDs not in the Musicmatch CD Lookup database.

Note that some older music rippers don't include ID3 tag information in the file, and many songs you find on file-sharing services lack this info as well. See Chapter 8 for details on how to fix missing ID3 tag information.

WMA songs have the same sort of tag information embedded in them, but the term ID3 refers specifically to MP3 tunes.

Advanced Options

The Recorder Settings window offers a number of other options, some more useful than others. Looking at the functions we haven't covered yet, starting from top right in the window, which we present as a reminder in Figure 4-8, we have

- **Advanced** Clicking this button brings up a group of settings that should be adjusted by advanced users. It allows you to adjust settings such as how Digital Audio Extraction takes place, or how much frequency bandwidth the encoder should use. We suggest leaving the settings in this window alone, as they can potentially affect the quality and accuracy of your CD rips.
- **Delayed Record** This feature lets you tell Musicmatch to start recording at a specific time. It's not really useful for ripping CDs, but could be handy if, say, you wanted to record a radio show using a stereo connected to your computer's Line In connector.
- **Add to Playlist Window** Songs will be added to the current playlist as they're ripped.

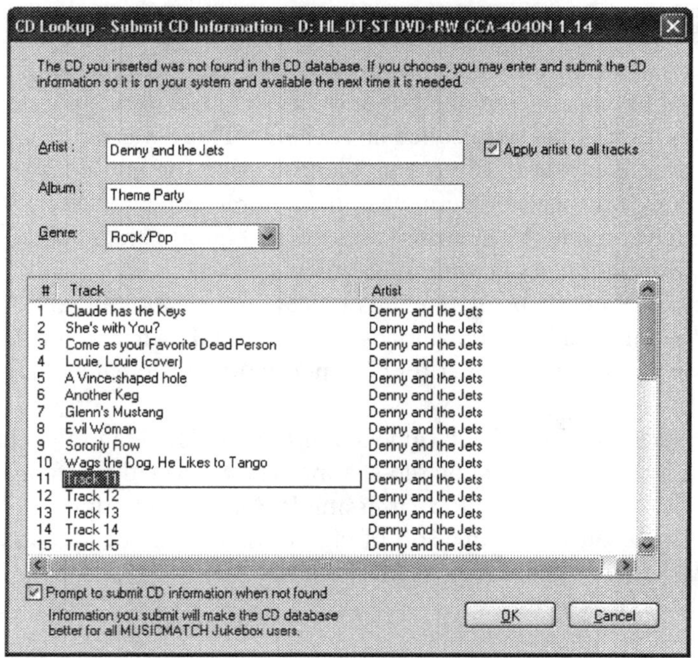

FIGURE 4-8 The Recorder Settings window offers options for choosing recording modes, volume leveling, and other advanced features.

- **Mute while Recording** Unless this is selected, Musicmatch plays songs while recording them. Note that deselecting this option (which is on by default) can dramatically increase the amount of time it takes to rip a CD.
- **Prepare tracks for volume leveling** This processes each song so that it can be played back with the volume leveling feature active. Volume leveling, used during playback and when burning songs to CD or transferring them to a portable player, ensures that songs from different sources play back with a consistent volume. If you've ever created a playlist and nearly jumped out of your seat because a song was twice as loud as the one before it, you'll appreciate this feature.
- **Make Track Clips** If you want to include short samples of songs for inclusion on a web site, enable this option and set your recording options to utilize a low bit rate. You can create clips of any length, starting at any point in the song.

- **CD Recording Mode** Under most circumstances, you'll want to use the default setting, Digital. This actually looks at the ones and zeroes on the CD, using an exact digital copy of the song to create the compressed music. Selecting the Error Correction checkbox helps eliminate distortion that can occur with some drives or scratched CDs, at the expense of longer recording time. The Analog option actually plays the CD and records the resulting sound, similar to connecting a microphone. Using analog both degrades the quality and makes the songs record at 1x speed, compared to an average of about 12x for digital recording using Musicmatch Jukebox Plus. You'll generally only use analog recording with very old CD-ROM drives that don't support digital extraction.
- **Recording source** This pop-up menu lets you choose between multiple CD-ROM drives for recording, and allows you to select Line In, Mic In, or System Mixer as a recording source. The latter options are primarily useful when doing live recordings or recoding from a tape recorder, record player, or other source. We'll cover those in the next chapter.

Picking a Recording Format

Recording formats are a very subjective thing. What sounds just fine to the average Joe or Joanne might make an audiophile cringe. So which formats and bit rates do Rick and Denny use?

Denny: I'm a big fan of MP3 myself. Though WMA and mp3Pro offer a size advantage, MP3 is the universal format that works for just about everything. When recording music with Musicmatch Jukebox, I use MP3 format with the Custom Quality (VBR) setting at 90 percent. That creates some pretty big files, but the least capacious device I use for playback is an iPod Mini. Even with "just" 4 gigabytes of storage, that's many hours of music despite MP3's more "bloated" file sizes.

Rick: Tough call. I'm a neat freak, and the idea of having both MP3 and WMA files littering my hard drive strikes me as, well, messy. That said, although the vast majority of my music collection is in MP3 format, I'm increasingly leaning towards WMA. That's because most of the music I purchase online is in that format, and I really think that a 128-Kbps WMA sounds better than a 128-Kbps MP3. In other words, between two songs files that are the exact same size, WMA is obviously the better choice. But I have to point out my distaste for the Draconian digital-rights management (DRM) features built into music-store WMA files. Bleh.

Chapter 5

Rescue Albums and Cassettes

How to...

- Identify audio connections on your PC
- Properly amplify record players and other analog sources
- Connect analog audio gear to your PC
- Ensure high-quality signals
- Set optimal audio levels
- Record LPs and 45s with Musicmatch
- Work with the Auto Song Detect feature
- Record cassette tapes
- Choose an audio editor
- Edit or split recorded audio files
- Remove noise from recorded files
- Add ID3 tags to album and cassette recordings

"After silence, that which comes nearest to expressing the inexpressible is music." —Aldous Huxley, English novelist

Anyone born prior to 1970 probably has a fairly substantial collection of record albums and/or cassettes stashed away in a closet or basement. This is perfectly good music you've bought and paid for, so why should it sit around collecting dust? Do you have to buy it again in digital format just to listen to it on your PC, a CD, or a portable player? Heck, no!

In this chapter, you're going to use Musicmatch to resurrect that idle media, to bring those beloved songs into the digital age once and for all. It's time for *Zenyatta Mondatta* (a Police album, for those of you wondering what the heck those two words are) to live again!

Before we proceed, it's important that you understand the distinction between ripping songs from CDs, which are digital, and copying them from albums and cassettes, which are analog. Indeed, the process of making a copy from an analog source—such as an LP record or cassette—is by definition imperfect. You'll get noise, imperfections in the analog media, and the inevitable degradation that occurs just by making a copy. Of course, analog is all we had in the "old days" before digital, and we all seemed to get along just fine. That said, let's take a look at what you need to make good-quality digital copies of analog material—and fix the quality of those that aren't so good.

Making the Connection

While we can talk about the science of analog recording all day long, the real difference between analog and digital recording is the way you hook everything together. Whereas CD ripping requires nothing more than the CD-ROM drive that's already inside your computer, copying records and cassettes requires, well, record and cassette players. You may also need an amplifier of some sort, plus the cable(s) required to connect the source (whatever it may be) to your computer.

NOTE *Although we focus primarily on records and cassettes in this chapter, there's nothing to stop you from resurrecting, say, old reel-to-reel tapes or even 8-tracks. However, we don't think you'll be happy with the latter; 8-track is a fairly low-fidelity format to begin with, and you'll have to contend with annoyingly loud "pops" when the tape changes tracks. If you just can't live without your Sly and the Family Stone collection, you may want to break down and buy the CDs—or purchase the songs from Musicmatch.*

Despite the veritable cornucopia of potential analog sources out there, the way you connect them all to your computer for digital recording is reasonably simple, standardized, and straightforward. Typically, you'll connect the audio source—such as a stereo receiver—to your PC's sound card input jack via an audio output jack. Things can get a bit squirrelly if your hardware is a bit nonstandard, but in general, that's pretty much it.

Sound Card Inputs

For us, one of the most frustrating aspects of connecting a PC to an analog sound system is decrypting the sound card—which is where your stereo, turntable, or cassette player is going to plug in. While sound cards vary from manufacturer to manufacturer and even from model to model, one thing is true about all of them: figuring out what each connector does is like making sense of an alien mothership's flight controls. The sound card's ports all look alike, and they all have miniscule

Resurrect Those Old Books on Tape

If you're like Rick (and heaven help you if you are), you love listening to books on tape while driving. However, most cars now have CD players instead of tape decks. And most portable audio players—well, they don't play CDs *or* tapes. So how are you supposed to enjoy Tom Wolfe's brilliant *A Man in Full* (and your other favorites) in this digital age?

Simple: Dig out your old Walkman tape player and sit for a spell at your PC. We'll discuss the full procedure later in this chapter (see the "Recording Cassettes" section), but for now here's a quick overview:

1. Find any portable tape player and put in a fresh pair of batteries.
2. Head to Radio Shack and buy a cable that has 1/8-inch stereo plugs at both ends.

3. Plug one end into the tape player, and the other into your sound card's line-in jack.
4. Use Musicmatch's Recorder feature to copy the tape to your PC in MP3 format.
5. Copy those MP3s to your preferred portable player, or burn them onto a CD.

symbols etched into the backplate in such a way that you can't tell them apart or even figure out which symbol lines up with which connector. And the whole thing is on the back of the PC, usually in the dark, requiring you to crane your head behind the desk and try to connect stuff with a flashlight in one hand and the cable in your teeth. Let's try to make sense of it all.

For starters, depending upon what kind of PC you have, your sound system may be on a separate sound card or integrated into the motherboard. An integrated sound system relies on an inexpensive sound chip to provide all the sound management features in your computer, and the inputs are typically located on the back of the case near all of the other connections, like the parallel, serial, USB, and PS/2 ports.

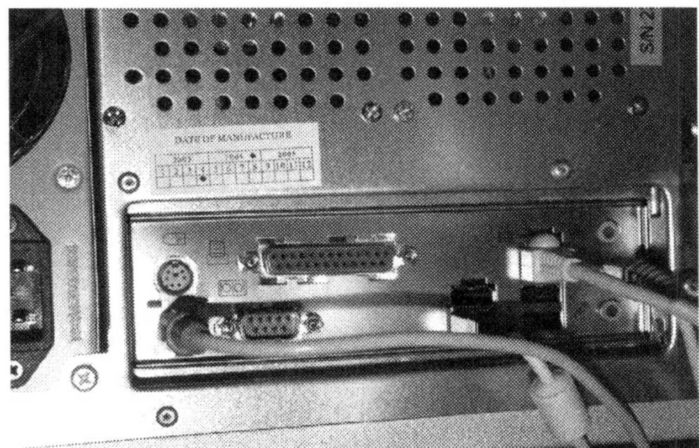

Some computers use a separate sound card, which resides in one of the PC's expansion slots. A separate sound card costs the manufacturer a bit more than integrated sound and takes up an expansion slot, but it has the potential to generate higher-quality audio.

Your sound inputs probably look something like the ones in Figure 5-1, which shows the back of a PC that actually has two sound cards installed (only for purposes of this book, we assure you) so you can see how differently various sound cards are marked. The easiest way to spot sound-card inputs is to look for a cluster of little round jacks. Or just look for where your computer's speakers are plugged in.

Sometimes you'll run into PCs that have both integrated audio and an add-in sound card. In those cases, the integrated sound is disabled and only the inputs on the sound card are active.

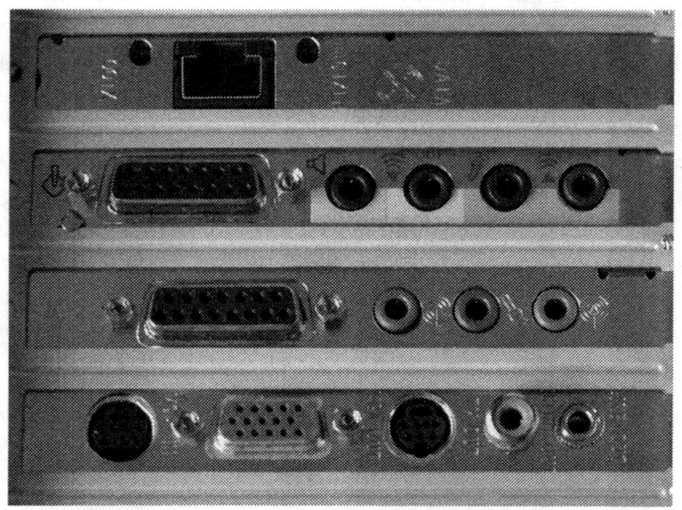

FIGURE 5-1 Typical PC sound-card connections

Your PC's sound system will have at least three jacks. Some have more. The key connectors are

- **Microphone** This is where you'd plug in a standard, unpowered PC microphone, like the little plastic boom mikes that often come with new PCs.
- **Line In** This is where you connect *line-level* components, such as stereo equipment.
- **Output** This is a line-level output most commonly used to send the audio signal to PC speakers. You can also use this connector to send audio to your home stereo or other analog gear. Some sound cards have two or more output connectors so you can attach speakers and still have an output available for other purposes.

To help make life easier, the majority of modern sound cards (and onboard audio systems) have color-coded jacks. Here's the breakdown:

- **Blue** Line-in
- **Pink** Mic (short for microphone, natch)
- **Green** Front-speaker output
- **Black** Rear-speaker output
- **Orange** Center channel/subwoofer output

NOTE *As noted previously, many sound cards have only the first three jacks. See Chapter 2 for information on sound-card upgrades if you're interested in increasing your output options. For this chapter, however, we're interested only in that little blue line-in jack.*

Record Players and Other Audio Sources

At the other end of the equation is your analog source equipment. Typically, this will be some sort of stereo system, though it could be anything from a record player connected to a simple amplifier to a Sony Walkman. To successfully connect the source to your PC, you'll need to use the right jacks. Here are the key considerations:

- **Pre-amplify the source material** You can't directly connect a *component-level* device like a turntable or microphone directly to the PC's sound card. The signal coming from those devices is too low to be properly utilized by the PC. Instead, connect the component to a stereo receiver or amplifier, and use the output connectors from *that* device to drive the sound card. Fortunately, most cassette decks are *line-level* devices, meaning they don't require any pre-amplification.

TIP *If you're trying to rescue old cassettes, don't bother with your tape deck. Instead, connect your old Walkman right to your PC. It's powered, so no pre-amplification is necessary. You just need a cable to connect the Walkman's headphone jack to your sound card's line-in jack.*

- **Use the Output, not the Input** Many stereo components have a pair of stereo connectors—one for input and another for output. Only components capable of playing *and* recording have both, though. That means CD players have output connectors only, but cassette players have input as well as output. You need to be sure you choose the right connectors when you make your connection. A typical amplifier, which is what you'll use to connect a record player to your PC, has a matrix of connectors that look like this:

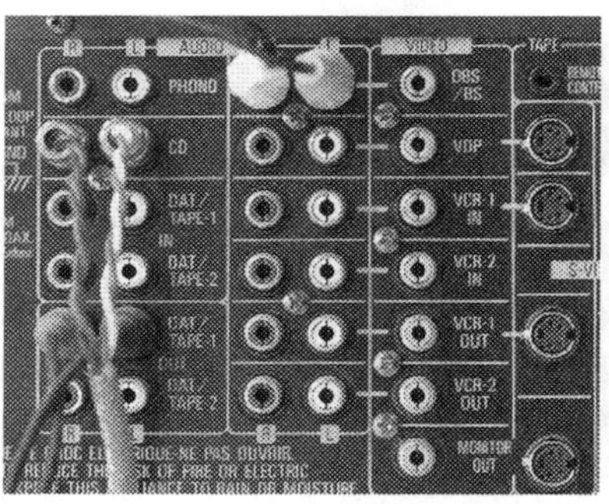

If you've dug an old turntable out of the garage to transfer LPs and 45s to Musicmatch but have no receiver to make it go, stop by your local Radio Shack. You can get an inexpensive phono pre-amp there that'll do the job.

Cabling It All Together

Great—you've got your analog source and your PC all ready to go. Now all you need is the right cable to connect them together. Here's the tricky part—your PC's sound inputs are one size and the analog gear is another.

- Your sound card requires 1/8-inch stereo mini-phone connectors, which are used to send both channels of audio information (left and right) through the same wire. These connectors are fairly common: they're used not just for computer sound cards, but also to connect headphones to portable music players. Beware, though: Mini-phone jacks come in two formats, stereo and mono. If you go to Radio Shack in search of a cable, make sure you get one that's stereo. Mono jacks are visually different, with only one insulating band around the metal plug instead of two. You can see them both, side-by-side, in the next illustration.

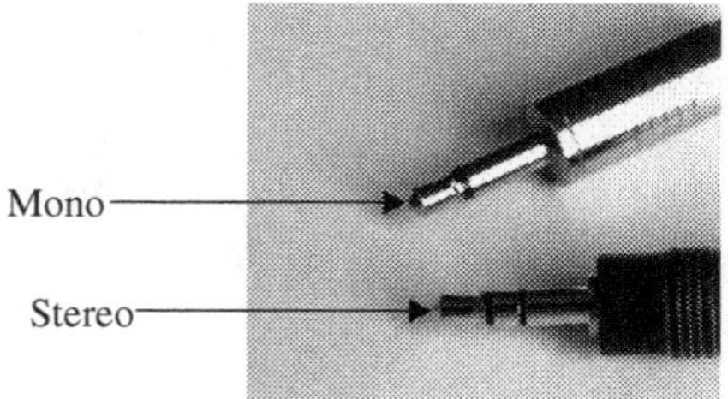

NOTE *A few high-end sound cards have RCA-style inputs instead of the more common mini-stereo jacks. If yours is one of them, just be sure to get the right cable. Your friendly neighborhood Radio Shack should be able to help you out.*

- Stereos and other analog gear traditionally have RCA jacks, which are larger than mini-phone jacks and always come in pairs; one each for the left and right channels. They're very, very standard—all home stereo and home theater systems use RCA jacks to connect various components together. Here is what a pair of RCA jacks look like:

Because the two ends of your setup require different plugs, the standard Y-cable is our best friend. Any electronics, computer, or stereo store can hook you up with a cable like the one in Figure 5-2. It's a Y-cable that features a 1/8-inch stereo mini-phone jack at one end and a pair of RCA plugs on the other.

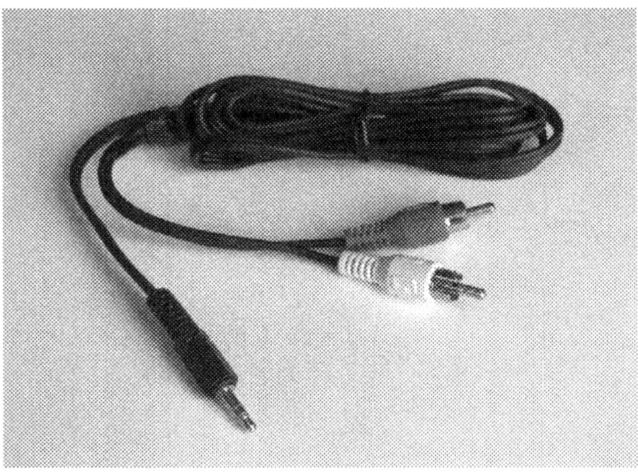

FIGURE 5-2 The standard RCA-to-mini-phone jack Y-cable allows you to connect your PC to most analog gear.

Cabling Accessories

There are a few other cable accessories that can help you get your gear hooked up as well. Your PC may be quite some distance from your stereo equipment, for instance. If you don't have a single cable that's long enough to reach, you can use several shorter cables, connected by a coupler that's female at both ends. This little gadget, which you can see next, is a real life-saver, and is available from electronics stores like Radio Shack.

Here's another common situation: your stereo may not have an extra output to dedicate to your PC for recording. If that's the case, you can "split" a single output so part of the signal goes to your PC and the other part of the signal goes to another component. There are a lot of Y-plugs around in electronics stores. You'll need a pair of them, of course, to re-route both stereo channels. In fact, there are cables, connectors, and adapters available at electronics stores like Radio Shack for almost every conceivable wiring quandary. You can convert an RCA jack into a mono or stereo mini-phone jack, for instance, or wire a device with a mini-phone jack output (like a headphone jack) directly to your PC's sound card with some of these gadgets:

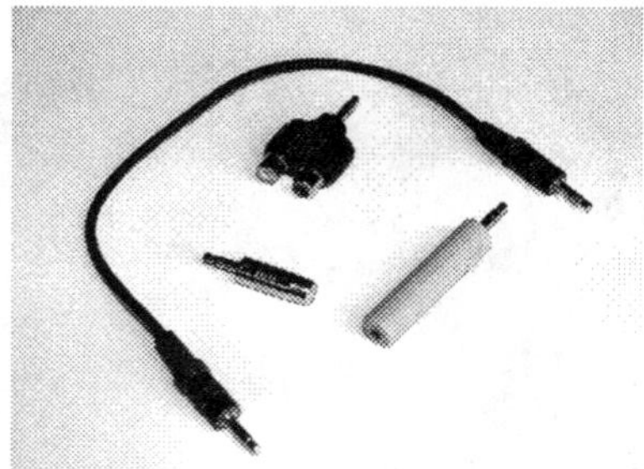

NOTE *If your stereo has a tape-out output, you can just as easily use that.*

Ensuring a High-Quality Signal

Though you can use accessories like the coupler, we actually don't recommend it. If you plan to make a high-quality recording, you need to keep the analog source material as high-quality as possible right up until the moment it gets sucked into the PC. Extremely long wires and gadgets like extenders and Y-plugs degrade the sound slightly, and if you degrade it enough it'll noticeably affect the final sound.

Indeed, the cabling is an important element in your overall sound. We recommend using quality, shielded cables instead of the standard rubber-sheathed stuff you get with most stereo gear. If you visit your local stereo equipment store, you'll find shielded cabling from companies like Monster Cable. Figure 5-3 shows the difference between quality audiophile cabling and run-of-the-mill cables.

In general, the thicker the cable is, the better it will sound. Thick cable is better able to transfer high-frequency sounds over long distance than thin cable; this is referred to as the cable's capacitance. The lower the capacitance (and the thicker the cable), the more full-bodied your sound will be. Thin cables tend to lose the high end of your music. Not surprisingly, quality audiophile cabling covers both bases: capacitance and shielding. While we're making a wish list of cable characteristics, it's worth noting that gold-plated jacks transfer electricity—and hence your audio—better than ordinary metal ones, and that's another benefit you'll get in higher-quality cables.

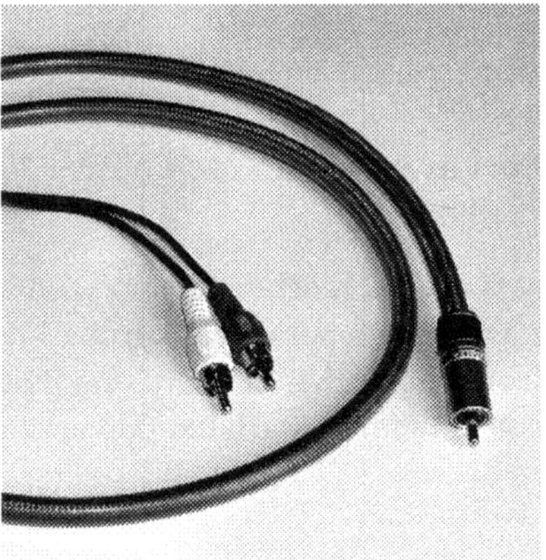

FIGURE 5-3 Audiophiles tend to use Monster Cable for most of their audio projects, but you can use less costly cables and still get good results.

Getting Closer to the Source

What if your PC is just too far away from the analog source material to make a reasonable connection? That's when you need to get creative. There are two easy ways to get the job done: borrow a notebook computer (and install Musicmatch on it) or use a portable MP3 player with recording capabilities (and skip Musicmatch altogether).

If you choose to use a notebook, you just need to make sure it has an audio input jack. Avoid using a microphone input since the voltage level is different and you'll distort the audio you're trying to record. You also need to install an audio editing program that can capture the music (like, oh, say, Musicmatch!), and the hard drive needs sufficient space for the data you're going to capture. Remember: you should have about 500MB available to grab a single LP (assuming you're recording in the uncompressed WAV format).

There's also the possibility of using a portable MP3 player with recording features. Rick has one he loves: the Archos Jukebox Recorder. It includes inputs for capturing hours of audio directly into MP3 format. Rick has used it to record both albums and cassettes—it's much easier than hauling a computer to where the stereo is set up (or vice versa). Of course, you still need to manually name the files and enter ID3 tag data yourself; there's no getting around that problem.

For the absolute best sound quality, here are a few other tips you might want to try:

- **Keep cables as short as possible** Don't use a 20-foot length of cable, for instance, if 6 feet will do.
- **Keep cables away from each other** If you run cables in parallel, right next to each other, you can generate background noise. Audiophiles try to run cables away from each other at sharp angles when they leave the components and not run them parallel to one another until they're a few feet away.
- **Don't lay the power cable and signal cables next to each other** The same basic premise as the previous tip, only this one is even more important because of how "noisy" power cords are.

The Best Films about Music

Rick: To me, music and movies go hand in hand. Just look at Charlie Chaplin's masterpiece *City Lights* if you need proof—the music tells half the story. Of course, there are movies that benefit from their music, and then there are movies that are *about* music (or are musicals). Here are my top five favorites from the latter category.

1. *The Commitments*
2. *The Blues Brothers*
3. *Almost Famous*
4. *High Fidelity* (but the book was better)
5. *Singing in the Rain*

Denny: There's a bit more comedy on my list than Rick's, but what else would you expect from a guy who owns the entire "Weird Al" Yankovic discography? At least I didn't list Al's *UHF* in my top five, despite the winning combination of top-notch musical parody and classic lines like "Badgers? We don't need no steenkin' badgers!"

1. *This is Spinal Tap*
2. *Pink Floyd: The Wall*
3. *High Fidelity*
4. *The Kids are Alright* (fun to watch before viewing Spinal Tap)
5. *A Mighty Wind*

Recording Audio with Musicmatch

With your analog source securely connected to your PC, it's time to fire up Musicmatch. The process of recording records or cassettes isn't much different from the process of ripping CDs, which we discussed at length in Chapter 4. Heck, that's *all* we discussed in Chapter 4, if you want to know the truth. Not that we have any regrets about the nature or content of Chapter 4, mind you, it's just that if you go back to Chapter 4 expecting to find something about, say, Internet radio, it just isn't there. Yes, it's high time we switched to decaf.

Anyway, here's the recording process in a nutshell:

1. Connect your record or cassette player to your PC (remember, record players require an amp in between).
2. Set the player's volume level to around the halfway mark.
3. Open Windows' volume controls and set the line-in volume to about the halfway mark.
4. Start Musicmatch and open the Recorder window.
5. Select the desired settings for your recording, making sure to choose Line In for the source.
6. Press the Record button in Musicmatch and the Play button on your analog source.
7. Edit the resulting files (if necessary) using a third-party audio program.

Let's look at these steps in a bit more detail, starting with LP and 45 records and then moving on to cassette tapes.

TIP *This would be a good time to mention that while Musicmatch does a fine job with records, it lacks the capability to remove pops, hiss, and other audio artifacts. If your record collection is in particularly bad shape, you may want to use a program that can filter out those unwanted noises. One good choice: Roxio Easy Media Creator 7 (www.roxio.com). It not only removes clicks, pops, and hiss, it also lets you edit the resulting sound files. Better still, choose a program designed specifically with audio restoration in mind, like Magix Audio Cleaning Lab 2004 (www.magix.com). Of course, whatever program you use, you can then organize and play the finished files in Musicmatch.*

Recording LPs and 45s

Okay, down to business. In this section, we'll walk you through the process of recording some vinyl with Musicmatch. We'll assume you've already got your turntable connected to your stereo receiver or amplifier, and the latter connected to your sound card's line-in jack—all of which we discussed a few sections back.

The next step is to "check the levels," which is music-industry slang for, um, checking the levels. In other words, we want to adjust the input and speaker volume for your turntable. Here's how:

1. Open Windows' Master Volume settings, which you can do by double-clicking the volume icon (represented by a little picture of a speaker) in the System Tray (lower-right corner of the screen). If you don't have a volume icon, click Start | Control Panel, double-click Sounds and Audio Devices, then check the box marked Place Volume Icon In The Taskbar. Click OK, and then go back to the beginning of this step and do as we instructed.

2. Start your turntable turning, put a record on it, and put the needle down anyplace. You should hear the music through your computer's speakers. In the Master Volume window, raise or lower the Line In slider so it's at the halfway point. You can then adjust the volume on your speakers so it's to your liking. (The line-in volume is independent of your speaker volume—that's why you can't just adjust your speakers to achieve an optimal recording level.)

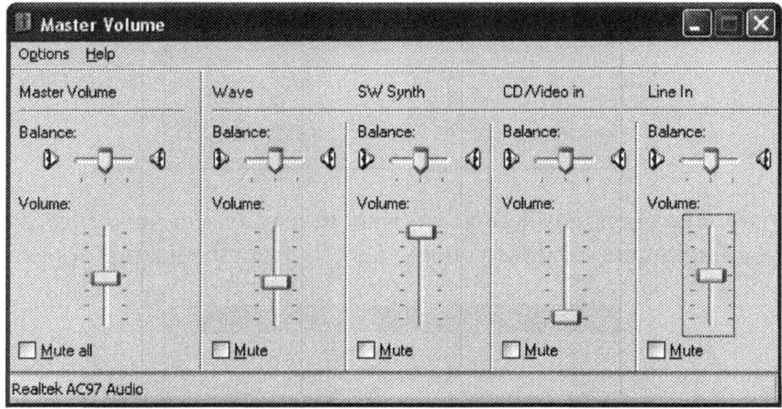

3. Close the Master Volume window and stop the turntable.

Obviously, your receiver or amplifier has a volume control of its own. As with Windows' line-in setting, you should set the volume at around the halfway point. That way you won't risk any distortion, but you'll produce a signal strong enough to overcome any line noise.

Now you're ready to bring Musicmatch into the mix. Fire up the program, and then open the Recorder by clicking View | Recorder. (If it already has a check mark next to it, then it should already be visible, so you're all set.) Now you have to tell the Recorder to record the audio that'll be coming from the sound card's line-in jack, rather than from your CD drive (which is the default). To do that, click the Recorder's Options button. This window appears:

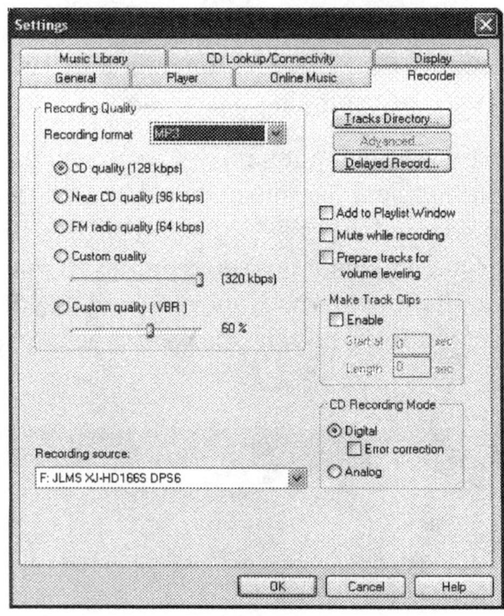

There are several options here you'll want to modify. For now, click the arrow under Recording Source, and then choose Line In from the list that appears:

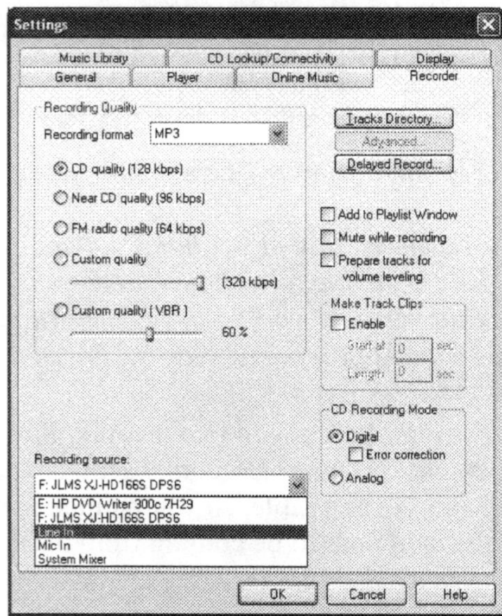

With this key step done, you could theoretically click OK and proceed to the actual recording process. However, let's take a closer look at some of the other options in this window and how you might want to set them:

- **Recording Format** Here's where you'll choose between MP3, mp3PRO, WAV, and WMA. The merits and shortcomings of these formats are discussed at length in Chapter 4. To recap, Rick is partial to WMA, while Denny prefers MP3. If you're planning to turn your albums into CDs, you may want to choose WAV, which records without compression and therefore without any loss of fidelity. You can always convert those WAV files into MP3s or WMAs later, as discussed in Chapter 12.
- **Tracks Directory** Click this button to select where to store the recordings on your hard drive and how to name the files. See the "Storing and Naming Your Music" section in Chapter 4 for a full explanation.
- **Advanced** Click this button to access some advanced recording settings. The crucial one for our purposes is Auto Song Detect, which Musicmatch uses to automatically divide an LP into individual tracks. Thus, if an album side has five songs, you'll get five MP3 files instead of one long one. See the "Working with Auto Song Detect" sidebar for details.

TIP *There's an argument to be made for leaving Auto Song Detect turned off. Yes, you'll wind up with one long audio file, which is probably something you don't want. But it's a relatively simple matter to load that file into an audio-editing program and split it up manually. That will give you much greater control, meaning you're less likely to wind up with tracks that are cut off too soon or split in half because of a quiet moment in the song.*

- **Mute while recording** Uncheck this box. Otherwise, you won't be able to hear your album while Musicmatch is recording it. This whole album-to-PC thing is a rather imprecise process, and you need to be able to hear if the needle jumps or the record skips or something. In other words, you should monitor the copy as it happens, and you can't do that if the audio is muted.

Once you've modified all the recording settings to your liking, you're almost ready to start the copy process. All that's left is to type in the name of the artist,

Working with Auto Song Detect

Let's say you're using Musicmatch to record the old Huey Lewis and the News album *Picture This* (we won't tell, honest). The album has a total of ten songs, five on each side. With Musicmatch's Auto Song Detect (ASD) feature enabled, you should be able to perform exactly two recording sessions and wind up with ten audio files. That's because ASD can automatically detect periods of silence—namely, the pause between songs—and create separate files accordingly.

To access ASD, click the Options button in Musicmatch's Recorder, choose Line In as your recording source, and then click the Advanced button. In the Auto Song Detect area, check the box marked Active, at which point the following two settings will become available:

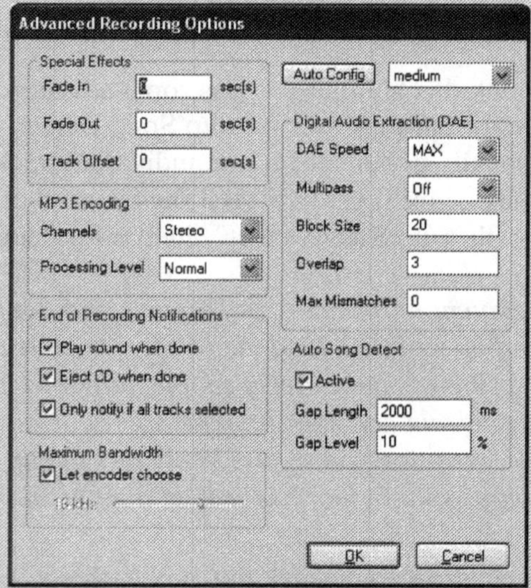

- **Gap Length** This is the amount of silence Musicmatch has to hear before it splits the recording and starts a new song file. The default is 2,000 milliseconds (two seconds), which is the usual amount of silence between tracks on an album. However, on some albums it's shorter, so you may want to decrease the setting to around 1,500 milliseconds (1.5 seconds). On the other hand, if you decrease Gap Length too much, Musicmatch may interpret short periods of silence *within* a song as the end of the song and split it in two. Experimentation is the word for this setting.

- **Gap Level** This setting is essentially the volume level that qualifies as a "gap." If you're recording an album that has a lot of quiet parts—like, say, classical music—Musicmatch will rely on Gap Level to determine whether the song is over or just at a low point. The default setting is 10 percent; you may need to raise or lower it depending on the nature of the album. A higher setting makes the ASD less likely to misinterpret a quiet passage as a gap, but too high of a setting could miss the gaps between songs.

Needless to say, getting ASD to work successfully can be a challenge. And the settings that work for one album may not work at all for another. That's why you may be better off without ASD. You can record an entire album side as a single file, and then use a third-party audio editor to split the tracks with manual precision. See the section "Post-Production: Fixing Your Recordings" later in this chapter to explore that option.

5

album, and track you're about to record. In the Recorder window, click next to Artist, and then type in the appropriate information:

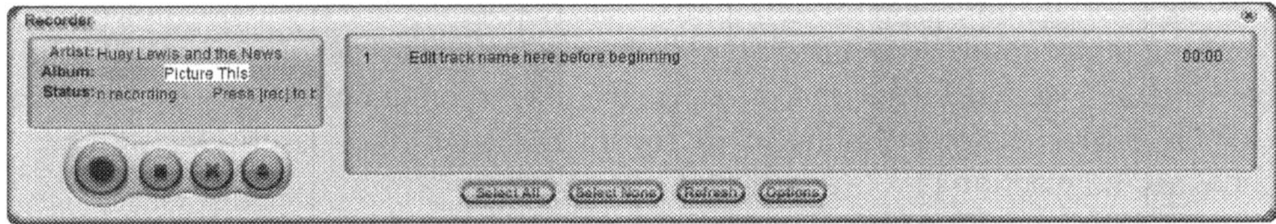

Next, click beside Album and type in that info. Finally, click where it says Edit Track Name Here Before Beginning, and type in the name of the song. Obviously, if you're recording an entire album side, there will be more than one song title. Don't worry about this for now—just enter the name of the first track. After the recording is done, you can add the appropriate song titles to the files.

Start Recording

The magic moment has finally arrived! Start your turntable turning, and then click the big red Record button in Musicmatch. Unlike CDs, which are copied as fast as your CD-ROM drive can move them, this recording will occur in real time (no, you can't set the turntable to a higher speed—unless you want your songs to sound like they were performed by Alvin and the Chipmunks). You'll have to wait it out—and you'll have to click the Stop button when the music's over.

When you reach the end of side A, you have two choices: you can either rapidly flip the album over and just let Musicmatch keep recording, which will result in one file containing the entire album, or you can click Stop, flip the album, and then start a new recording for side B. If you're going to be splitting the file in a third-party audio program anyway, you might as well take the first approach.

Recording Cassettes

As many people as there are who have milk crates full of old records, there are probably twice as many with shoeboxes full of old cassette tapes. Fortunately, it's even easier to convert those relics to digital audio (and then dump 'em at your next garage sale—people will buy *anything* for a quarter).

The process of recording audiotapes with Musicmatch is almost identical to recording records. However, we have a recommendation that can save you a lot of time and effort: instead of dealing with your old tape deck and the stereo it's connected to, just dig out (or borrow from someone) a portable tape player. You'll get very close to the same sound quality you'd get from a tape deck, without the hassle of moving a lot of equipment around (unlike records, which leave you no choice).

For our tape-to-PC conversions, we used two simple items: an old Sony Walkman (see Figure 5-4) and a cable that connects the player to our computer's sound card (see the earlier section "Cabling It All Together" for a further description of the cable and connection).

Before you go any further, be sure to install a fresh pair of batteries in your tape player. You don't want it to run out of juice in the middle of a recording.

At this point we're going to refer you back to "Recording LPs and 45s," as the steps you need to follow to record cassettes are just about identical. Just read through that section and substitute the word "tape" for "record." You'll do fine.

Once you've finished copying a record or cassette, you'll probably need to do some "post-production." That's music-industry slang for "fix all the boo-boos." In this case, post-production means splitting big files into smaller ones (if necessary), adding or fixing ID3 tags, and cleaning up any noise that may be present in your digital audio recordings.

FIGURE 5-4 All it takes to convert old cassettes to digital audio is a portable player like this one.

A Tape Deck for Your PC

Wouldn't it be cool if you could plug those old cassettes right into your PC without having to mess around with external players, special cables, and all that? Now you can, thanks to the PlusDeck 2. This unique device resembles the tape deck that's in your car, but it installs in one of your computer's open drive bays. With it you can not only listen to cassettes through your PC's speakers, you can "rip" cassettes almost as easily as you do CDs. It can even record from your PC to blank tapes.

At press time, the only U.S. distributor we could find for the PlusDeck 2 was ThinkGeek (www.thinkgeek.com), a site that carries all manner of cool gadgets. The device sells for $149.99.

Post-Production: Fixing Your Recordings

There are a few problems inherent in copying albums and cassettes to your PC. For starters, when you capture music from an analog source, your computer has no way to know exactly when a track starts or ends (hence the presence of the Auto Song Detect feature discussed earlier in the chapter). Nor can it identify the music being recorded and assign ID3 tags to the files. In other words, all that automation that occurs during a CD rip (see Chapter 4) goes out the window when you're copying analog music. Now, like the *U.S.S. Enterprise* in the last ten minutes of any *Star Trek* episode, it's all about manual control.

The solution to the first problem—giant audio recordings that need to be split up into single song files—lies in any number of audio editing applications (alas, Musicmatch isn't one of them). There are a lot of these programs available, and in general, any one that can save your music as either an MP3 or WMA file will get the job done. To be useful, the program should be able to

- Load an MP3, WAV, or WMA file
- Let you select, cut, copy, and paste segments of the audio
- Save selected audio bits as new files
- Save in MP3 and WMA formats

If the program also lets you record audio from the PC's line-in port, you can use it for the entire project, leaving Musicmatch out of the mix altogether. But this section is about post-production, not, um, beginning-middle-and-end-production, so let's focus on editing the files you recorded with Musicmatch.

We recommend these programs, though you may find others that suit you better:

- **Sound Forge** This excellent Sony program has just about every editing and recording feature you could ask for. The downside? It costs about $400. Fortunately, there's a "lighter" version available: Screenblast Sound Forge 7.0. This consumer version of the program comes with a few less features and a much reduced price tag (about $60). Even so, we highly, highly recommend it.
- **Adobe Audition 1.5** Every bit as elaborate as Screenblast Sound Forge, this program is also handy for video editing. Unsurprisingly, it also costs quite a bit more: $299. But if you're serious about editing audio, you may want to check it out. There's a trial version you can download from Adobe's web site (www.adobe.com).
- **Audiotools** If all you're looking for is audio capture without all of the cumbersome editing features in other programs, look into Unrelated Inventions' Audiotools. This excellent capture program is smart enough to

automatically split songs into separate tracks based on sensing the silence between songs (much like Musicmatch's Auto Song Detect feature).

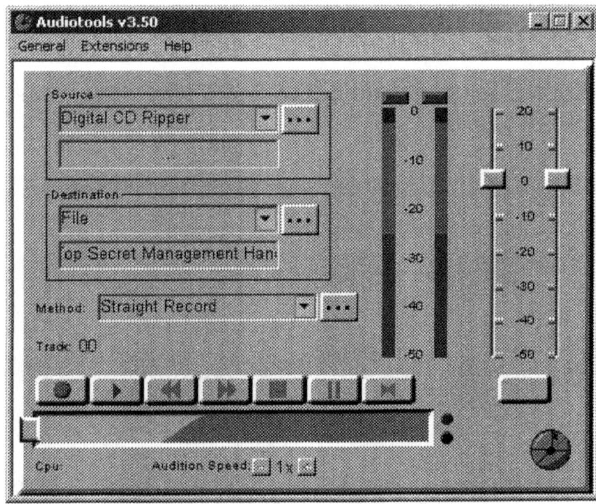

- **Goldwave** This shareware classic can't be beat for the simple task of splitting up audio files and saving them in a variety of formats (it supports every format we've ever heard of and a few we haven't). The program costs $55 to register, but you can do a lot even with the freely available shareware version.

You can use Windows' built-in Sound Recorder app (which has the benefit of being free) to cut files if you absolutely don't want to spend any money. You record your music as WAV files, then you use the "cut before" and "cut after" menu commands to isolate individual songs. Afterward, use Musicmatch to convert the resulting WAV files to MP3 or WMA format.

Editing Your Music

So, if you followed our advice, you have an album sitting on your hard disk in the form of one, huge, uncut file, with a dozen or more tracks all stuck together—and possibly a whole lot of noise in the middle where you flipped the tape or LP over and kept recording. Now it's time to break them up into individual files.

Thankfully, this is little more than a simple cut and paste job. Audio editors let you cut and paste sections of your music files just about as easily as working with text in a word processor. Let's demonstrate the process in Adobe Audition, but you can do this in any audio editor:

1. Open Audition or another audio editor and load the big audio file. It should look something like this:

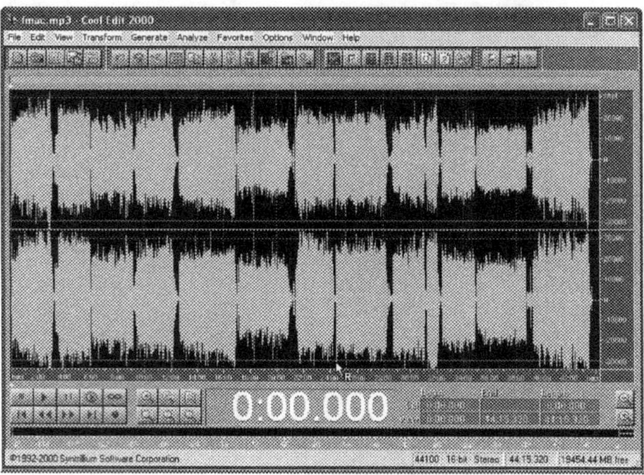

2. You'll need to use the program's zoom control to zero in on the start of the first track. Many audio editors let you zoom by rolling the mouse's scroll wheel, which is very handy.

3. Start playing audio (often you can toggle Play/Pause with the Spacebar). Watch the scrubber (that's the vertical line that moves across the audio waveform) and see where you need to cut to start the first track. You should look for, and try to skip, any initial audio pops, such as when the tone arm goes down on the vinyl. It can help to isolate that initial pop and select it with the mouse. Then press the DELETE key to erase it from the track.

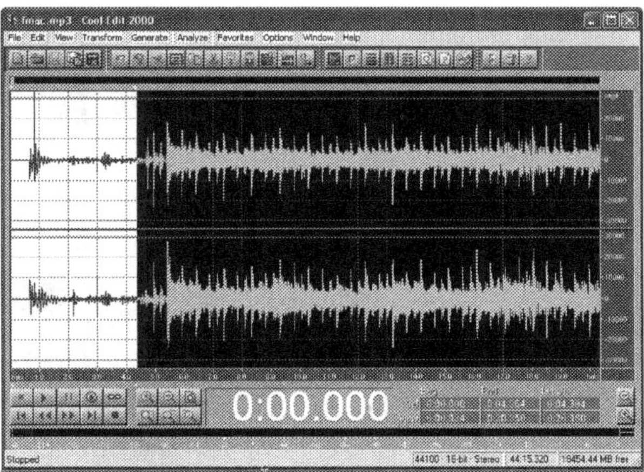

4. Now cruise ahead (use a combination of the zoom tool and the slider to advance through the song) to find the end of the first track. When you find the end, select it and drag the mouse back to the left, highlighting the entire first song.

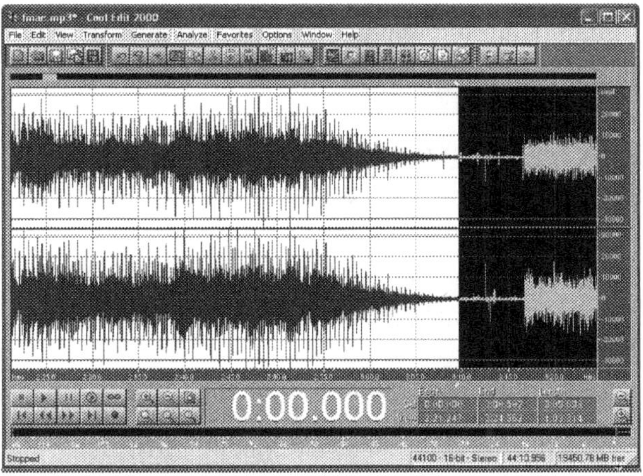

5. With the first song selected, choose File | Save Selection. Save the file according to a logical file-naming scheme. We recommend naming it with the track number and song title, and save the file inside a folder named after the album, which itself is saved inside a folder for the artist. Example: 01-Come Together.mp3

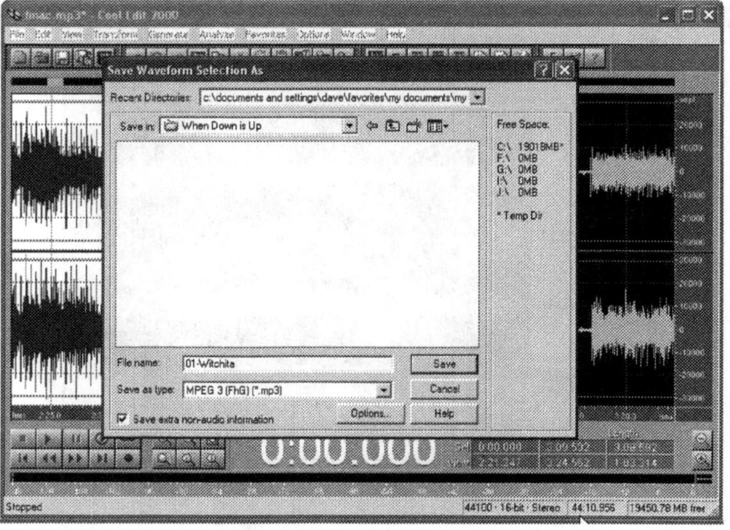

6. After saving the file, delete the selected waveform from the file you're working with. Now find the end of the second song, select the entire song, and save it just like you did with the first song.

7. Lather, rinse, repeat. It's slow, it's boring, but it's the only good way to break your songs down from a single album-long file.

Cleaning Up Noisy Audio

Songs ripped from digital sources like CD generally don't have to worry about capturing noise in the ripping process. But analog captures can include all sorts of glitches, including hiss and crackle sounds from LP recordings, popping sounds from a scratched record, and background rumble from noisy equipment or dirty electrical lines.

There are a lot of products available that are designed to clean up your music. In general, your choices are determined largely by which audio editing software you're already using. Here's an overview of a few popular programs:

- **Audio Cleaning Lab** This standalone capture and editing program is an inexpensive alternative to some of the pricier products out there. It does a good job for most folks who don't want to spend a lot of time or money creating a digital music library, but need to do a little audio cleanup.

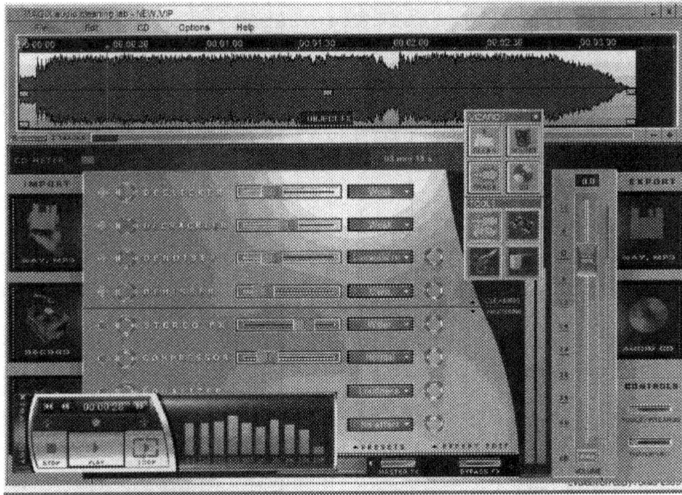

- **Ray Gun** Ray Gun is a bit more expensive ($119 for the Windows version), but it has the added benefit of being a Direct X-compatible plug-in (look in the Plug Ins section of the company's web site), meaning you can use it directly with programs like Sound Forge and Goldwave. Ray Gun is also able to run on its own, so you can use it to clean up songs even if you don't own a separate audio editor. In standalone mode, though, it can import only WAV files.

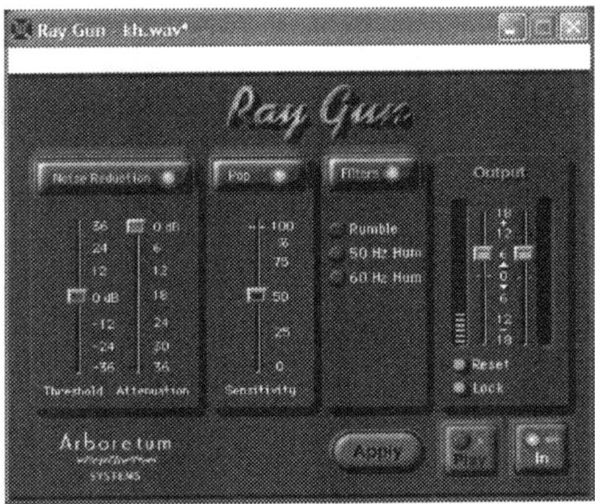

No matter which audio cleanup tool you use, there are certain steps you can take to get the best results. Be sure to consider these tips:

- Many noise reduction filters need to sample the silent *leader* (the period of silence before the music begins) to establish a baseline for how much noise is on the track. If you plan to perform noise reduction, do it before you cut away all of your silent leader.
- If you have *clipping* (a kind of distortion that results because the audio was recorded at too high of a level), there's no easy fix: discard the selection and re-record the audio.
- If there are multiple filters you can use to eliminate noise, such as a pop remover, hiss remover, and hum remover, follow any directions the program offers about which order to perform the steps in. It can make a difference.
- Noise reduction is interactive—you generally have to use your ears to see which settings work best for the music you're cleaning. Listen carefully as you tweak the settings, because you can easily clean too much and end up damaging the music.
- Compare the cleaned-up song side-by-side with the original dirty version and make sure you like the result before you over-write the original or delete it from your hard disk, losing it forever.

Giving Your Music the Gift of ID3

Now that your songs are broken down into individual tracks and saved with appropriate filenames, you're almost done. We still need to give these songs their ID3 information so that Musicmatch can properly organize tracks and display their artist, album, and name information. ID3 tags are also vital for portable audio players. Here's how to finish off the project:

1. Open Musicmatch and find the album you just edited in the Library. If it isn't there, you can choose File | Add New Tracks To Music Library or just drag and drop the files from a folder into the Musicmatch window. No matter how you do it, select all the tracks from the album.

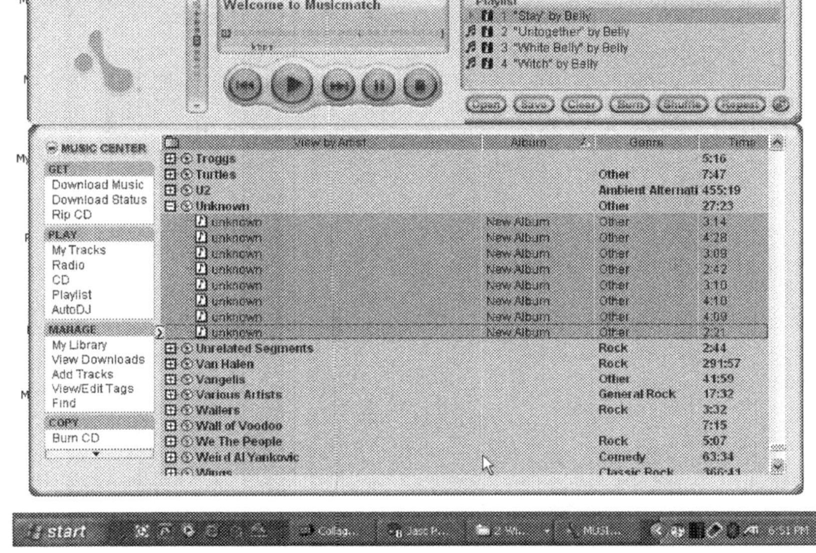

2. Right-click the selected tracks and choose Edit Track Tag(s). You should see the Edit Track Tag(s) dialog box.

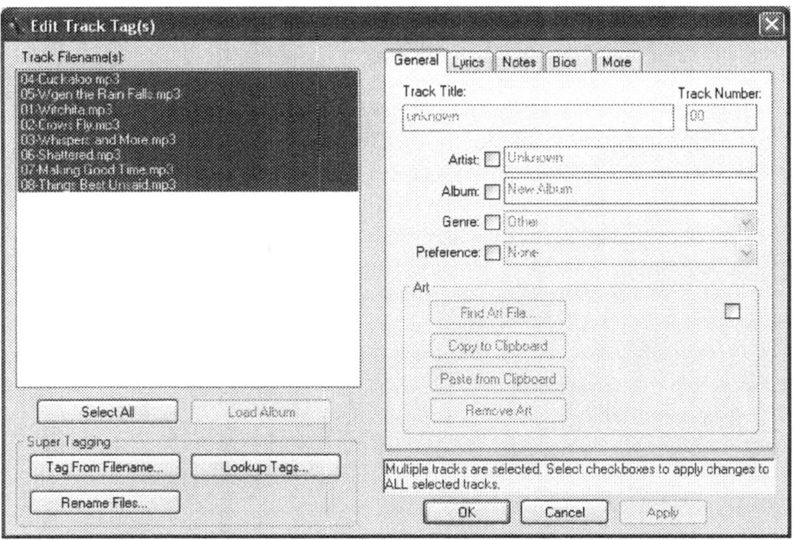

3. Assuming that all the tracks share a common artist, click the checkbox for Artist and enter the artist name. By placing a checkmark there, you tell Musicmatch to change the Artist tag for all the selected songs.

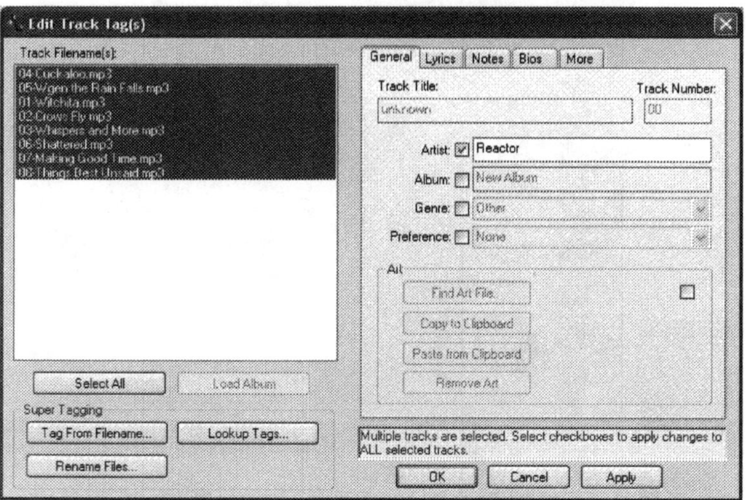

4. Do the same for other common elements, like Album and Genre.
5. Now click the tracks one at a time (they're listed on the far left of the dialog box) and change the track title to match the actual song title from the album.

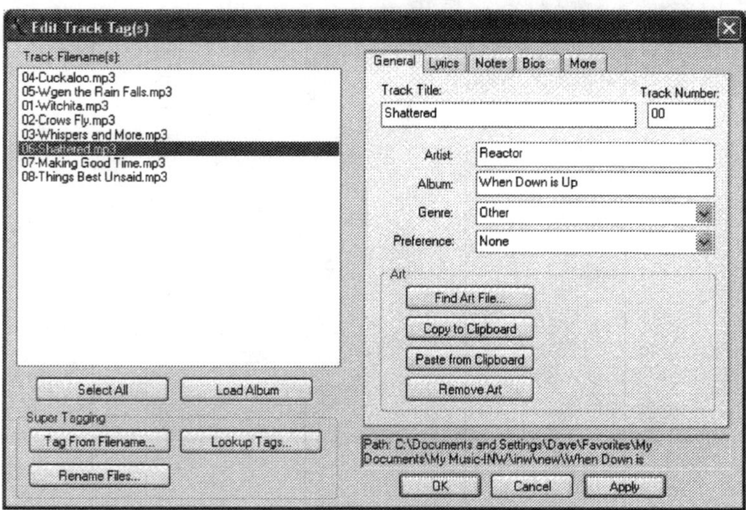

6. When you're done, click OK.

After a few moments, the tags will be updated and you can look for that artist entry in the Library.

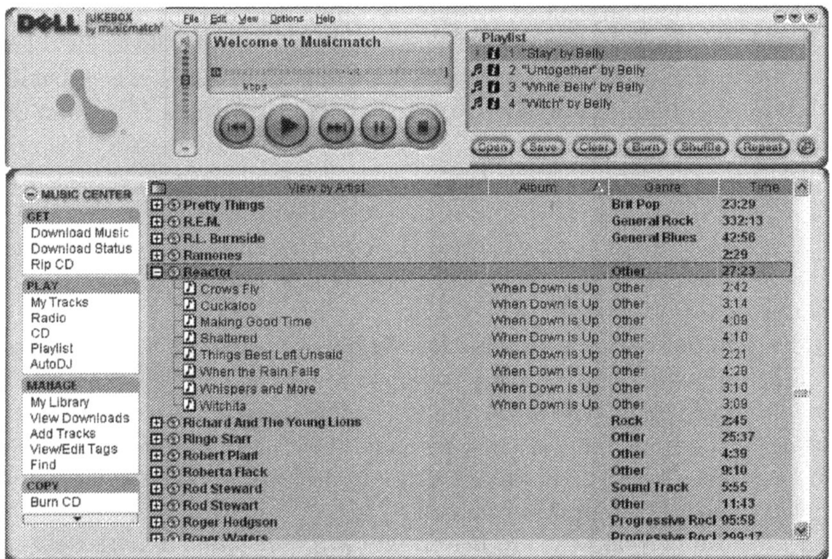

Jimmy Stewart Tells All

Yes, Rick knows Jimmy Stewart personally. Not the famous dead actor, alas, but the guy who kept Rick out of trouble (mostly) during college and now consents to be his friend. Funny thing is, he prefers to go by James, but we won't hold that against him—especially since he took the time to answer some serious and silly questions for this book.

Q: You're something of a musician. Discuss.

A: As musicians go I'm kinda like a decent fishing lake. I'm wide, long, of average depth, except for a few "holes" where my abilities go deeper. I'm no "monster," which I would say would be like an ocean—deep everywhere. I have a degree in music composition and theory, played trumpet nearly every day for 15 years, have been playing guitar since I was in high school (and I'm a young and studly 38 years old now), and listen to a wide variety of musical styles.

Q: How long have you been a Musicmatch user and what made you choose that program over something else?

A: I've been a legal, license-holding user of Musicmatch Plus for two years now. Before that I tried Microsoft's Windows Media Player and a few others. I loved how quick and easy it was to rip CDs using Microsoft's player, but didn't like that I could only rip to Microsoft's own WMA format. I decided on Musicmatch Plus because it seemed to organize my library the way I would do it—simply, using nonproprietary means, and with great ease for the basic tasks I needed: Ripping CDs to MP3s or WAV files, playing MP3s and WAV files, and playing CDs. I was hoping it would also sync with my Creative Nomad Jukebox 3 device, but they seem to have overlooked that one. Anyway, I found another program that does a fine job there.

Q: Do you use Musicmatch on a daily basis or just for certain tasks?

A: The big luxury here is that I've ripped my entire CD library to MP3 and no longer have to fiddle with single discs. I end up using Musicmatch whenever I'm using my computer and want to listen to music. More often than not I'm on the phone or listening to news (TV or radio) in the background, but when I want to listen to "tunage" I ping Musicmatch.

Q: Suppose you had the chance to jam at a live concert with the band or singer of your choice. Who would you choose?

A: I'm not big into worshipping idols. When I see a great concert with phenomenal musicians I become exhilarated and partly nauseated. It's because I know that if I had stuck with it and dedicated myself to composing and performing, I could have been pretty good and might have been able to make a living doing something I love. So, to sit down with Chick Corea or Stevie Ray Vaughn would be pointless, unless they needed a cup of coffee or something. On the other hand, there are a number of songwriters I'd love to collaborate with, such as John Hiatt, Marc Cohn, David Gray, John Mayer, David Bowie, Lennon & McCartney (shhhhh!—my list, my rules), Elvis Costello, Jackson Browne, Bonnie Raitt, Cat Stevens, Dave Barnes, Jeff Buckley, Jonathan Brooke, Joni Mitchell, Patty Griffin, Sarah McLachlan, Shawn Colvin, Sheryl Crow, Toni Childs, Alana Davis, and Alison Krauss. That's my short list and my long list. Oh, and in case any of those artists are reading this and want to write a few strong tunes together, you can get my number from Rick.

Of course, the truth be known, I've had more than my share of fun and success writing and playing music with my good friend Roberto. So, line up some cats who can play and Roberto and I will play a set or two of originals. It'll be a cross between *American Idol, America's Funniest Home Videos,* and *Survivor.*

Q: After the gig, the plane carrying you home crashes on a deserted island. What five albums would you want to have with you?

A: I'd never survive with just five, so I'd gladly trade in my CDs for a decent acoustic guitar and a few extra sets of strings. Besides, it was a trick question. What good are albums without a record player? Not bad for someone with a liberal arts degree, eh? Now, if you were to twist my arm I'd say *The Glory of Gabrieli,* Empire Brass Quintet; *David Russell Plays Bach; Cat Stevens Greatest Hits; Kind of Blue,* Miles Davis; and *Aja,* Steely Dan—but I wouldn't be at all happy about it.

Q: Record stores: doomed to extinction or permanent fixture in society?

A: Record stores are doomed. Electronic distribution is quickly becoming a no-brainer, though I refuse to buy music online until licensing and audio quality are clearly on the same level as CDs.

Where to Find It

Web Site	Address	What's There
Adobe	www.adobe.com	Adobe Audition
Arboretum	www.arboretum.com	Ray Gun
Goldwave	www.goldwave.com	Goldwave
Magix	www.magix.com	Audio Cleaning Lab
Sony Pictures Digital Media	mediasoftware.sonypictures.com	Screenblast Sound Forge
Unrelated Inventions	www.unrelatedinventions.com	Audiotools

Chapter 6

Buying Music from Musicmatch Downloads

How to...

- Set up a Musicmatch Downloads account
- Find album and artist info
- Buy and download your first song
- Buy songs you hear on Musicmatch Radio
- Understand digital rights management

"People don't buy plastic and paper, they buy emotions." —Scott Young, Executive, Wherehouse Entertainment

"American music is something the rest of the world wants to listen to. Our job is to make sure they pay for it." —Jason Berman, Recording Industry Association of America (RIAA)

Sit down, kids, and hear a story about when your old grandpas Denny and Rick had to *go to the mall* to buy music. If we heard a good song on the radio (an ancient device that actually broadcast music for miles, using energy waves, which was used in the days before streaming Internet audio), we actually had to go to something called a "record store" and recite a few lyrics for the clerk, hoping he or she could point us to the right record album. If you've ever seen the superiority complex of the clerks in the movie *High Fidelity,* you know what a pleasant experience that can be.

Then came a day when music became freely available on the Internet. You could download virtually any tune using programs like the original Napster and KaZaa—all for free! But all was not well. First of all, downloading songs without paying for them was illegal in most countries, including the U.S.A. It was also a lousy thing to do to your favorite artists, who lost royalties if you didn't buy their music. And "lousy" describes the sound quality of many of the files found on file-sharing services—that is, *if* the files were even what they claimed to be, and weren't incorrectly named. And last, but certainly not least, even if you were just trying albums before buying them, if you left the "upload" feature turned on, you could have been the next target for the RIAA's music piracy lawsuit team. (For more on the ins and outs of file-sharing services, see Chapter 7.)

Then along came Musicmatch Downloads (and iTunes, and Napster 2.0, and a few others, but you'll have to wait for the next chapter to read about those), with legal music downloads. The songs were guaranteed high-quality (160-Kbps Windows Media

Audio files), and full albums generally cost less than they did in music stores. Best of all, you could buy songs individually. Just try going into the record store and telling the clerk you only want to purchase "Bohemian Rhapsody" without any of the rest of *Queen's Greatest Hits.* (What, you really tried it? That was just an example. They laughed, didn't they?) Best of all, it was completely legal.

NOTE *The Musicmatch Downloads service is currently only available to residents of the U.S.A.*

Today, there are a bunch of other features that make buying tunes from Musicmatch Downloads appealing. You can listen to 30-second clips of songs before buying—saving you from buying The Carpenters' "Close to You" when you meant to purchase the Cure's "Close to Me." You can also use the tunes you download to create custom mix CDs, or download them to supported portable players. The thing you can't do is give them away to friends and family. The songs are protected using digital rights management (DRM), a copy protection scheme that limits the number of computers you can play them on, how many times a playlist of songs can be burned to CD, and so on. We'll cover DRM in detail later in this chapter in the section titled "Understanding Musicmatch's Digital Rights Management."

Signing Up for Musicmatch Downloads

The first thing you'll need to do before using Musicmatch Downloads is to sign up for an account. Don't worry, just signing up won't cost you anything—you'll only pay if you download a song or album, or sign up for one of the Musicmatch MX streaming music services. (More on Musicmatch MX in Chapter 8.)

NOTE *Though you can upgrade to Musicmatch Jukebox Plus by mail using a check, you absolutely must have a credit card to use Musicmatch Downloads.*

To sign up, just follow these easy steps:

1. If the Music Center is displayed on the left side of the Musicmatch window, click the Download Music button. Otherwise, click the View pull-down menu and choose Download.
2. Click the Account button, which you'll find just below the "previous track" arrow on the Player. You'll see the screen shown in Figure 6-1. Click the Create Account button.

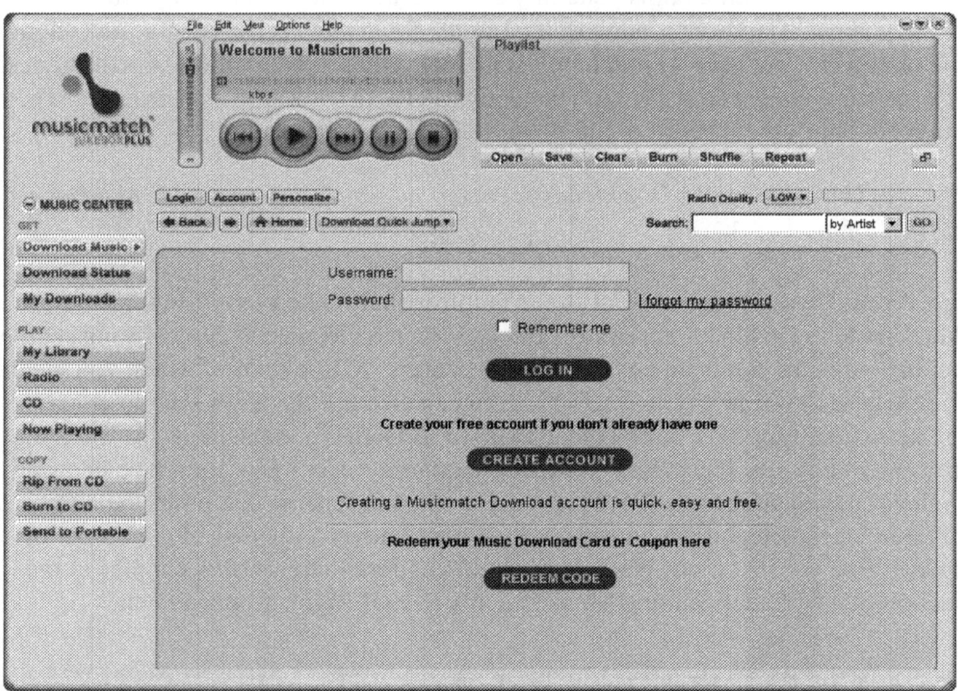

FIGURE 6-1 Click the Create Account button to start creating your Musicmatch Downloads account.

3. Fill out the requested account information, as seen in Figure 6-2. Be careful when choosing a security question. If all of your friends know that you followed Phish around to 16 cities on their 2002 world tour, "Who is your favorite artist/band" might not be the best choice for security questions.

4. Next you'll be asked to enter your personal and billing information. Again, your card won't be charged anything until you buy a song. Musicmatch merely keeps the number on file for future purchases.

5. If you used a different e-mail address than the one you used to register with Musicmatch, you'll now once again be prodded to upgrade to Jukebox Plus. We got this offer even though we were running the Plus version already. You don't need to upgrade to Jukebox Plus to utilize Musicmatch Downloads, though the faster burning speed will be appealing if you plan to copy your downloads to CDs.

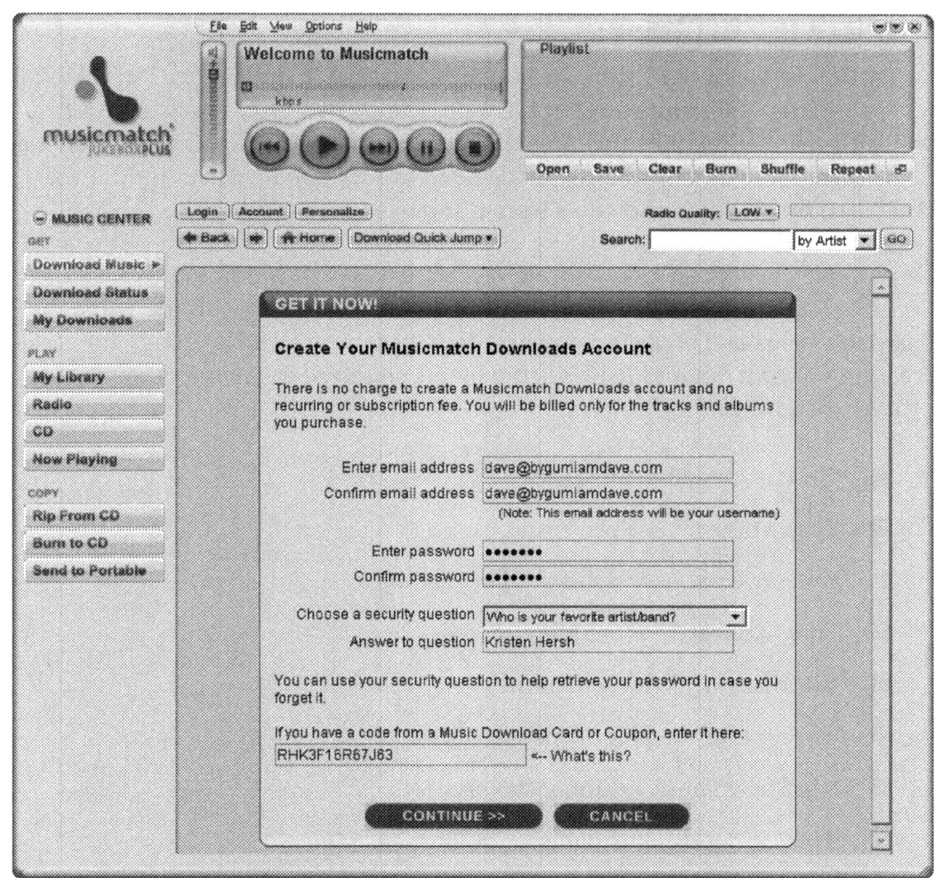

FIGURE 6-2 Your e-mail address will serve as your login name.

6. Finally, you'll be taken to the Account Information screen, where you can make changes to your e-mail address, password, and billing info, or add a subscription to Musicmatch Radio. If you've received any Musicmatch Downloads coupons or gift cards, you can enter them here by clicking Redeem Coupon.

7. Click the Done button at the bottom of the account information screen and you're ready to download! You'll receive an e-mail confirming your new account.

Our Own Purchases

So what have Denny and Rick spent their Musicmatch dollars on? After buying a copy of Dido's *Life for Rent* for his wife, Denny decided to re-establish his waning geek cred by downloading all the great tunes he'd heard while watching *Smallville.* Rick, on the other hand, decided to supplant his Rick Springfield collection by buying some tunes from a show grown-ups watch.

Denny: Hey, what can I say? *Smallville* has the best music soundtrack since *Melrose Place* went off the air. So I Google-searched up an episode guide that listed the songs and ended up downloading these wonderfully moody tunes and creating my own *Smallville* playlist, which I preferred to the selection on the official soundtrack CD.

- "So Far Away" —Staind
- "Just Another" —Pete Yorn
- "Wherever You Will Go" —The Calling
- "The Scientist" —Coldplay
- "No Blue Sky" —The Thorns
- "Kryptonite" —Three Doors Down
- "No Such Thing" —John Mayer
- "Nuclear" —Ryan Adams
- "What Do I Have to Do?" —Stabbing Westward

Rick: It's a good thing your teeny-bopper taste in television doesn't match up with your taste in music. *Smallville?* I didn't realize anyone over the age of 15 watched that show. Anyway, it's ironic that you mention TV-show soundtracks, because just the other day my wife and I were watching *Third Watch* (the most underrated show on television) and heard a song we really liked. A quick Google search later revealed the tune "Road" by Nick Drake. And herein lies the beauty of Musicmatch Downloads: after we looked up the Nick Drake song, we were given a list of similar artists, many of which we sampled and liked! You can't do that in a record store. But I digress; here's my list of recent Musicmatch purchases, not all of which were sparked by TV shows:

- "Road" —Nick Drake
- *Songs About Jane* —Maroon 5
- *Left of the Middle* —Natalie Imbruglia
- "Everything Reminds Me of Her" —Elliott Smith
- *Welcome Interstate Managers* —Fountains of Wayne
- "Owner of a Lonely Heart" —Yes

You can use this account on more than one computer, but keep in mind that Musicmatch will only allow you to activate five computers per account to play your Musicmatch Downloads.

Now that your account has been established, just click the Login button located above the Downloads browser window before purchasing music; you'll see the screen we saw back in Figure 6-1.

If you're the only one who uses your computer, you can click Remember Me after entering your username and password and you won't need to re-enter that information every time you log in.

Finding Album and Artist Information

Now that your account is established, you're ready to download some music! But first, you'll need to find some tunes to purchase. If you know what you're looking for, Musicmatch's search feature will help you find specific albums, artists, or songs. Just type a name or title in the Search box on the right side of the screen, above the Downloads browser window, and choose the appropriate search type—Artist, Album, or Track—from the drop-down menu, as seen in Figure 6-3.

If the item isn't found, you'll see a list of close matches in the Downloads browser. If you see what you're looking for in the list, just left-click it. Otherwise, click the Back button above the browser window to try again.

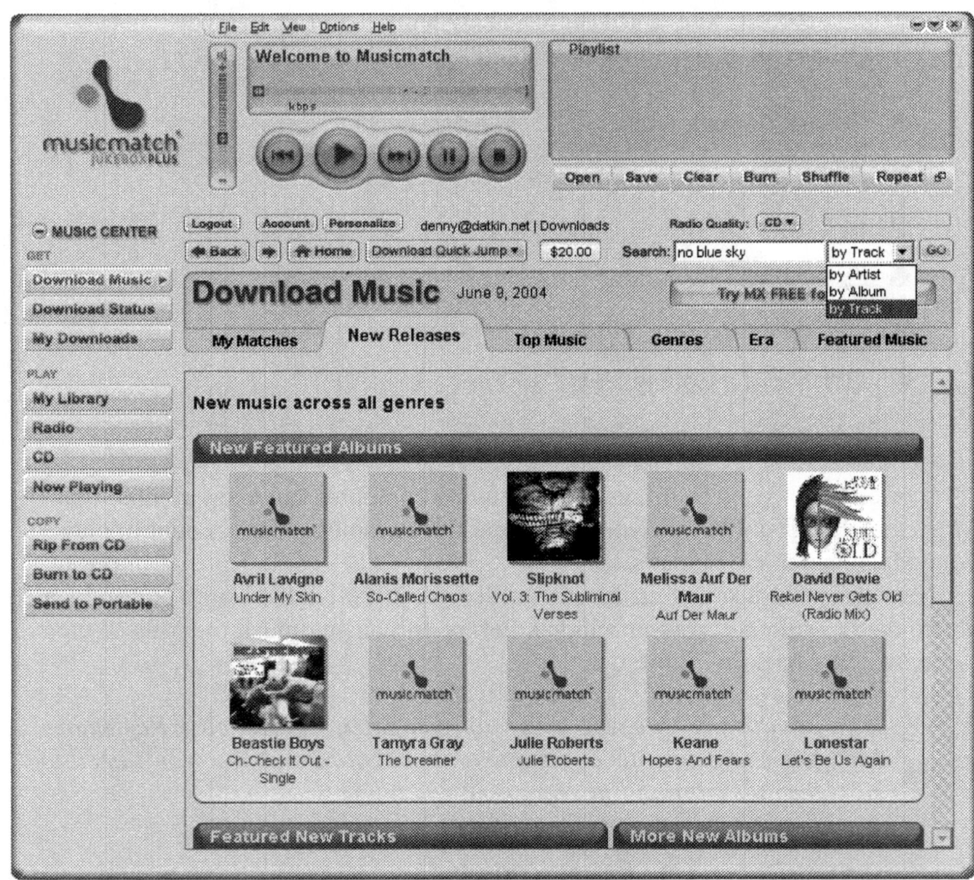

FIGURE 6-3 Search for music by Artist, Album, or Track

If the artist, album, or song was located, you'll see a results window similar to the one in Figure 6-4. Here you can browse through individual tracks or entire albums, discover similar musicians, or read more about the artist. Searching by song title is a great way to find cover versions of favorite songs, though Denny managed to resist the burning temptation to download John Tesh's cover of "Red Rain."

TIP

Musicmatch's database includes information on far more than the 500,000-plus songs currently available for download. Even if a major-label band doesn't have its music available for purchase, chances are you can still find a biography, discography, and often even album reviews and track listings for the group or artist.

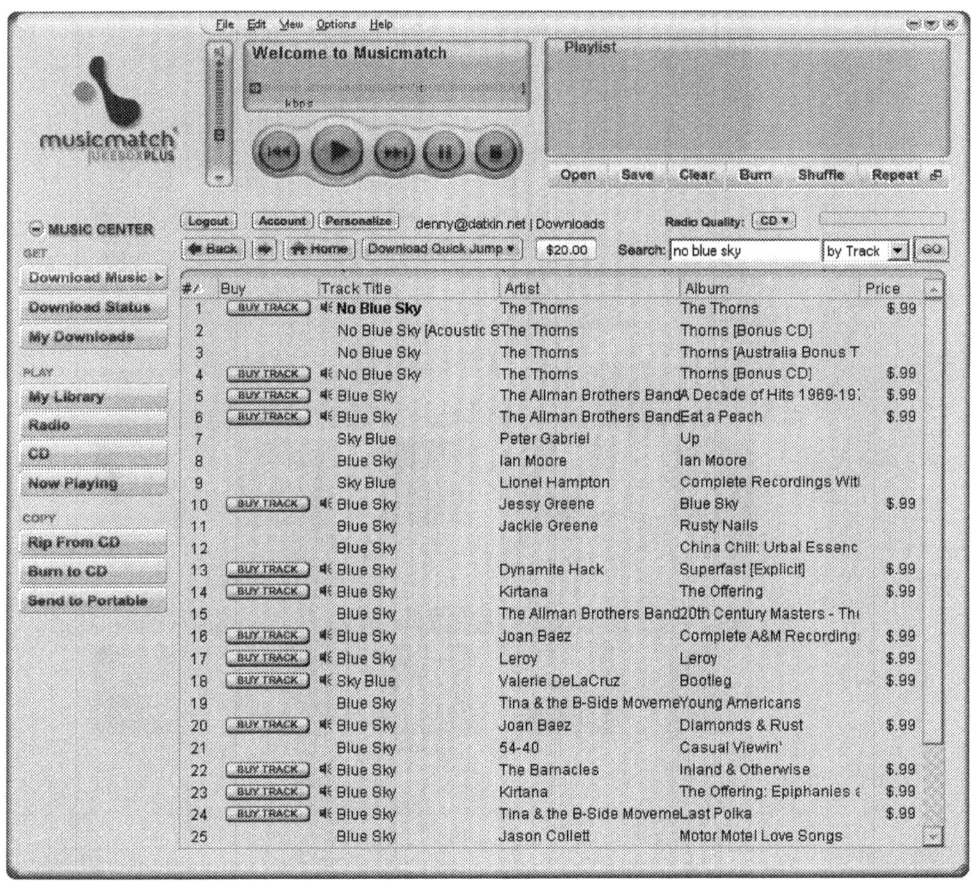

FIGURE 6-4 Musicmatch lists exact matches for your search first, and then it follows with similar titles.

The Related Artists tab, combined with the ability to hear 30-second samples of any song in the Musicmatch library, is an excellent way to discover new bands and singers that fit your tastes. And even if you think you know all there is to know about your favorite musicians (such as Rick, who has an unrivaled collection of Raffi biographies), you should still check out the Artist Info tab. The biographies are often packed with hotlinks, which can point you not only to related artists, but also to albums and songs the musician has guested on. You might also find links to earlier bands that the artists were members of. A little exploring can quickly empty the wallet of musical completists looking to add to their collections.

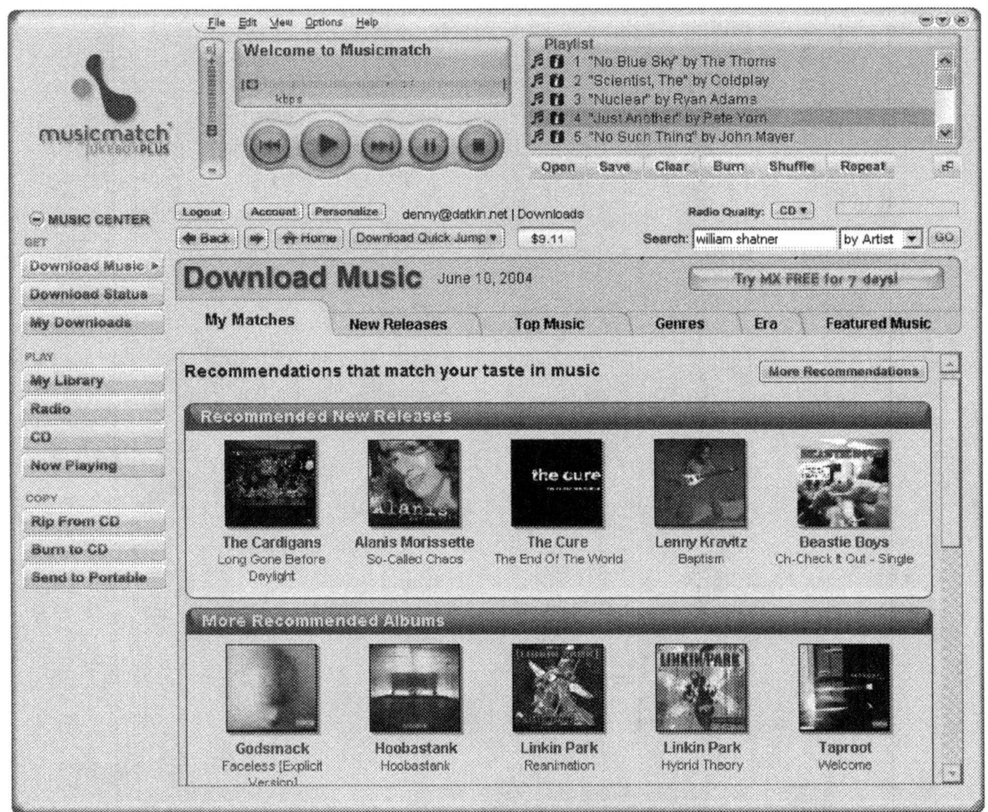

FIGURE 6-5 Musicmatch can recommend music based on your current music library.

If you're in a more exploratory mood, Musicmatch offers a variety of ways to browse its extensive music library. Click the Download Music button in the Music Center bar and you'll see a screen that looks something like Figure 6-5.

Musicmatch Downloads offers six different approaches to browsing its library; just click the appropriate tab at the top of the Downloads browser to start browsing. The tabs are

- **My Matches** Musicmatch examines the contents of your music library and recommends similar artists, as well as other albums by the artists in your collection. You can fine-tune the recommendations by clicking the Personalize button above the music browser and entering up to ten of your favorite artists, as seen in Figure 6-6.

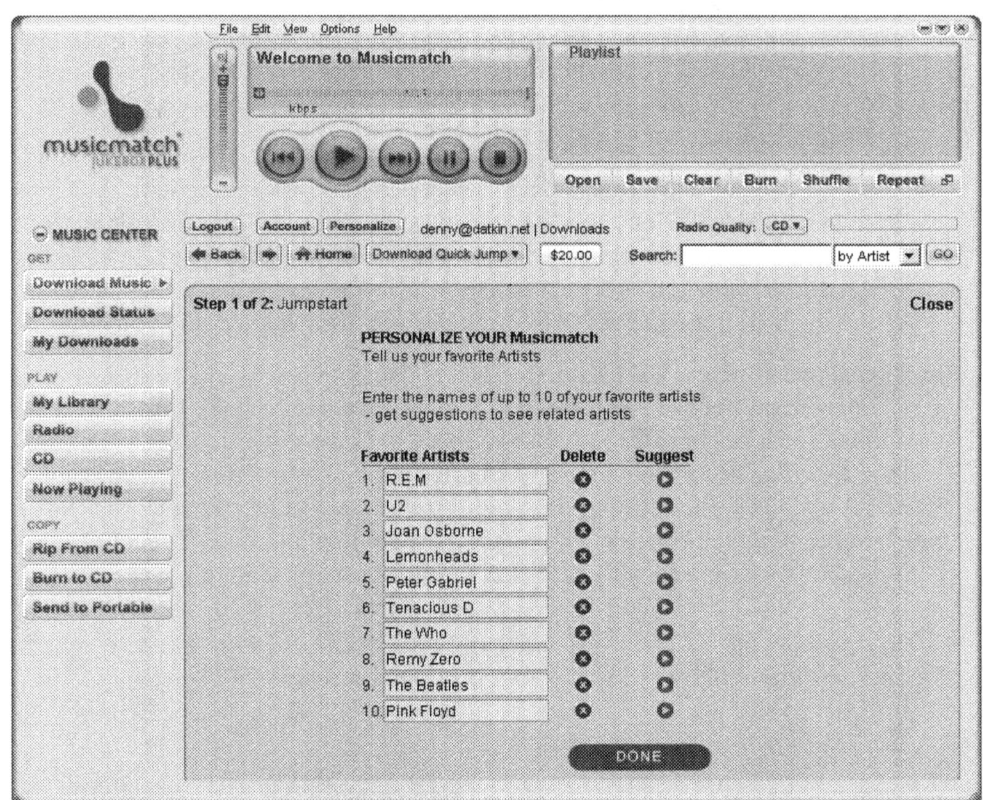

FIGURE 6-6 Click the Personalize button and enter up to ten of your favorite artists in order to improve Musicmatch's music recommendations.

- **New Releases** As you'd expect, this page lists albums and singles recently added to the Musicmatch Downloads library.
- **Top Music** See what all the cool kids are downloading! This page lists the most-played or downloaded albums, songs, and artists on Musicmatch's Downloads and Radio services. Check it out—you don't want to be the only person in the crowd who thinks "Hoobastank" is an insult, when it's in fact an extremely popular group among Musicmatch listeners.

6

- **Genres** Looking for West Coast rap? Having trouble finding new Ska tunes? Want to impress that cute Irish girl (or guy) who just moved into the apartment down the hall by playing some Celtic Fusion tunes? Musicmatch breaks down its library into 17 main genres and over 200 subgenres, making it easy to find certain styles of music.
- **Era** Though the Members Only jacket has long since been retired, Denny has an unhealthy affinity for '80s music, so he was quite pleased to find that the 12-inch remix version of Animotion's "Obsession" was just a few clicks away in Musicmatch's '80s category. You'll find sections for every decade from the '60s through the 2000s, broken down by decade or individual year.
- **Featured Music** This section is where Musicmatch highlights a few hot or new bands, as well as artists in the news. Each entry may link to a new album, or it might offer a chance to listen to some of the musician's tunes for free. For instance, when Ray Charles passed away, Musicmatch made its Artist On Demand streaming radio station available to all its users for free for a limited time, in his memory. (We'll touch on Musicmatch Radio later in this chapter, and you'll find the full scoop in Chapter 8.)

Okay, by now you should have found more than a tune or two that you're anxious to add to your digital library. So let's go spend some money!

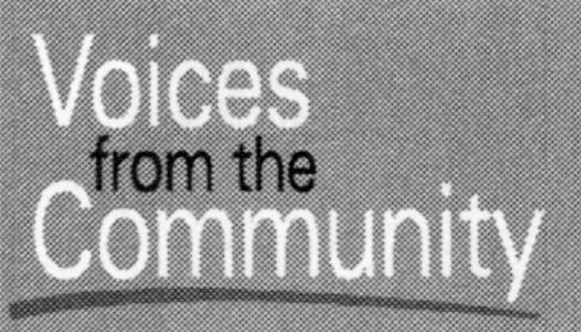

How Serious Users Use Musicmatch

Tom Pettigrew is "VP Global Sales Partners" (we're not sure what it means either, but it sounds pretty cool) for Isilon Systems, "the premier provider of intelligent clustered storage systems for digital content" (nope, don't know what that means either, but it sounds just as cool). Turns out, even high-powered executives at high-tech companies use Musicmatch.

Q: How do you use Musicmatch?

A: I have a laptop with a USB sound interface from Creative Labs hooked up to my centralized house stereo system. My family (my wife and two teenage daughters, ages 16 and 18) uses this with my Musicmatch Plus account to play music throughout the house. If it's a hot afternoon by the pool, we might have the Classic Rock station on. If it's a dinner party, we might pick Smooth Jazz.

If I'm having a discussion with my daughters about the history of rock, I might pull up a specific group and play several of their songs or punch through several of their songs to get to the one we want to listen to. For example, Queen has been a hot topic lately, so I've been pulling up their songs… and a lot of my daughters' teenage friends who know Queen only for "Bohemian Rhapsody" now know a considerably larger repertoire. My youngest daughter has a PC in her bedroom and she uses a Musicmatch account to play selected music pretty much all the time. Thanks to the "artist" and "similar artist" categories, she's really expanded on the number of groups she listens to and has a very broad appreciation of a number of music styles as a result.

Finally, I have Musicmatch on my laptop and I travel with a pair of Sony portable speakers in my bag. I logged over 200,000 miles last year. As miserable as all that travel can get, many hotels now have broadband Internet access in their rooms. I've found that a great way to relax and handle all the stress is to boot up, attach the speakers, log into Musicmatch, and stream some relaxing new-age or jazz music into the room. It really creates a nice ambience and makes staying in a hotel alone just a little bit more bearable.

Q: What's your favorite Musicmatch feature or capability?

A: Our favorite feature by far is to select a specific artist and related artists. It's great to see where it takes the music. There are always some nice surprises and some exposure to songs and artists that we wouldn't have thought of.

Q: How big is your music collection?

A: Between me and my daughters we must have 600 to 700 CDs, and (don't tell the RIAA) my oldest daughter has to have at least 40GB of MP3s that she downloaded (someone at Musicmatch can do the math on how many songs that would be—but I know it's a lot!).

Q: Name some of your favorite bands and musicians.

A: Yes, Queen, Sheryl Crow, a lot of classic rock (Jethro Tull, Led Zeppelin, Stones, Beatles, etc.), generic new age, and smooth jazz.

Buying and Downloading Your First Song

Once you've established an account and browsed or searched for a song or album you'd like to buy, the actual process couldn't be easier. If a song is available for purchase, Musicmatch will place a Buy Track icon to the left (in the browser window) or right (in the playlist) of the song title. If the current browser view lists albums, you'll see Buy Album buttons next to available album names as well.

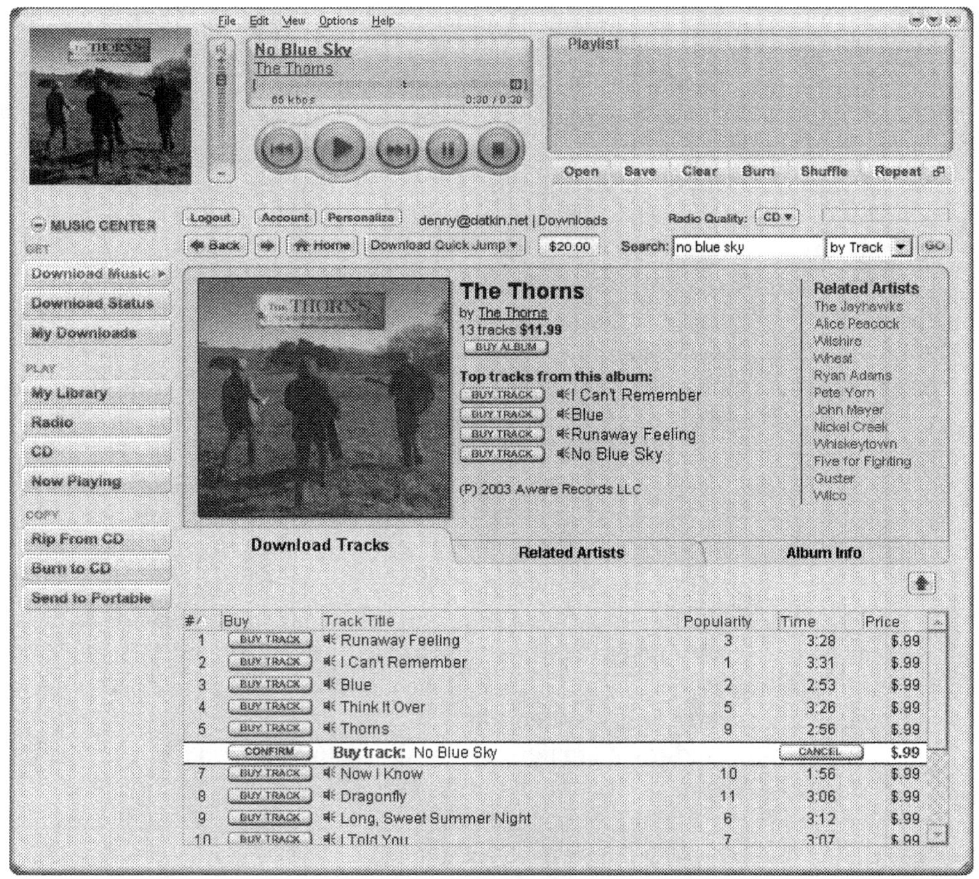

FIGURE 6-7 After clicking a Buy Track button in the track list, the button will change as seen here; click Confirm to buy the track, or Cancel to abort the purchase.

Buying a track or album couldn't be easier. You simply click the Buy Track (or Buy Album) button next to the music you're purchasing. If you've clicked in the track list, the Buy Track button will change to read Confirm, as seen in Figure 6-7. If you're sure you want to buy the track, just click Confirm. If you've changed your mind, or you clicked the wrong button, just click the Cancel button, which you'll find, oddly, under the Time column in the same row.

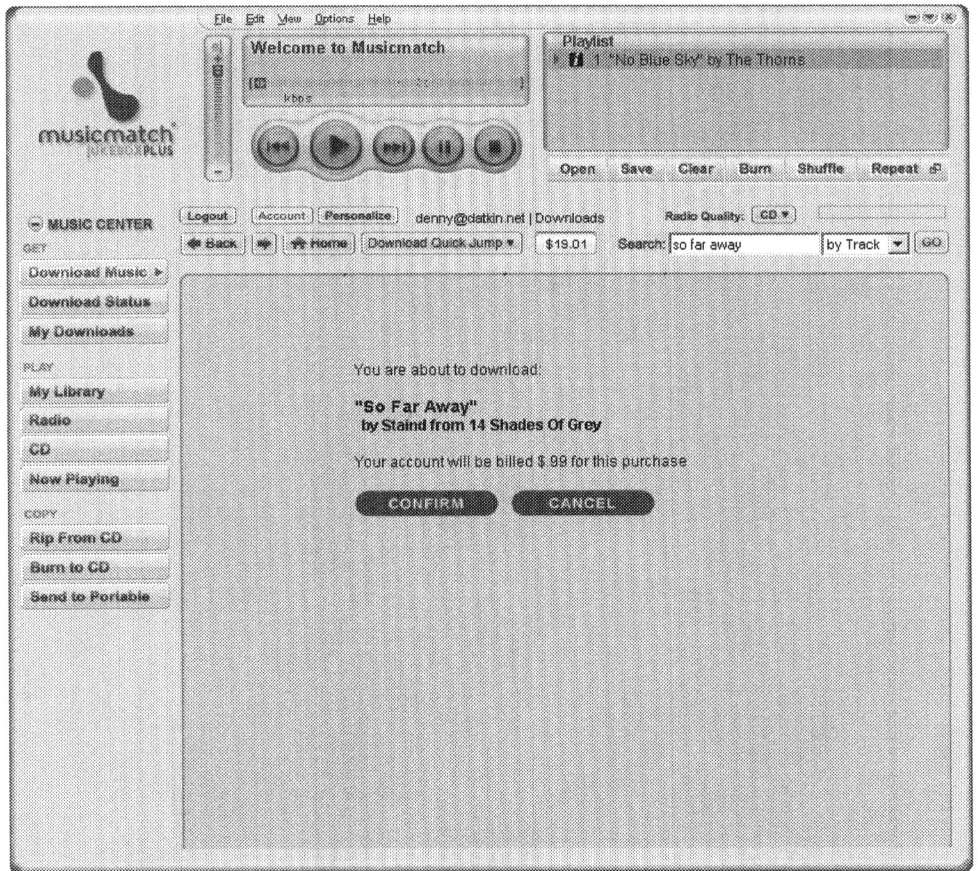

FIGURE 6-8 Depending on where you click to buy a song, you may see this confirmation window instead.

If you buy an entire album, or you choose a track from the list at the top of the browser, you'll see the confirmation window in Figure 6-8 instead. It works just as you'd expect—click Confirm to buy the track, or Cancel to abort the purchase.

That's all there is to it! After you confirm the purchase of a song, it will automatically be downloaded (as seen in Figure 6-9) and added to your library, and to the current playlist. (See Chapter 9 for the full scoop on playlists.) If you bought an album, Musicmatch will download all of the album's songs automatically.

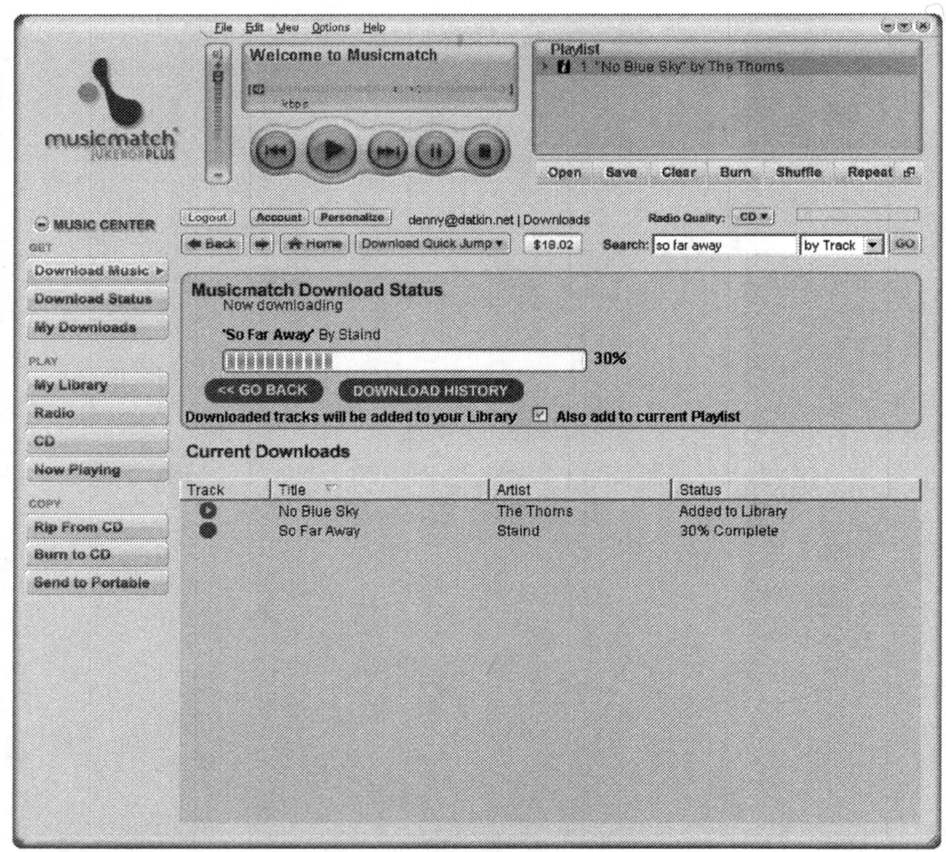

FIGURE 6-9 A Musicmatch download in progress

Musicmatch won't let you re-download a song you've paid for after the initial download. You should back up any songs you purchase to CD to protect them against hard drive crashes and other PC disasters.

Songs you download will be stored in a folder called Musicmatch Downloads within your Tracks Directory. If you didn't change the default assignment for this directory, you'll find the songs in My Documents/My Music/Musicmatch Downloads. (See Chapter 4 for information on changing the directory where tracks are stored.)

Did you know?

You Can Buy Songs off the (Musicmatch) Radio, Too!

When you're listening to Musicmatch Radio or the premium Musicmatch MX premium radio streaming music service, you can often purchase the song you're listening to. Just look for the Buy Track button next to the song name in the playlist, and click it if you want to purchase the tune. Note that you'll be charged the usual 99 cents for buying the song even if you're a listening to it on the premium MX radio service. Your monthly fee covers only music that's streamed down over the Internet (in other words, that aren't recorded on your hard drive), not downloads. Still, Musicmatch's radio offerings are a great way to find new (or forgotten) tunes to download. Just start the radio service playing in the background while you do other work on your computer, and if you hear a song you'd like to add to your Music library, just return to Musicmatch and download the tune. Note that not all tunes on Musicmatch's radio services are available for purchase.

Understanding Musicmatch's Digital Rights Management

As part of the effort to curb the rampant sharing of songs prevalent in the early days of Napster (and the modern days of KaZaa and Morpheus), Musicmatch protects its music using the Digital Rights Management (DRM) features built into the Windows Media Audio format. The DRM restrictions are far from Orwellian: You can play tunes on up to three computers, download them to supported portable players, and burn up to five copies of each CD playlist you create. Still, they do limit your flexibility compared to MP3, mp3Pro, or unprotected WMA files.

Musicmatch authenticates over the Internet your right to play each song the first time you play it. After that, you can play that song on that computer with no restrictions, and there's no need to be connected to the Internet.

Let's take a look at just what you can—and can't—do with songs you purchase from the Musicmatch Downloads store.

What You Can Do with Musicmatch Downloads WMA Tunes

Musicmatch's Digital Rights Management isn't draconian—you're able to replicate and transfer the songs in a number of ways.

1. Play them on up to three PCs. The first time you play a DRM-protected WMA song on a computer, you'll need to log in to your Musicmatch account so that the song can be authenticated.
2. Play them using Windows Media Player, Winamp, and a number of other player applications that support WMA files. Once your tune has been authenticated over the Internet on the first play, it will play back using any WMA-capable program.
3. Burn them to CD. Musicmatch lets you burn songs to CD in standard, unprotected CD audio format. You can only burn a particular playlist (say, an album with songs in the original order, or a custom mix CD) up to five times, though there's no limit to how many times an individual song can be burned to disc as long as you vary the playlists it's used in.
4. Download them to supported portable players and PDAs. You can transfer your downloads to portable players that support DRM-protected WMA files, such as the Dell Digital Jukebox, a variety of Rio and Creative Nomad players, and PDAs running the Windows Mobile for Pocket PCs operating system. The procedure is the same as with unprotected songs. See Chapter 11 for everything you need to know about downloading music to portable music players.

What You Can't Do with Musicmatch Downloads WMA Tunes

On the other hand, the DRM does limit what you can do with Musicmatch tunes compared to more flexible unprotected songs. Here are some of the things you *can't* do with songs you buy.

- Give them to friends. If you try to play the tune on someone else's computer, they'll get a message that they need to download Musicmatch and log in—using your account. And sharing your account information isn't an option, since you're limited to five computers, not to mention the fact that your friends could use the account to purchase music you'd have to pay for.

- Burn 50 copies of your compilation CD for all your friends. Musicmatch only lets you burn up to five copies of a playlist containing protected songs.
- Play them on a computer without an Internet connection. You must be able to connect to the Internet the first time you play a tune so that Musicmatch can authenticate your right to play the tracks.
- Play them on a Macintosh or Linux system. Though earlier versions of Musicmatch were available for Mac and Linux computers, the program is now exclusive to Windows, and Musicmatch Downloads tunes can only be played in Windows systems.
- Play them on an iPod, Palm OS handheld, or any other portable that doesn't support DRM-protected WMA format. But take heart, Palm users: The developer of the Pocket Tunes audio player for the Palm OS says that a future version of the program will support DRM-protected WMA files.
- Play them on most networked or wireless media players, such as the D-Link DSM-320 and Hauppauge MediaMVP. At press time, none of these players supported DRM-protected WMA files.

These restrictions can be worked around with a bit of extra effort, as seen in the How To… sidebar that follows. But the procedure we outline takes a fair amount of time and effort, and likely causes a slight degradation in sound quality. So keep the DRM restrictions in mind when choosing to buy an album from Musicmatch rather than purchasing it from a record store.

Moving Your Music to a New Computer

Everyone buys a new computer from time to time. Given Musicmatch's stringent DRM protections, should you be worried that you won't be able to play your library of paid-for tunes on the new machine? Fear not—Musicmatch employs a method known as *deactivation* that will keep you listening happily until computers are actually implanted directly in your brain.

Put simply, deactivation is the process of telling Musicmatch that you're relocating your tunes. When you deactivate the old PC, it will no longer be able to play the songs you've purchased from Musicmatch Downloads. This is a permanent move (unless you reformat the computer's hard drive, that is), so don't do it until you've activated Musicmatch on your new PC and checked to make sure your tunes play okay. (Remember, Musicmatch allows you to have up to five "active" computers at a time, so you can easily have both your old and new machine active simultaneously.

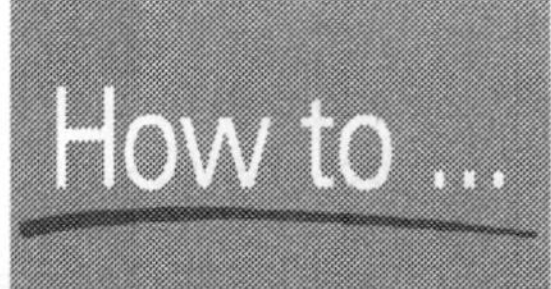

Use Musicmatch Downloads on Unsupported Devices

There's actually a trick you can use if you want to listen to your Musicmatch tunes on equipment that doesn't support DRM-protected Windows Media files, such as an iPod or a non-Pocket PC PDA. With a little effort, you can convert the songs to standard MP3 format. There's nothing illegal about doing this—Musicmatch doesn't even prohibit this procedure in its license agreement—but it's not something that the company (or the music industry) supports since this procedure could be used to share copyrighted music by unscrupulous users. But we know you're the honest type, so we'll share the trick with you:

1. First, burn the tunes you want to convert to MP3 to CD. (See Chapter 11 for full details on how to burn CDs using Musicmatch.) If you're just using this CD for conversion purposes and don't plan to use it for standalone play, use a CD-RW rewriteable disc, which you can erase and reuse after this procedure is complete.
2. Now, leave the CD in the drive and rip the contents to MP3 format, as outlined in Chapter 4. In order to maintain the quality of the 160-Kbps WMA files, we suggest using a custom MP3 quality of at least 192 Kbps, or a VBR setting of at least 80 percent. Note that unless you're ripping a downloaded album in its original order, Musicmatch will likely need you to enter the artist, title, album, and other information for each song after you rip it.
3. You'll now have a second copy of your song in MP3 format, which can be used on virtually all portable players, as well as on Macs, Linux systems, and other more "unusual" players. Note that this gives you two copies of these songs in your Musicmatch library; you may want to move the original WMA versions to another directory or burn them to a CD to avoid the duplication.

We've entrusted you with great power. Please use it wisely. We'd hate to see abuse result in future program releases disabling this useful procedure and eliminating this added flexibility.

The reason to deactivate the old one is to make sure you don't inadvertently get stuck years down the road.)

You can work around all this DRM nonsense by burning your downloads to CD, and then ripping them back to your PC as an MP3 or as an unsecured WMA format file. See the sidebar "Use Musicmatch Downloads on Unsupported Devices" to learn how.

Buy, Burn, Rip, and Run!

A Speedy Journey Through Musicmatch's Major Features

In this spotlight section, we'll walk you through all of Musicmatch's major features, showing you how to do just about everything Musicmatch lets you do with music. We'll find an album from a favorite artist and buy it online. After giving it a quick listen, we'll burn it to CD for listening in the car or on the home stereo.

But we won't stop there! The next step is to turn around and rip the CD we've just burned, converting the songs to MP3 files. Why bother? Because many devices, such as Palm PDAs, Apple iPods, and home media players don't currently support the copy-protected Windows Media Audio (WMA) files you purchase from the Musicmatch Downloads service.

Finally, we'll take the album we purchased and download it to a portable player for on-the-go listening. And even though we'll be doing everything short of folding, spindling, and mutilating (much to the disappointment of Rick, who has destructive tendencies) the album that we purchased, the entire process of buying, burning, ripping, playing, and downloading happens with surprisingly few clicks.

Shopping at the Record Store

First, let's head to Musicmatch Downloads and buy an album. (You'll need to set up a Musicmatch Downloads account to do this; see Chapter 6 for details.)

To get started, click the Music Store button on the left side of the screen. In our example, we'll find the newest album from Coldplay (though obviously you can substitute any album you might want to buy). Click in the Search box in the top-right corner of the Music Store window, type **Coldplay** in the box, and make sure Artist is selected as the search type, as seen in Figure 1. Then click Go to begin the search.

The Results window will appear, with the most popular tracks from Coldplay highlighted. We want to purchase an entire album, so click the Album tab, as shown in Figure 2, to bring up a list of available Coldplay albums and CD singles. *Live 2003* sounds like a good collection for a fan new to the group, so we'll double-click that in the list.

Figure 1. Looking for instant gratification? Buy an album from the Musicmatch Downloads Music Store.

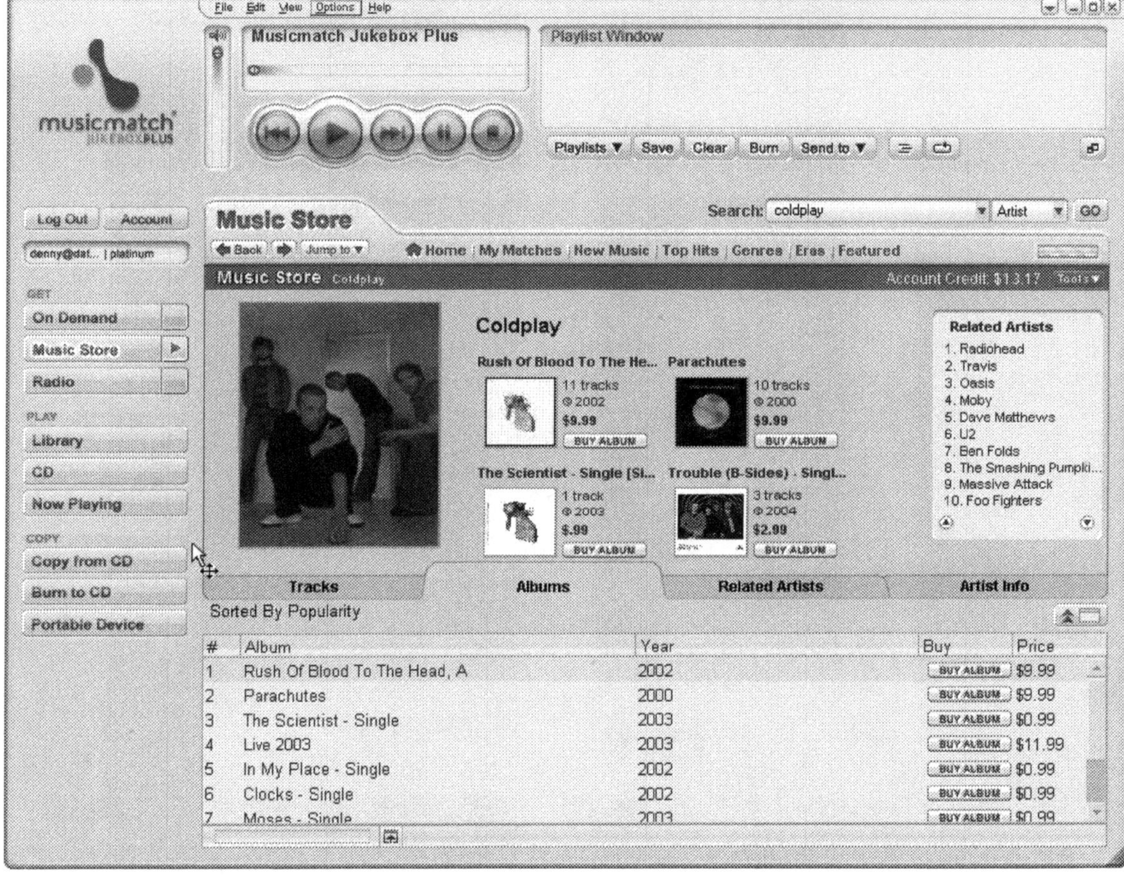

Figure 2. The Music Store features a variety of albums, as well as CD single collections.

Double-clicking the album brings up an image of the album cover, as well as a track list. Let's double-click a few of the track titles to listen to 30-second samples, just to insure this is the album we want. In Figure 3, we're listening to a sample of "Amsterdam."

Okay, we've now officially decided that Coldplay can not only play more than the basic three chords, but that the band officially "rocks." (Well, in a mellow way.) So we're ready to buy. Just left-click the Buy Album button next to the album cover and a window will appear, asking you to confirm the

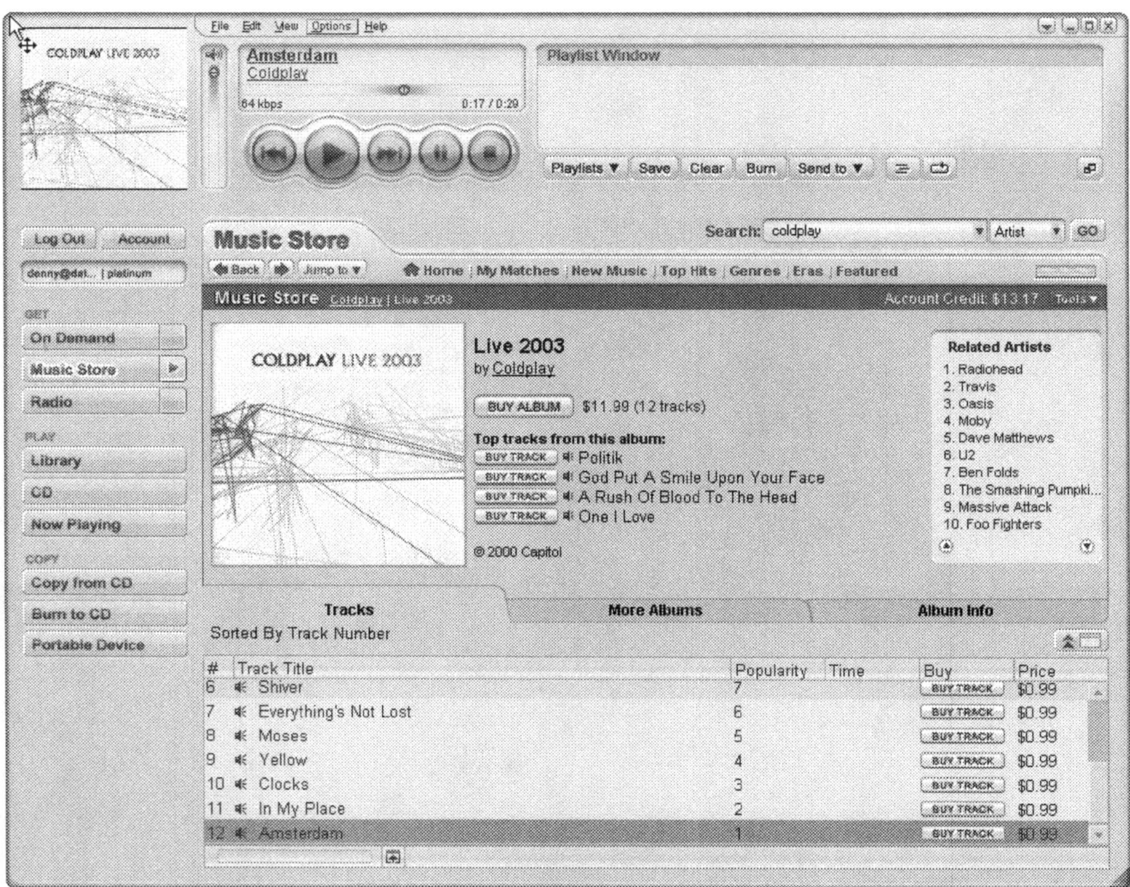

Figure 3. You can listen to 30-second samples of songs to ensure that you want to buy the entire album.

purchase, as seen in Figure 4. Left-click the Confirm choice to buy it, or Cancel to abort the purchase.

Once you confirm the purchase, the album will start downloading automatically. If you haven't changed the defaults on Musicmatch's General Settings tab, each song will be added to the music library and the current playlist upon completion of the download. Once the first song is downloaded, the playlist will automatically begin playing. If you look at Figure 5, you'll see that the first two songs have been added to the Playlist Window, the first song is currently playing, and the third song's download progress is indicated at the bottom of the Music Store window.

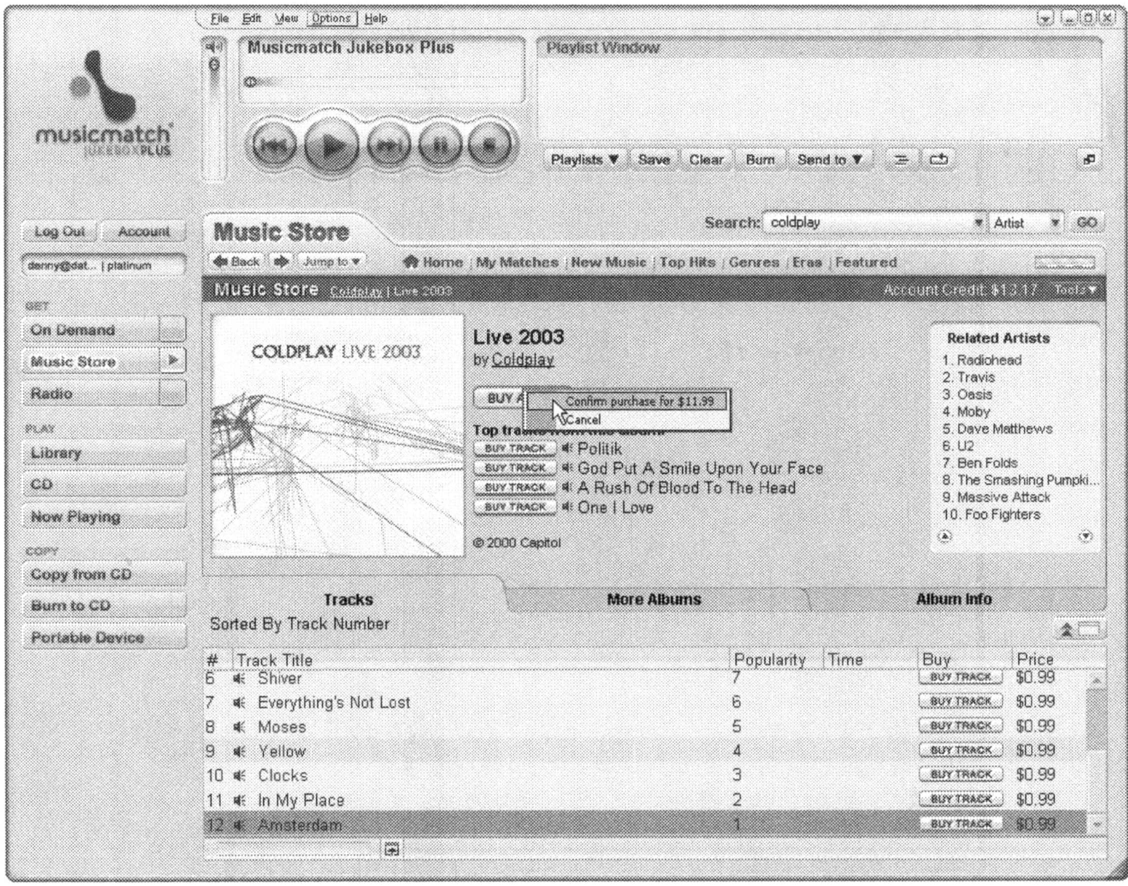

Figure 4. Musicmatch gives you the opportunity to confirm or cancel a purchase.

Once the album has finished downloading, Musicmatch will have automatically created a playlist containing all of its songs. Occasionally, we found that Musicmatch downloaded songs out of the original order; to fix this, you can drag the song name in the playlist around using the left mouse button until they match the order shown in the album description in the Music Store window. Rather than having to re-create that playlist later, let's save it for future use. Click the Save button in the Playlist Window and you'll see a window like the one in Figure 6. Enter the name of the album and click the OK button.

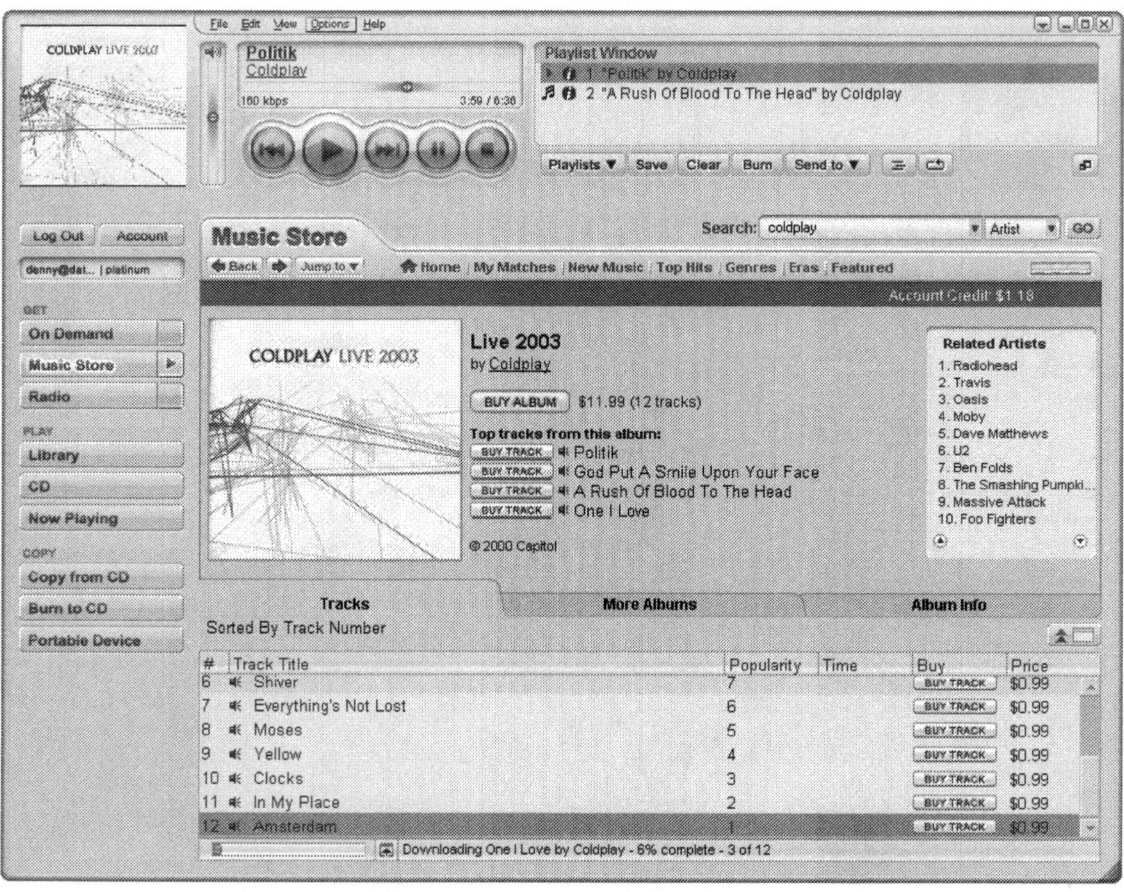

Figure 5. As each song is downloaded, it's added to the current playlist.

That's all there is to it! You've now purchased and downloaded an album, and created a playlist to allow easy playback later. Depending on the speed of your Internet connection, the entire process likely took just a few minutes—far quicker than running down to the local music store.

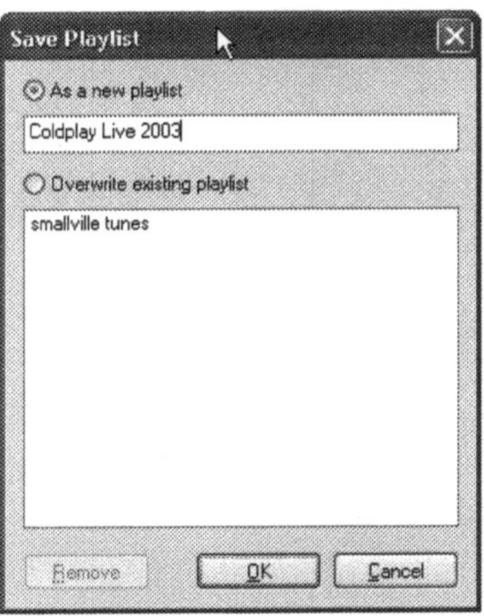

Figure 6. Choose a name for the current playlist; the album name is the logical choice.

Burn, Baby, Burn

Of course, if you had run down to the local music store, you'd have a physical CD to show for your trouble. Assuming your PC has a CD or DVD burner installed, you can easily create your own CD version of the album you just purchased.

If you're continuing from the last section, you'll already have the album loaded as the current playlist. If not, click the Playlists button at the bottom of the Playlist Window and choose the Playlist you created earlier. Now click the Burn button below the Playlist window to begin the CD creation process.

When the Burner window opens, the first thing you'll see is a status window, as shown in Figure 7, as the program verifies the presence and integrity of the songs in the current playlist.

Once all the songs are verified, the burner window will show the current playlist. At the top of the window, you'll see a generic album name consisting of numbers. Click this and enter the actual album name, as shown in Figure 8.

NOTE

Be sure to click the Burn button in the playlist window, rather than the Burn to CD button you'll find in the sidebar on the left side of the screen. That way, Musicmatch will burn the current playlist to the CD.

If you have more than one burner on your computer (such as a PC equipped with both CD-RW and DVD+RW drives), or if you want to change the burning speed, click the Tools button to activate the settings menu shown in Figure 9.

You can hold down the left mouse button and drag songs up and down in the list in order to change the order in which they're burned to CD. If you want to omit songs from the disc, de-select the checkboxesnext to the songs' names, as shown in Figure 10. (This capability is especially useful for removing in-between-song skits that, while funny at first, can grow tiresome with repeated listening. We're talking to you, Tenacious D.) In this case, however, we want to create an exact copy of the CD you'd buy in a store (so we can rip it in the next step), so don't change the song order or deselect any tunes.

Now insert a blank CD in your CD burner and click the Burn button near the top-left corner of the burner window. You'll see a progress window like the one shown in Figure 11, indicating which track is currently being burned, and the percentage of the overall burn process that's been completed.

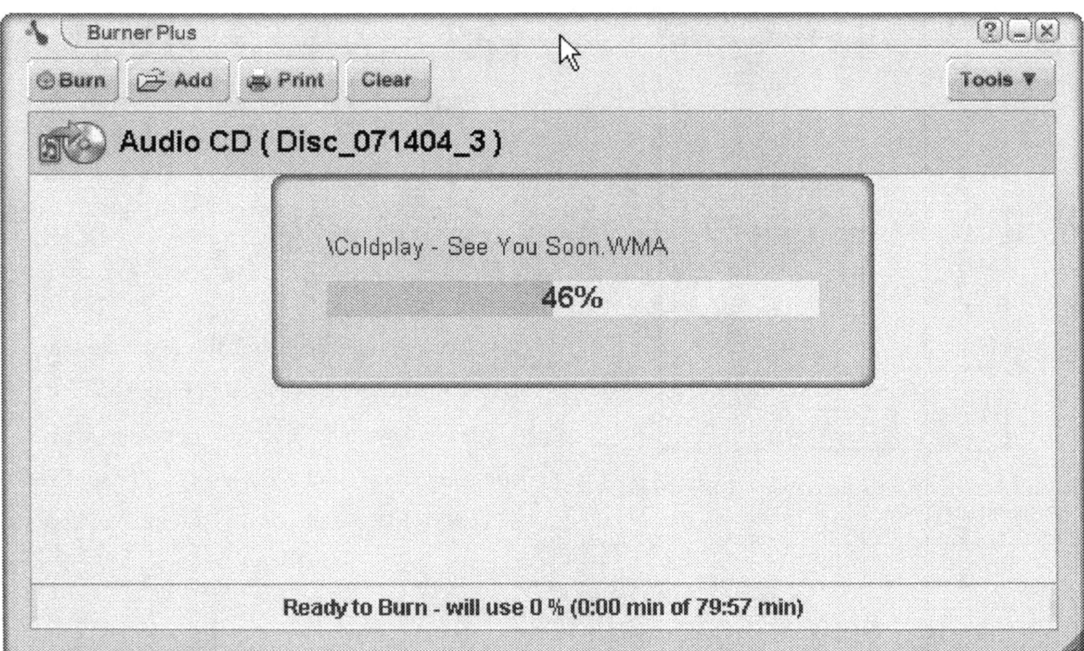

Figure 7. Musicmatch first verifies that all of the songs you want to burn are present and accounted for.

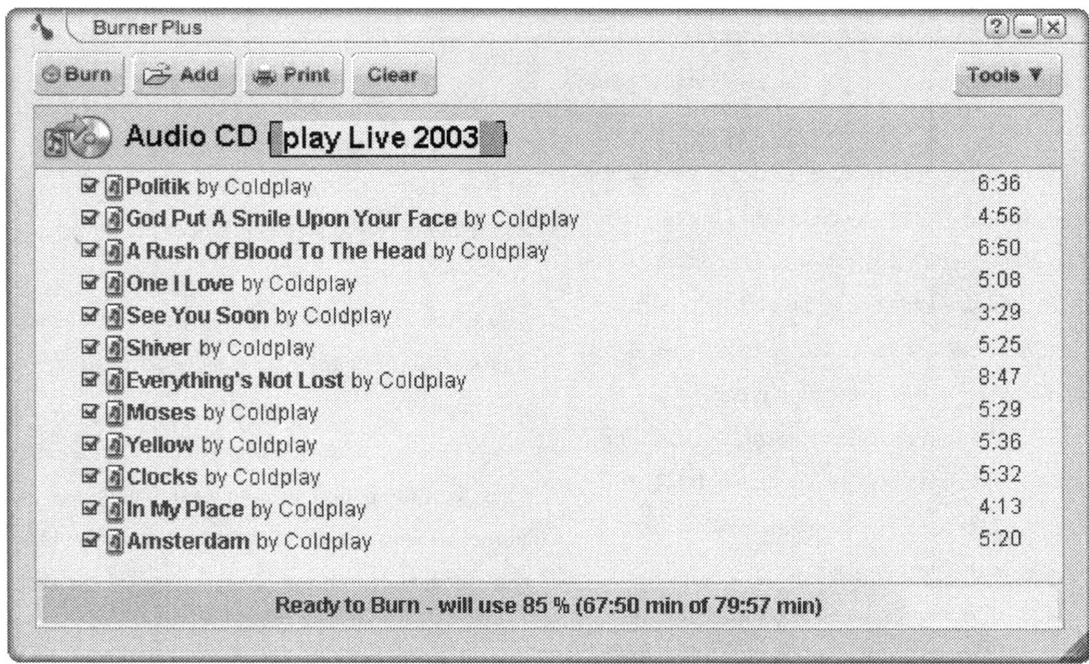

Figure 8. Entering the actual album name helps you identify which CD is loaded if you later play the CD on a computer or CD TEXT–enabled CD player.

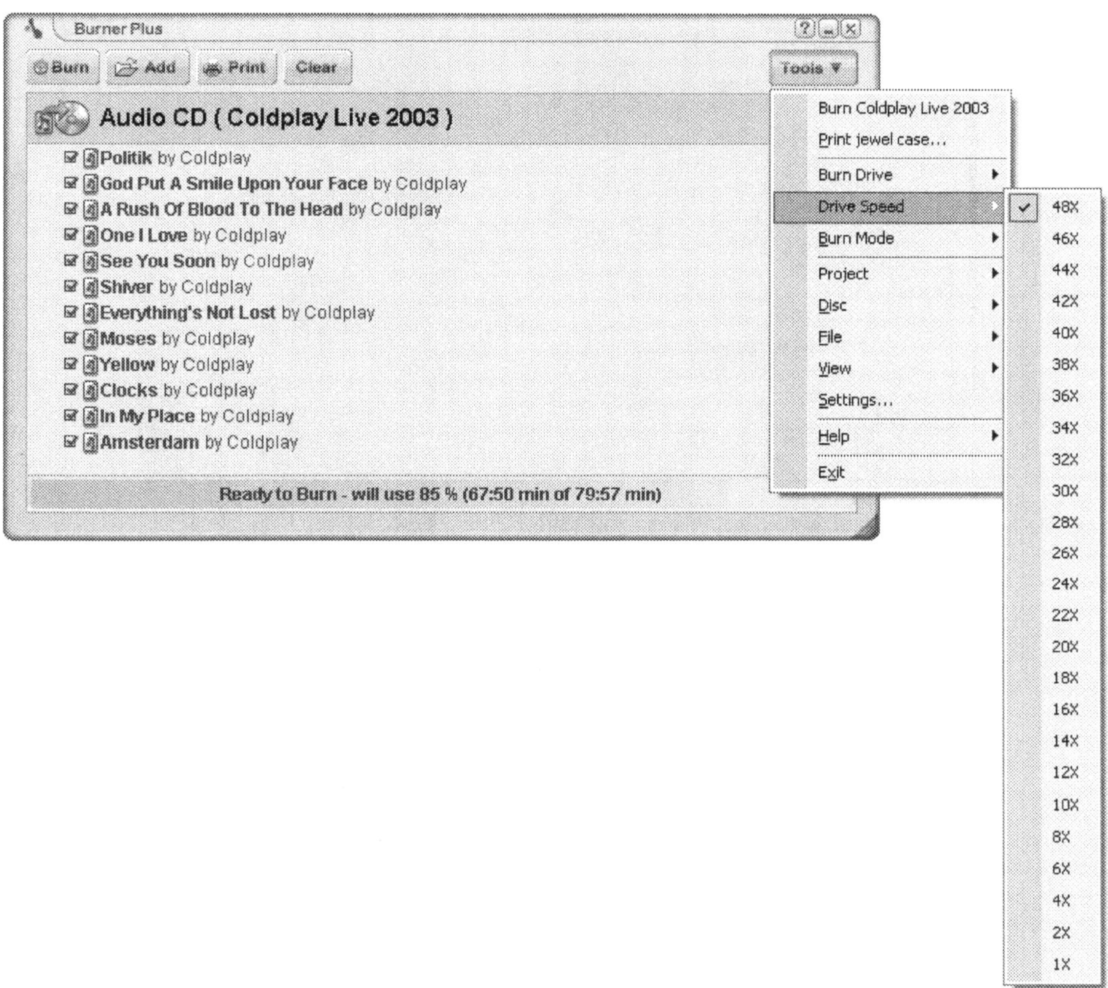

Figure 9. Choosing the speed at which Musicmatch will burn your CD; if you get burn errors, you may want to try a slower burn rate.

Once the burn has been completed, the disc will be ejected and you'll see the window shown in Figure 12. If you want to create another copy of the CD (note that Musicmatch limits you to five copies of any one playlist of music purchased from its Download Music store), click Burn this Disc Again. Otherwise, click Return to Musicmatch Burner to exit, then close the Burner window by clicking the *x* in the top-right corner. Congratulations, you now have an actual CD to show for your purchase!

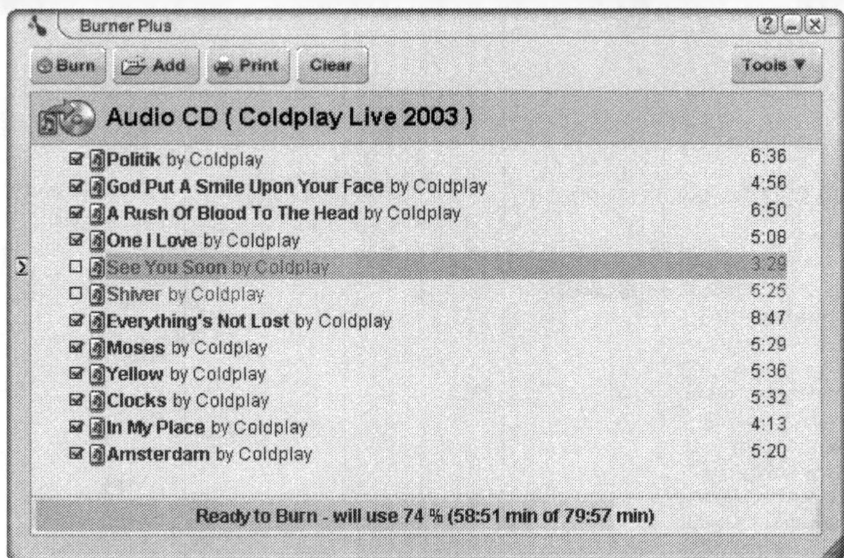

Figure 10. You can de-select individual songs so that they won't be burned to disc.

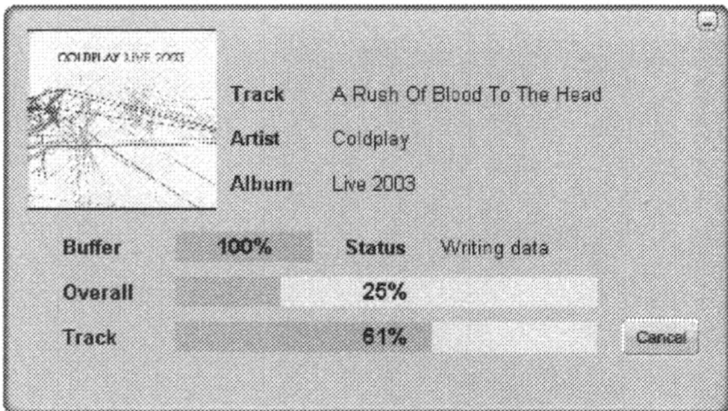

Figure 11. The status window shows you how far your CD burn has progressed.

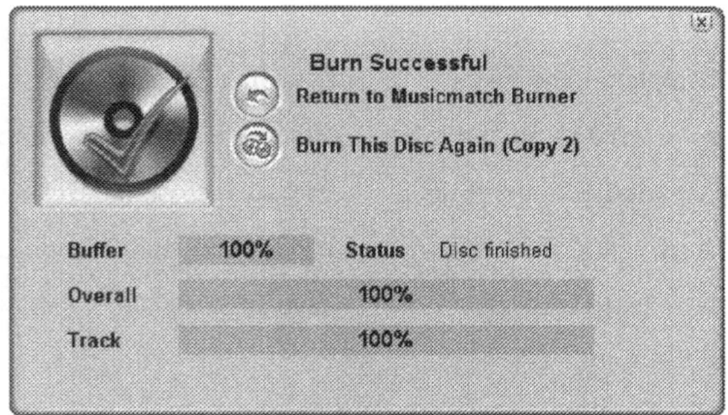

Figure 12. Though "Burn Successful" sounds like something you'd hear an astronaut say, it signifies that your CD burn has completed.

Rip-Tide

Now that we've burned our album to CD, we're going to turn right around and rip it back to digital format! Why would we do such a thing when we already have the digital music files we bought from the Musicmatch Store? Because there's still a lot of hardware, unfortunately, that doesn't support the WMA format that songs you buy from Musicmatch are stored in. By ripping the CD we purchased, we'll have copies in MP3 format, which will play on just about everything out there. These songs can be included on MP3-format CDs, which play on many modern DVD players, car stereos, and portable CD players, and offer about ten hours of music on a single disc.

First, let's start by making sure our songs get recorded in MP3 format. Choose Settings from the Option pull-down menu, then click the Recorder tab. Be sure that MP3 is selected as the recording format, and choose Custom Quality (VBR) for the quality setting. Drag the VBR slider over to about 85 percent, which will maintain most of the original quality of our downloaded files. The window should look like the one in Figure 13.

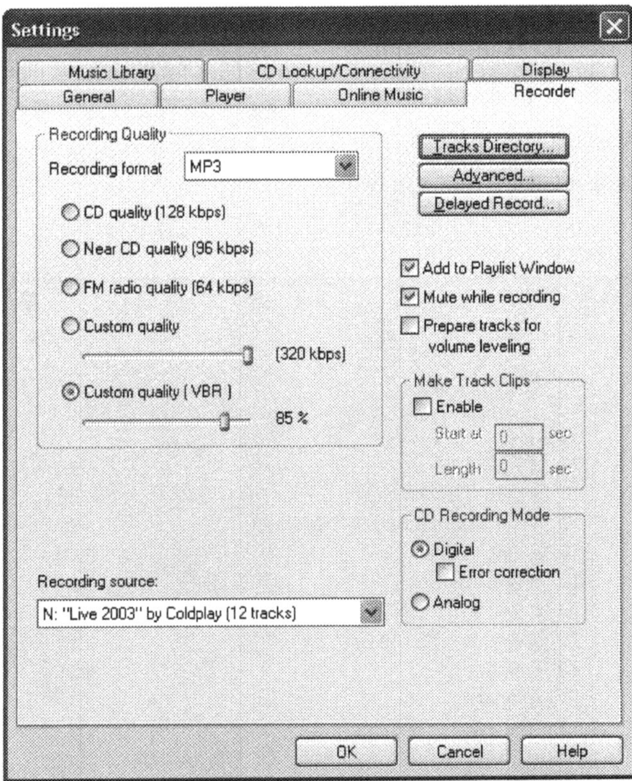

Figure 13. Using these settings will insure that the MP3 songs you rip will sound as good as the WMA songs you originally burned to disc.

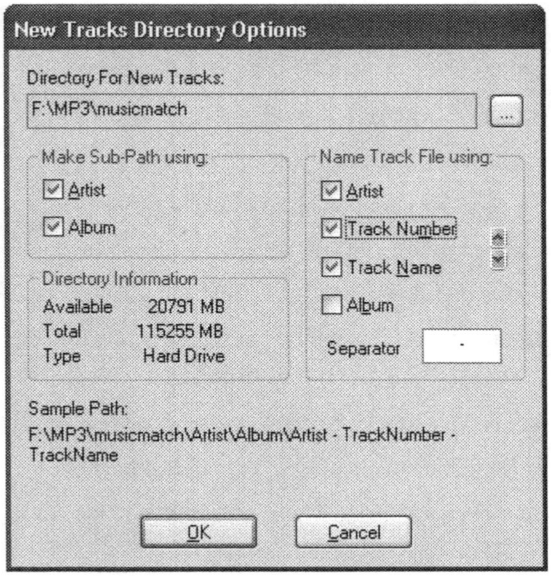

Figure 14. Choose a different directory if you don't want the MP3 songs you rip to mix with your Musicmatch downloads.

Now click the Tracks Directory button. You'll want to store the songs you rip in a different directory than the one you used for your Music Store downloads so you don't have duplicate copies in two different formats sharing a directory. In the example shown in Figure 14, we've set our directory to the Musicmatch subdirectory in the MP3 directory on drive F:. You'll want to set this to a directory that matches your PC's hard drive setup—perhaps create an MP3 directory in the My Documents folder. Click OK when you've finished setting the directory.

Now that you've finished the setup process, put the CD we burned back in the drive. Assuming you're connected to the Internet and that you have CD Lookup enabled (see Chapter 4 for details), the program will recognize the CD (since the song length and layout are identical to a store-bought version of the disc) and download the album and track info, and you'll see a screen like the one in Figure 15.

If there are songs you don't want to rip from the CD, simply click the checkbox next to them to remove the checkmark. Now click the Start Copy button to begin "ripping" the CD to MP3 format.

Figure 15. If you leave the tracks in their original order, Musicmatch will recognize the CD and download song info from its CD Lookup service.

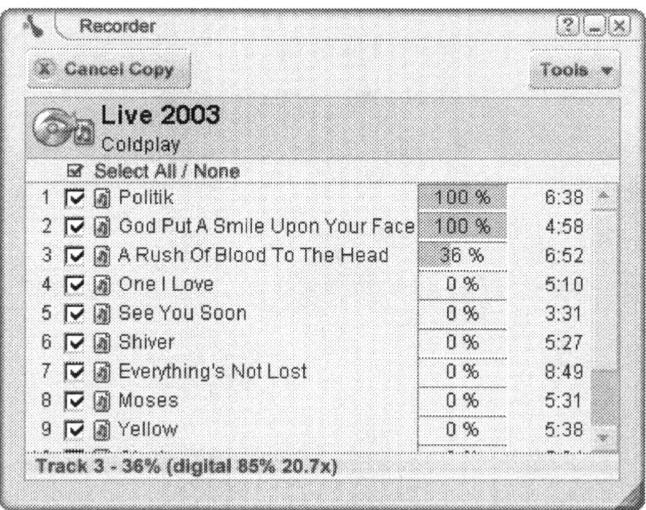

Figure 16. The status line shows you which song is being ripped, and how fast; in this case, track 3 is being ripped at 20.7x speed.

You'll see a progress meter next to each song, and a line at the bottom of the window shows the current track progress, the recording format, and the current recording speed, as shown in Figure 16.

After the CD has been ripped, all of the songs should be listed in the current playlist. You'll want to save a new version of the playlist to reflect the MP3 version of the tunes. In Figure 17, we just change the playlist name to reflect that it contains the MP3 versions of the songs.

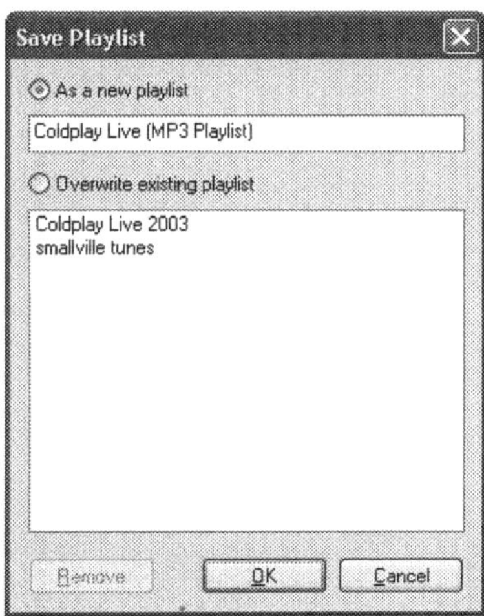

Figure 17. Since this playlist contains different versions of the same songs as the original downloaded album, we'll change its name to note that it's composed of MP3-format tunes.

Figure 18. Re-ripping an album can create duplicate listings in your music library.

Now we have two copies of the album on our computer, one in protected WMA format and the other in the more flexible MP3 format. Unfortunately, clicking the Library button in the left-hand sidebar shows that we also have two copies in our music library, as you can see in Figure 18. Musicmatch automatically adds songs to the library as it rips them.

To solve this problem, let's remove one set from the listing. By default, it's not really obvious which entries are the WMA songs and which are the MP3s. However, if you click the View Library By button and choose View By File Types, as shown in Figure 19, you can separate the two copies of the album.

Now scroll to either the MP3 or Musicmatch Downloads section, depending on which version of the album you want to remove from the library. Click the word "Album" at the top of the file listing to sort by album, and then use the mouse to highlight all the songs in the album, as shown in Figure 20.

Figure 19. The View Library By File Types command will separate songs recorded in different formats.

Figure 20. Hold down the left mouse button and drag the mouse to highlight all of the songs you want to remove from the library.

Figure 21. Click the right mouse button on your highlighted songs and select Remove Tracks to remove the duplicates from your music library.

Now click the right mouse button and select Remove Tracks, as shown in Figure 21. As long as you don't click the box labeled Also Delete The Selected Files From My Computer when Musicmatch pops up a window to confirm the removal, the songs will be removed from the library listing but the files will remain on your hard drive.

The Song Remains the Same

With these simple steps, we've bought an album, created a CD, and made copies of the songs that can be played on virtually any digital music player. You can use the CD in your car or home stereo, but there's no need to dig it up to listen on your PC. Just click the Playlists button and select the album from the pull-down menu that appears!

Chapter 7

Download Songs from Other Online Services

How to...

- Work with online music stores other than Musicmatch Downloads
- Make sure Musicmatch remains the default music player on your PC
- Download free music from Download.com
- Work around the problem of different file formats
- Find and download live concerts
- Keep the RIAA off your back
- Fix filenames and ID3 tags in songs you've downloaded
- Record Internet radio with Replay Radio

"Without music, life is a journey through a desert." —Pat Conroy, author

"I don't think anybody steals anything; all of us borrow." —B.B. King, legendary blues guitarist

As we began work on this book, the world of digital music was undergoing a rather massive revolution. It began in August, 2002, when Apple introduced the iTunes Music Store—not the first online store to sell music, but the first one (with a decent song library, anyway) to banish all the ridiculous restrictions that hampered previous efforts, and the first one to sell songs for a flat rate of 99 cents each.

In the interim, the Recording Industry Association of America (RIAA) unleashed its dogs (that is, lawyers) on several thousand music fans who engaged in illegal song-swapping via services like Morpheus and Kazaa. The lawsuits seemed to have their intended effect, as these services reported fewer users in the aftermath. Or maybe it was the serendipitous arrival of numerous iTunes-like stores—Musicmatch Downloads among them—that offered users a fair, affordable alternative to pilfering songs online. Either way, people are now buying music online in record numbers and abandoning risky file-sharing services.

In this chapter, we're going to look at online music stores other than Musicmatch Downloads (which was covered at length in Chapter 6). It may surprise you to learn that you can use Musicmatch to organize and play tunes purchased elsewhere.

You'll even learn how to work with the iTunes Music Store and songs purchased in Apple's proprietary AAC format.

We're also going to talk about file-sharing services like Kazaa and Morpheus and how they fit into today's digital-music landscape. Are you at risk by using them? Under what circumstances, if any, is it legal (and ethical) to download songs? For answers to these and other compelling questions, read on.

Downloading Music from Other Online Services

Musicmatch Downloads isn't the only game in town. At press time, services such as iTunes, Napster, Real, and even Wal-Mart were offering online music stores. Can you buy songs from these services but use Musicmatch to play, organize, and manage them? In some cases, yes. In some cases, no—but there's usually a workaround. Let's take a look at what these services have to offer and how they compare with Musicmatch Downloads (see Table 7-1). 7

As you can see, songs delivered in the AAC format aren't immediately compatible with Musicmatch. As for WMA-formatted tunes, they should play just fine—though you'll need to be connected to the Internet when you first try to play them in Musicmatch so the software can download the necessary DRM license information (see Chapter 6). We purchased some tracks from Wal-Mart (see Figure 7-1), for instance, and had no difficulty playing them in Musicmatch.

Service	Address	Price per Song*	File Format	Compatible with Musicmatch?
Apple iTunes	www.apple.com/itunes/store	$.99	AAC	No
BuyMusic	www.buymusic.com	$.99	WMA	Yes
eMusic	www.emusic.com	N/A	MP3	Yes
Napster	www.napster.com	$.99	WMA	Yes
RealPlayer Music Store	www.real.com	$.99	AAC	No
Wal-Mart	musicdownloads.walmart.com	$.88	WMA	Yes

*Song prices may vary. At BuyMusic, for instance, some singles are available for 79 cents each. eMusic has only subscription plans, which start at $9.99 per month.

TABLE 7-1 Music Download Services Compared

FIGURE 7-1 Even Wal-Mart is getting in on the digital downloads act, offering songs for the competitive price of just $.88 each.

The obvious advantage to buying songs individually instead of an album at a time is that you're paying for only the songs you want. That said, you can usually lower your price-per-song ratio by buying the entire album. At BuyMusic, for instance, Natalie Imbruglia's White Lilies Island *sells for $9.49. If you were to buy each 99-cent track individually, you'd pay $11.88. So before you make the decision to buy, say, four or five tracks off an album, see if it doesn't make more sense to just buy the whole thing.*

So, what about services that don't utilize the MP3 or WMA format? How can you play, say, the AAC-format songs purchased from the likes of iTunes and RealPlayer Music Store? The answer lies in a simple trick that's a bit time-consuming, but also perfectly legal and totally effective.

How Download Services Deliver Songs

A few points of clarification are in order. When you purchase music from, say, BuyMusic or Wal-Mart, all you're doing is downloading song files to your PC. There's no additional software required, so you're free to add the songs to your

Musicmatch Library and do with them what you will (though each service has its own restrictions regarding how many times you can burn each song to a CD, how many PCs you can transfer it to, and so on—so read the fine print before you buy).

Services like iTunes, Napster, and RealPlayer, however, are more like Musicmatch in that you're required to download and install their software before you can buy music from them. In fact, these three programs are really Musicmatch competitors, offering music-library management, CD ripping and burning, and so on. Should you avoid them and stick with Musicmatch exclusively? That's up to you. For simplicity's sake, we think working with a single program is the way to go. But if you want to maximize the number of songs and albums available for purchase, you may want to install one or more additional services.

NOTE *When you install any music manager, be it Musicmatch, iTunes, or whatever, that program will try to become the default player for all music stored and played on your PC. For instance, if you have Musicmatch installed and then install iTunes, the next time you double-click a song file or insert an audio CD, it will play in iTunes instead of Musicmatch. Fortunately, if this happens without your knowledge or just by accident, it's an easy matter to make Musicmatch the default player again. See the following section titled "Making Musicmatch the Default Music Player on Your PC."*

Ultimately, you still wind up with song files stored on your PC—but as you already know, only those in the WMA format can be played directly in Musicmatch. If you buy AAC-format songs from iTunes or RealPlayer, you'll need to perform a few extra steps if you want to get them into Musicmatch. See "The Format Workaround" section later in this chapter for details.

NOTE *The oddball in the group is eMusic, which does require you to install its Download Manager in order to receive your tunes, but you wind up with everyday MP3s you can load straight into Musicmatch.*

Making Musicmatch the Default Music Player on Your PC

So you installed iTunes, Napster, or some other music-related program (perhaps one that came with your portable audio player), and suddenly Musicmatch is no longer the program that loads when you try to play tunes or CDs. That's because the new program has told Windows that *it* is now the default music player, not Musicmatch. The impudence!

This is easy to correct. In fact, in most cases Musicmatch will automatically try to reclaim its status as the default player—but you may need to help it along. Here's how.

1. Close any other open music programs, and then start Musicmatch.
2. Click Options | Settings, and choose the General tab if it's not already selected.

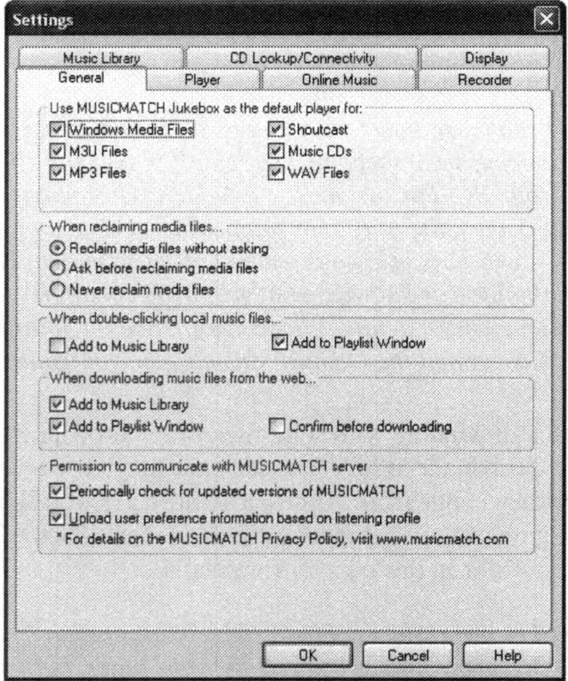

3. At the top of the tab, where it says Use Musicmatch Jukebox As The Default Player For:, make sure the Windows Media Files, MP3 Files, and Music CDs boxes all have checkmarks in them.
4. In the next section, When Reclaiming Media Files…, click the radio button marked Reclaim Media Files Without Asking. This way, Musicmatch will reestablish itself as the default music player even if you install another program that sets itself as the default.
5. Click OK. Now restart your computer so the changes can take effect.

Free Music from Download.com

A bit later in this chapter, you'll hear the wrenching story of MP3.com, a site that was originally created to help independent bands and musicians distribute their songs and, hopefully, find an audience. There were thousands of songs you could download absolutely free—and then pay a relatively low price if you wanted an entire album from a particular artist.

Unfortunately, MP3.com was shelled with litigation like Normandy was shelled with artillery in World War II. It was bought and sold several times, eventually landing in the hands of CNET. (In the interests of full disclosure, this book's authors are CNET contributors, and its tech editor is a CNET employee.) The good news is, the free music downloads are back—and they're well worth checking out.

NOTE *Actually, the original MP3.com song library was sold to GarageBand (www.garageband.com), and many of the tunes still reside there. The current iteration of MP3.com is actually a price-comparison, artist-info site. To find free downloads, you'll need to head to Music.download.com—a site owned by CNET but effectively separate from MP3.com. Yes, this is all just as confusing as it sounds.*

The site is home to over a dozen categories of music, from Blues to Rock to Children's Music. (If you've ever spent 20 or 30 bucks on CDs for the kids to listen to in the car, you'll appreciate being able to download some quality tunes that don't cost a penny—and maybe expose the tykes to something a little more substantial (and tolerable) than Barney.) All the songs are in MP3 format and have no restrictions, meaning you can play them in Musicmatch, burn them on CDs, or whatever. This is a great way to expose yourself to new music and musicians.

You can find this free music-download goodness at music.download.com.

The Format Workaround

Music services like iTunes and RealPlayer Music Store deliver their tunes in a format called AAC, which Musicmatch doesn't support. (As you recall, it supports only MP3 and WMA, by far the two most popular digital music formats—at least for the moment.) But what if, say, iTunes carries a tune that you can't buy elsewhere? Perfect example: right around press time, iTunes had an exclusive Green Day cut of "I Fought the Law." Rick scoured the other services for the track but couldn't find it. Thus, he either had to buy it from iTunes or live without it.

Fortunately, there's a way around this issue. iTunes and RealPlayer enable you to burn CDs, just like Musicmatch. And when you burn one, it effectively becomes like any other audio CD, free of format and compatible with any CD player. See where we're going with this? As discussed in Chapter 4, it's a simple matter to rip songs from audio CDs and turn them into MP3 (or, for that matter, WMA) files. Presto: problem solved. Buy your tunes from iTunes or RealPlayer, burn them to CD using that service's software, and then rip the songs back to your PC in your preferred Musicmatch-compatible format. This might seem like too labor-intensive a workaround, but if you think about the fact that you end up with a burned CD for safekeeping, car use, and so on, it doesn't seem so inefficient.

TIP *This trick also works with Listen.com's Rhapsody service, which doesn't actually download files to your PC but does let you burn songs to CD. The good news is, Rhapsody charges just $.79 per song. The bad news: that's on top of a monthly subscription charge. Bleh.*

TIP *Use CD-RW media, which is rewriteable, for this procedure, unless you're planning to burn a CD anyway. If you use CD-R to burn just a track or two, now you've more or less wasted that CD.*

One-Stop Shopping for Music

So many music services, so little time. Suppose you're looking for the new Alanis Morissette album. Naturally you'd check to see if it's available from Musicmatch Downloads—but what if it's not? And even if it is, could you find a better price at another store? You'll have to do a lot of Web surfing if you want to find out.

Or you could head to MP3.com. This newly revamped web site is kind of like those services that give you airfares for all the major airlines. When you search for an artist like, say, Ms. Morissette, you get a discography, a biography, and links to great goodies like photos, music videos, and interviews. Better still, the site tells you which online music stores carry any given album or track, what format it's in (MP3, WMA, and so forth), and whether it has DRM protection. You also get a link to MySimon.com, where you can shop for the lowest price on the CD version (if you're the old-fashioned sort).

At press time, MP3.com was still in the beta stage, so certain features weren't working. But it's quickly shaping up to be a way-cool destination for music lovers and convenience-minded shoppers alike.

We should note for the record that this PC-to-CD-to-PC process takes a small toll on audio quality. Although you're starting with relatively high-quality audio files to begin with, they've already been compressed once (in this case, in the AAC format). Decompressing the files (which happens when you burn them to CD) results in a slight loss of fidelity, as does recompressing them when you rip them back to your PC. Hey, it's an imperfect world.

Live-Concert Downloads

Back in the bad old days, the only way to get a bootleg recording of a live concert was to get a copy from someone who had one or buy one from a less-than-scrupulous source. These days, it's much easier (and legal, even) to obtain concert recordings, thanks to a couple of nifty Internet locales.

The first is Live Downloads, which at press time was offering concert recordings for about two-dozen artists—George Clinton among them. Most albums are priced under $10, though something like a package of all 16 Lollapalooza 2004 concerts will run you over $100. (Of course, when you consider the price of a couple of tickets to just one show, that's a pretty good deal.)

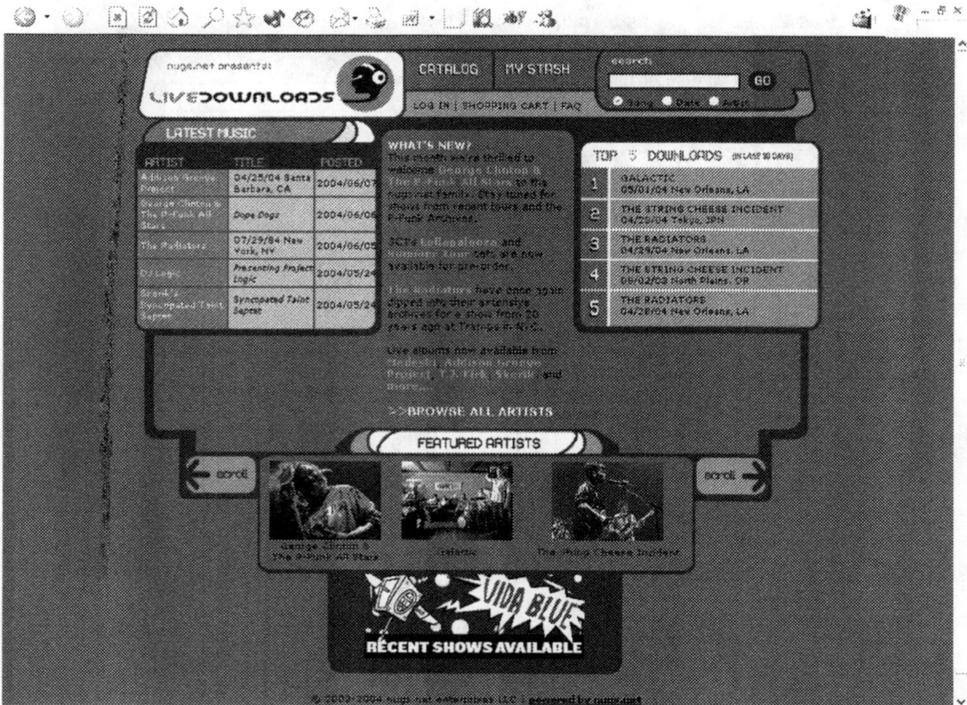

Live Downloads sells recordings in both MP3 and FLAC formats. The latter is a *lossless* format (see Chapter 4), meaning you'll enjoy better fidelity than with the MP3s. However, they're also much larger files, so they take longer to download. And Musicmatch doesn't support FLAC, so you'll need a third-party program just to listen to the files (to say nothing of burning them to CD). You can use a program like Winamp (a freeware classic) and its corresponding FLAC plug-in, or the popular Nero 6 Ultra Edition suite (for which there's also a FLAC plug-in).

For a more varied selection, check out the treasure trove at the Internet Archive (see "Where to Find It" at the end of this chapter). This site is home to a whopping 10,000 concert recordings—all free for the download! Yes, free. Among the artists you'll find there: The Grateful Dead, The Gin Blossoms, Tenacious D, and Toad the Wet Sprocket. Sweet!

And now for the catch: most of the recordings are in a format called SHN, which, like FLAC, is lossless and therefore high-quality, but an even bigger hassle to work with. Once again you'll have to use the freeware program Winamp—and a special plug-in—to listen to these files. And if you want to burn them to CD, you'll need yet another third-party program (mkwACT, another freebie, thankfully) to convert the SHN files to WAV format. You can find out more at the Internet Archive's FAQ page: www.archive.org/about/faqs.php#Audio. Although Musicmatch really isn't part of the equation for Internet Archive recordings (unless you convert the files to WAVs, MP3s, or what have you), we thought it was too cool to leave out of the book.

File-Sharing Services

In its original incarnation, Napster earned notoriety around the world for enabling computer users to share MP3 files with one another—quickly, easily, and free of charge. Needless to say, the music industry went insane, filing lawsuits, trying to shut Napster down (it eventually succeeded), and crying a whole lotta foul.

Consumers, for their part, were pretty pleased. Hey, free music! No more paying exorbitant prices for CDs! No more lining the pockets of greedy music executives and overpaid, under-talented artists (ahem, *Britney,* ahem).

Wait, wait, we're getting ahead of ourselves. This is a story worth telling in detail, as it relates to our opinion regarding modern-day file-sharing services.

A Brief History of the MP3 Controversy

Just what made MP3 technology so controversial, anyway? After all, WAV files, which employ a similar audio-recording technology, existed for years before MP3 hit the scene, so why all the fuss? The answers can be found in three pivotal lawsuits, an act of Congress, and perhaps the Betamax VCR.

Before we go any further, we must point out that we're not lawyers. We're not married to lawyers. Our pets aren't lawyers. We have never even played lawyers on television. Denny did date one in college, and they had nothing *in common. The bottom line: We've written this section to spell out some of the legal and political issues surrounding the MP3 debate, but nothing we say constitutes actual legal advice.*

Blame It on Rio

In 1998, Diamond Multimedia Systems introduced the Rio PMP300, a pager-sized descendant of the Sony Walkman that could play MP3 files downloaded from the Internet or ripped from audio CDs. Ironically, before the device ever reached store shelves, the Recording Industry Association of America (RIAA) filed an injunction to prevent its release. The claim? That the Rio promoted the illegal distribution of copyrighted music.

NOTE

Just to set the record straight, the very first MP3 player was the Eiger Labs F-10. But it was Diamond that got sued, most likely because Eiger Labs is a Korean company, and suing them would have been more of a hassle (and less likely to produce a large settlement, as it's a smaller company).

The RIAA was aware that people were downloading copyrighted songs from the Internet and felt that the Rio player would encourage that behavior. Fortunately, the courts were smarter and allowed Diamond to ship the Rio. It became such a smash hit that Diamond eventually spun off a separate division devoted to the Rio line. (That division was later acquired by SonicBlue, which later filed for bankruptcy and was acquired by Digital Networks.)

In the interim, the courts ruled that portable MP3 players did not fall within the "digital recording device" definition used in the Audio Home Recording Act of 1992. (See the sidebar "Congress Gets into the Act.") Thus, other companies were free to make their own MP3 players, and make them they did. At press time, we counted hundreds of different models—and those were just the Rio clones. (The market now includes CD/MP3 players, in-dash car players, home-stereo players, MP3-playing cell phones and PDAs, and more.)

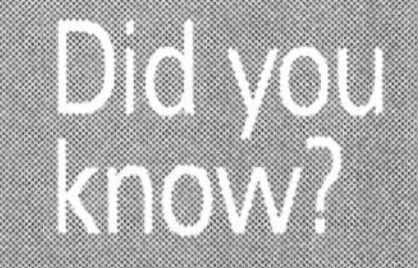

Congress Gets into the Act

The Audio Home Recording Act of 1992 was enacted long before MP3 hit the scene, but its doctrines are being examined for current legal actions. According to the AHRA, individuals cannot be prosecuted for making copies of copyrighted digital material, as long as they do so only for personal use. That clause enabled Diamond Multimedia to sell the Rio portable MP3 player—but it wasn't enough to keep Napster operating following the RIAA's lawsuit. Interestingly, analog devices such as cassette decks and MiniDisc players are covered in the AHRA, but multipurpose devices (like computers and CD-RW drives) are not. That's one reason the waters are still so murky. You can find the full text of the AHRA at www.virtualrecordings.com/ahra.htm.

Having failed to stop the hardware (which, to our thinking, has nothing to do with copyright issues), the RIAA then set its sights on the Internet services that were making an MP3 splash. The first target: MP3.com.

The Rise and Fall of MP3.com

MP3.com began life as a service that let unknown bands and artists promote themselves. Users could download free songs from these musicians and then buy their CDs if they liked what they heard. Great concept, and it worked: the service thrived, and Rick and Denny both discovered several cool bands.

Despite its name, MP3.com had nothing to do with the creation of the MP3 format, nor is it ground zero for all things MP3. It just happens to have a name that reflects what it is. Not quite onomatopoeia, but close.

Over the years, MP3.com evolved to offer a much broader range of music-related services—and turned into a lawsuit magnet in the process. In early 2000, the RIAA sued to put a stop to MP3.com's Instant Listening Service and Beam-it service, citing the creation of an unauthorized digital music catalog. (Instant Listening Service made it possible for users to listen immediately to CDs purchased from MP3.com's partner e-tailers, while Beam-it enabled users to listen to their existing CD collection on any Internet-connected computer. Ironically, these features are now widely available from other services.)

In a nutshell, MP3.com was storing a library of copyrighted material on its own servers and potentially making money from it (though both services were free upon their launch). MP3.com lost the lawsuit and had to pay roughly $160 million to various record companies, but was able to reinstate Beam-it and Instant Listening Service.

MP3.com was later acquired by Vivendi Universal, which planned to use the service as a backbone for the now-defunct Pressplay, a music-subscription venture with Sony Music Entertainment. At press time, MP3.com had been picked up by CNET Networks and was effectively shut down pending the launch of a new digital-music service (which at press time was close to launching—see the earlier sidebar "One-Stop Shopping for Music"). Yes, things continue to evolve rapidly in the ol' music biz.

Our Favorite Songs from the '80s

The songs may seem cheesy to today's kids, who think that Avril Lavigne invented angst and that OutKast was the first band to misspell its name (hint: "Led Zeppelin"), but Rick and Denny both came of age during the '80s, a strange decade of very large hair and an MTV that actually played music. So sit back while they take you down to Funkytown with these lists of faves from the days of Huey Lewis and Oingo Boingo.

Rick: Yeah, I took a lot of abuse from my college buddies for my bubble-gum taste in music. But at least I can say I evolved. I destroyed my Cyndi Lauper albums and now recognize the true gems of the '80s.

- "Don't You Forget About Me" —Simple Minds
- "Bang the Drum All Day" —Todd Rundgren
- "What I Like about You" —The Romantics
- "Rebel Yell" —Billy Idol
- "Melt with You" —Modern English

Denny: My '80s music collection features an odd mishmash of very danceable tunes, cool and New Wave tunes, and a few pop songs that I'd never have admitted liking to my more Gothic college friends.

- "Turning Japanese" —The Vapors
- "If You Leave" —Orchestral Maneuvers in the Dark
- "Bizarre Love Triangle" —New Order
- "True" —Spandau Ballet
- "Tainted Love" —Soft Cell
- "I Don't Like Mondays" —Boomtown Rats
- "Cool Places" —Sparks
- "The Metro" —Berlin

The Napster Effect

History will record Napster as the service that really put MP3 technology on the map—and as the catalyst of a litigation firestorm. The service debuted in 1999, the brainchild of college student Shawn Fanning, and quickly became popular on college campuses, where students used it to share—and augment—their MP3 collections. About a year later, a media frenzy erupted seemingly overnight, followed closely by high-profile legal action.

Unlike MP3.com, which ostensibly dealt with authorized songs, Napster enabled music lovers worldwide to exchange copyrighted songs in the form of MP3 files. The software was free, the service was free, the songs were free. This polarized the music industry like nothing before (not even Michael Jackson). Many artists—heavy-metal band Metallica the most notorious—denounced Napster as enabling theft of their work (the phrase "copyright infringement on a massive scale" was used regularly). Other artists came out in support of Napster, citing the possibilities of a wider audience for their music. The RIAA, unsurprisingly, went ballistic—and went to court.

See, the record companies don't make any money when you download songs from a file-sharing service like Napster. Even worse, the artists don't make anything either. Put simply, you're getting for free what you normally would have to buy, and that raises no end of legal and moral questions.

On the other hand—and this is where things get murky—the Audio Home Recording Act of 1992 gives consumers the right to make copies of commercial media, as long as it's for noncommercial use. (This is the very act that helped Diamond Multimedia win permission to make MP3 players.) Because Napster members weren't making money from the exchange of their MP3 files (even though they contained copyrighted material), one could argue that the law wasn't being broken. Hmmm.

While the record companies ply the courts with legal arguments, the rest of us must grapple with knotty ethical issues like these:

- **The One Song Argument** If you like a particular song but would never consider buying the entire album it's on, what's the harm in downloading it? The artist wasn't going to get your money anyway.
- **The I-Already-Own-It Argument** Suppose you have a batch of albums, 45s, 8-tracks and cassettes. You've already paid for the music, so why shouldn't you be able to download the digital versions? The artists and record companies did get your money, after all.
- **The Lost Song Argument** Suppose there's a song—or even an entire album—that you'd gladly buy, but you can't because it's out of print. If you can find it online as an MP3 file, why shouldn't you be able to download it? The artist wouldn't be getting any money anyway because the material is out of print.
- **The Greater Exposure Argument** In the old days, we were exposed to new music via the radio (or MTV, depending on what qualifies as "old days" for you). By being able to download a wide variety of music, you gain greater exposure to artists you might not have discovered otherwise—and you may wind up buying an album as a result.
- **The Bootleg Argument** Trading bootleg concert recordings is older than David Crosby, so there's no harm in doing it electronically, right?
- **The VCR Argument** When you record a TV show or movie on your VCR, you're effectively copying copyrighted material. But a famous Supreme Court case held that movie studios could not outlaw a technology (in this case, the Betamax VCR) just because it was capable of copyright infringement. Most people, they ruled, would use it for non-infringing purposes. So, you can record whatever you want, and keep it for your personal use or share it with friends (or even strangers)—just as long as no money is changing hands. The same rules should apply to MP3 recording and sharing, right?

- **The Mix-Tape Argument** People have compiled their favorite songs and "burned" them onto cassette tapes for friends for as long as the cassette deck has existed. How is sharing songs online fundamentally different? A computer is just an updated cassette recorder—albeit one that can make perfect copies.

How to Not Break the Law

Concerned that the RIAA is going to send its thugs (that is, lawyers) to your house for downloading Britney Spears' latest? Fear not, Denny, that's extremely unlikely. As we write, the RIAA's lawsuits are targeting those people who share large libraries of songs, not those who merely download the occasional few.

That said, we've compiled the following lists of legal and illegal activities so you know exactly what you're dealing with.

Definitely Legal Activities

Here's a list of stuff we know for sure is legal—this week, anyway.

- **Internet radio** As discussed in Chapter 8, Internet radio is one of Musicmatch Jukebox's coolest features. But whether you listen to it in Jukebox, Windows Media Player, or a site like Beethoven.com, Internet radio is absolutely legal.

File-Swapping Ethics

Rick: You and I have had more than a few debates on this subject. My feeling is that if I own or have ever owned an album, a 45 record, an 8-track tape, or whatever, then I've already paid my money to the artist, and am therefore entitled to download those songs—regardless of where they come from. Anything else I download is piracy, plain and simple.

Denny: I don't disagree with you, except for possibly the last sentence. I just add that I think downloading live concert bootlegs is a normally victimless crime. It's not like you can buy CDs of these versions of the tunes even if you want to spend the money—unless you're a Pearl Jam fan, since that band put out a series of 9,254 live CDs a few years back. I think there's an entire CD of nothing but Eddie Vedder snoring on the tour bus. Anyway, the kinds of fans who are looking for the live version of Weird Al's "It's Still Billy Joel to Me" or Pat Boone's surprise live acoustic cover of "Cornflake Girl" are already likely to own the artist's entire library anyway.

- **MP3 players** As the courts ruled in the landmark Diamond Multimedia case, there's nothing wrong with carrying music in a portable player. (Hadn't the RIAA ever heard of the Sony Walkman?) Thus, your Apple iPod or Dell DJ is as legal as your toaster.
- **CD burners** The drives that enable you to burn and copy CDs are legal; otherwise, you wouldn't have been able to buy one at your local CompUSA. However, if you stand outside CompUSA selling copies of Donald Fagen's *The Nightfly* that you burned yourself, don't be surprised if you wind up serving 5 to 10. Remember, anything that qualifies as *personal use* is okay. You can copy your own CDs to play in your car and make music compilations for friends—you just can't make money from it.
- **Downloading authorized songs** Legitimate music sites like Musicmatch and iTunes have extensive libraries of songs you can download legally, because the artists and record companies that hold the rights gave their permission.
- **Downloading for free with permission** If an artist or label owns the copyright to a song and decides that it's OK for you to download it for free, then that's okay—over a file-sharing network, e-mail, a web page, or whatever.

Definitely Illegal Activities

Here's a list of stuff we know is illegal:

- **Posting unauthorized songs online** If you run a web site and make any authorized song available for others to download, you're breaking the law.
- **Selling MP3s** Hopefully this goes without saying, but if you try to sell copies of your CDs, songs, albums, and the like, you're breaking the law.

The truly gray area is swapping MP3 songs using file-sharing services like Kazaa and Morpheus. On the one hand, you're getting copyrighted music for free. On the other, no money changed hands, so you didn't break the letter of the law. Yes, this issue keeps us up nights. It's a toughie. Our advice: let your conscience be your guide. Artists deserve to be paid for their work. Even if they're annoyingly rich.

Legal File Sharing?

By the time the courts got around to shutting down Napster, a flotilla of similar services had already arrived to take its place. You can still download just about any song you want using a service like Grokster, Kazaa Media Desktop, LimeWire, or

Morpheus. How is it that these services can deliver Napster-like functionality without incurring the wrath of the legal system?

The answer lies in a twist of technology. You see, Napster operated around a central server, meaning it facilitated the exchange of copyrighted material. That's why it could be held liable for copyright infringement. The competing services rely on what's called *peer-to-peer* file sharing, meaning there's no central server in between your computer and everyone else's.

Here's another way to look at it. When you mail a letter, it goes through the post office before reaching its destination. Now, imagine taking the post office out of the equation: when you mail a letter, an unmarked truck picks it up and drives it to the recipient. That's peer-to-peer file sharing: no central office involved, just a direct exchange of data.

Semantics? Yes, one could say so. While courts have ruled that the services themselves aren't liable for copyright infringements, the RIAA has sued some users of these services. In other words, while the services themselves are above litigation, you may not be.

Artists Speak Out on File Sharing

Is it theft? Is it a form of free promotion? Does it pay for itself or cost the artist money? Does debate even matter, because it's inevitable anyway? We decided to get the opinions of the only people who really count—the artists who are routinely being infringed through MP3 trading.

Kristin Hersh [formerly of Throwing Muses]: You're lucky to be working at all. Yet, if I didn't have enough money to be in the studio, I would be arguing for the other side. I am happy to be able to make music and get paid for it. I'm not in this to get rich. I know some people are, but that's not what this is about, really. It's just music. I never expected to get rich from all this.

Billy O'Connell [Kristin's manager]: The artist should be in charge of giving away his or her own music.

Peter Himmelman [solo artist and musical director for TV's *Judging Amy*]: First, intellectual property is property. It's theft. It's exactly the same as taking a can of carrots you didn't pay for out of a store. A lot of people don't have a problem with stealing, but I want to call it what it is. Second, though, artists with a lot of fame and wealth, ironically, are the ones that put the clamp down on MP3s most readily, because they have the most to lose. Lots of people want to tape my shows. I'm all for it, as long as I get a copy. I don't look at that as a form of theft—it's like it's being preserved somehow. If I filmed that show and it cost $350,000 and you started trading that, I might feel differently, though.

Cherish Alexander [lead singer of The Painkillers]: Copyright is important and you want to make sure your music is protected. At the level we're at, I'm just grateful that we have the access to give people the opportunity to download and listen to a song. It is about the music and getting the music out to people. At this point, we just want to get our music out there. Any kind of promotion we can use to get it out there we welcome with open arms. It's like free promotion—you have to give up something to get something, you know? We could sit here and complain, but we're willing to do what it takes.

Dana Mase [solo artist]: If someone just takes music, it's stealing. It's one thing if I post songs on my own web site in MP3 and let people download them, but I'm totally against stealing. Artists have to survive. If you're trying to make a living from your music, if you're giving it away for free, it's free. If not, it's for sale.

Diana Darby [solo artist]: I don't have an adamant position. On the one hand, I'm against it because people should have to pay for other peoples' music. But on the other hand, when an artist is first starting off, there's nothing wrong with exposing people to music. I just hope that if one of my songs is up there and they download it, they'll like the song enough to go buy the record.

Mark Linn [Diana's producer]: When we talked, Napster was still in its glory [*Mark is referring to a radio show that Diana, Mark, and writer Dave Johnson appeared on in the fall of 2000 to discuss MP3 piracy*]. It was great for new artists to get publicity. I liked the underdog aspect, the way you could rip off Metallica just as easily as Diana Darby. Not that I like the idea of indiscriminate theft! But I liked the fact it was really able to open doors for people who didn't have publicity resources. It has been said that in the future the only way an artist will make money is through merchandise, and the music itself will be free. I don't really believe it, and I hope it doesn't come true, but well-placed people in the industry have said that.

And in the End…

Perhaps you're wondering why we've devoted so many pages to the controversial issue of file sharing. This is, after all, a book about Musicmatch, which offers a very decent *legal* method for downloading songs. Well, folks, most of the people we know have used a file-sharing service to download music for free, and that's something we oppose. The simple fact is that musicians deserve to be paid for their work—even if it means putting more money into the coffers of record companies. We think looking at the history and evolution of this issue helps to shed some light on its present and future.

Fortunately, the present now includes some decent alternatives to file sharing. Musicmatch is the perfect example, offering songs for just 99 cents each and entire albums for $9.99. The downloads are fast, easy, and legal, and they're not restricted in any meaningful way. You can copy them to portable players, burn them on CDs, and even listen to them on more than one PC. Services like this just plain didn't exist a few scant months ago. Now that they do, there are few acceptable justifications for using a file-sharing service.

Fixing Filenames and ID3 Tags in Songs You've Downloaded

Okay, so you used Kazaa, Morpheus, or even the old Napster to download a rock star's ransom in MP3 tunes. What's done is done—we hereby (and without any actual authority) grant you amnesty. Just don't do it anymore, okay?

Of course, one of the problems inherent to file sharing (and another reason you should rely on legal downloads from now on) is that there's no consistency. Song names are often misspelled, ID3 tags are messed up or just plain inaccurate, and usually the formatting of both differs from how you've organized the rest of your library. It's like someone dropping off a stack of LPs at your front door, only the albums are in the wrong sleeves, some sleeves are missing altogether, and the Beatles' *White Album* is pink for some reason.

These goofs aren't necessarily limited to songs downloaded from file-sharing services. You may also find that the tracks you get from, say, eMusic or iTunes have filenames that are inconsistent with the rest of your collection, or ID3 tags with incomplete or oddly formatted data.

Fortunately, Musicmatch makes it quite easy to fix filenames and ID3 tags. In fact, you can do it in one fell swoop for a whole batch of tunes.

NOTE *If you need a refresher course in ID3 tags, see Chapter 4.*

What's the Difference Between a Filename and an ID3 Tag?

This is probably the single most confusing aspect of working with digital music. Every song stored on your computer is a file, and every one of those files has a name. Makes sense, right? Every document you create with Microsoft Word has a name, too. Ah, but there's a difference between the filename of a Word file and what's contained within that file. It's a similar story with songs and their ID3 tags.

For example, let's say you download a copy of the Devo classic "Whip It." The filename might be Devo-Whipit.mp3. Meanwhile, the ID3 tag info might look like this:

- Track title: whip it
- Artist: Kid Rock
- Album: <blank>
- Genre: Disco
- Track number: 12

As you can see, the filename and ID3 tag can contain disparate information, and either one (or both) can be formatted incorrectly or just plain wrong. In our example, the filename does accurately reflect the song title and artist, but it doesn't match up with the rest of our files. (If it did, it would be Whip It - Devo.mp3—song name first, then a hyphen, and then the artist name.) Meanwhile, the ID3 tag has incorrect data for the artist, genre, and track number, and no album info at all. If you're like Rick, these kinds of organizational mistakes can lead to cold sweats.

Thankfully, Musicmatch can come to the rescue by fixing ID3 tags *and* filenames, and it can do it quickly and almost automatically. Read on.

Editing ID3 Tags

As discussed in Chapter 4, when you rip a song from a CD, a program like Musicmatch will look up all this information from an Internet-based database and store it in the music file for later use. The ID3 tag information is used by Musicmatch and portable audio players to display pertinent information and organize your music. (As you'll learn in Chapter 8, Musicmatch can sort your songs by virtually any ID3-tag criteria, such as artist, album, genre, and so on. That's why it's crucial that the ID3 tags be accurate.)

When you download a song from a file-sharing service, you never know what kind of ID3 tag information you're going to find in there. If our experience is any indication, it'll be a hodge-podge of misspelled and/or inaccurate data. Maybe you'll find that the album title is in all-caps, which is the kind of thing that drives Rick absolutely insane. Or the tag won't have album information at all, only the song and artist name.

To fix an ID3 tag in Musicmatch, do this:

1. If you haven't already, add the song to your Musicmatch Library, as discussed in Chapter 3.
2. Find the song in the Library list, right-click it, and choose Edit Track Tag(s).
3. Now you have two choices. You can modify the tag information manually, which is done in the right side of the Edit Track Tag(s) window. Or, you can click Lookup Tags, which will search the Internet for correct ID3 tag information for this file. This is definitely the best bet—assuming, of course, that at least some of the existing tag info (like song title) is accurate. If the tag is really messed up, the Lookup Tags option might not be able to find matching data. In that case, fix a few of the fields (such as track title and artist) manually, and then click Lookup Tags again.
4. Hopefully, you'll wind up with something like the following window, which found a match for our Huey Lewis sample track, "Couple Days Off."

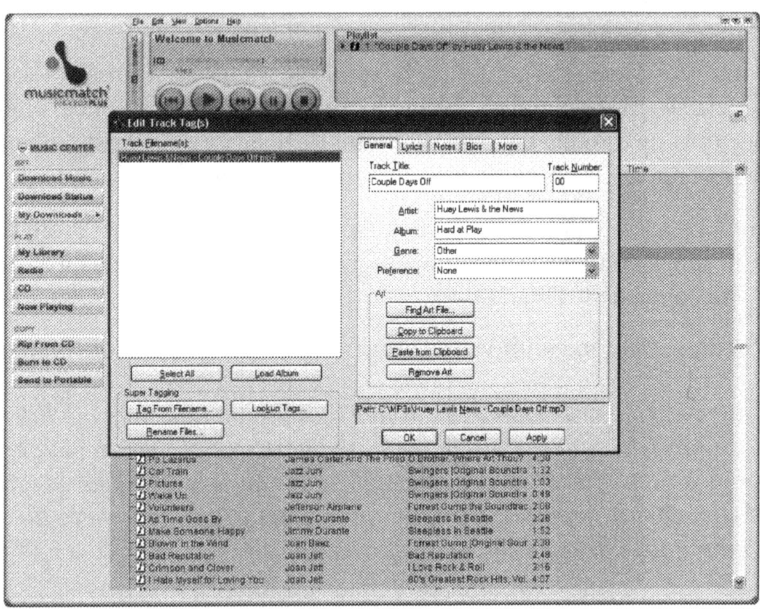

5. The highlighted line with the green arrow pointing to it is Musicmatch's best guess for accurate ID3 tag info. (We find that more often than not, the system gets it right.) All you have to do now is click Accepted Selected Tags. If, on the other hand, Musicmatch has come up with an incorrect tag, which has been known to happen, you can click Cancel and edit the tag manually.
6. Notice that updated info has been plugged into the Edit Track Tag(s) window. When you click Apply (or OK), the song's ID3 tag will be updated accordingly. If you want to make any minor tweaks, you can do that, too.

Bear in mind that these changes have no impact on the filename for the song—only its embedded ID3 tag. If you want to fix (or just change for consistency's sake) a filename, see the "Fixing Filenames" section later in this chapter.

Fixing Several Tracks at Once

What if you want to make a global change to a bunch of tracks at once? Perhaps you've got an album's worth of songs that all need updated ID3 tags. Here's what you should do in Musicmatch:

1. Start by selecting all the tracks you want to edit in your Musicmatch Library. (To select multiple tracks, hold down the CTRL key while clicking each track name.)
2. Right-click any of the selected tracks and choose Edit Track Tag(s) from the menu.
3. In the Edit Track Tag(s) dialog box, all the tracks are initially selected on the left. To make a global change to all of these songs at once, click the checkbox next to the tag data you want to change (like Artist, Album, Genre, or Preference). Type your change in the text field.
4. To make automatic changes, click the Lookup Tags button. Note that the more songs you've selected, the longer it will take Musicmatch to download all the suggested ID3 tag info.
5. When you're done with your changes, click OK to close the dialog box.

You can access Musicmatch's Edit Track Tag(s) and Rename Files functions (the latter is discussed in the next section) via the Super Tagging menu, which appears when you right-click any song. Super Tagging is just Musicmatch's umbrella term for editing track tags, renaming files, and creating tags based on a song's filename.

Brilliant Reasons to Manually Edit Your ID3 Tags

Here are some ways you can use ID3 tags to streamline and organize your MP3 files—and get more enjoyment from your music:

- **Correct errors** Online music databases aren't perfect, and you will sometimes run into albums with typos, incorrect capitalization, and other annoying glitches.
- **Turn double albums into single albums** Double albums don't have to be two separate albums when they're digital files. Select Pink Floyd's *The Wall Disc 1* and *The Wall Disc 2,* for instance, and edit the album's ID3 tags so the album title is just *The Wall.* Then change the track numbers on disc two so "Hey You" becomes track 14 instead of restarting at track 1, and "Outside the Wall" becomes track 26. It'll consolidate the album into a single set of songs and play each one in sequence, the way Roger Waters would surely have intended if LPs could hold 80 minutes of music.
- **Consolidate onesies** If you download a lot of songs, you may end up with a half-dozen tracks from the same artist, but they're all stored in different folders since each song came from a different album. If you prefer, make your own *Greatest Hits* album—select all the individual tracks and change their album titles to *Greatest Hits* (or, better yet, *Bandname Greatest Hits,* so you don't wind up mixing together multiple groups when sorting your music). All the songs will consolidate into a single folder.

Fixing Filenames

While you're in the process of fixing ID3 tags, you might as well correct those messed-up filenames as well. It's not vital that you do so—Musicmatch relies on ID3 tags, not filenames, for sorting and organizing music—but there's something to be said for getting all your musical ducks in a row. Or something like that.

After you've completed the Lookup Tags process (or you've manually changed a song's ID3 tag info), click the Rename Files button. Musicmatch enables you to create a new filename based on the corrected ID3 tag. Therefore, our "Huey Lewis & News—Couple Days Off.mp3" sample becomes "Huey Lewis & The News—Couple Days Off.mp3."

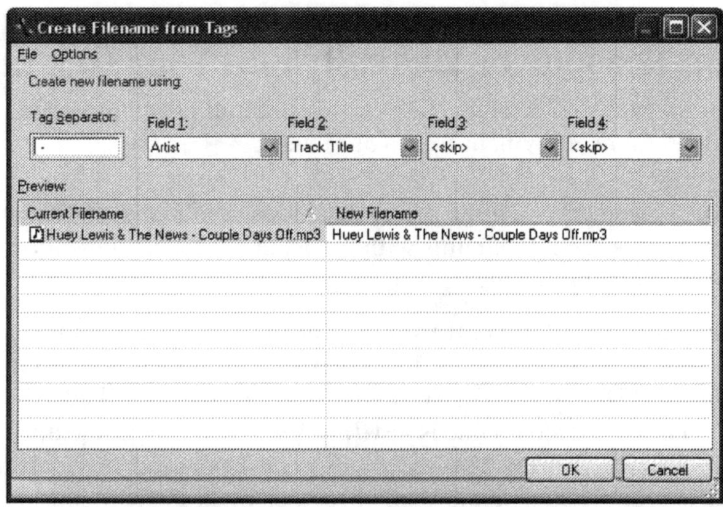

That's just one filename option. Musicmatch lets you assign up to four fields of information to each filename, and in whatever order you choose. Here are some examples:

- Artist—Track Title
- Track # - Track Title—Artist
- Artist - Album—Track # - Track Title

It's entirely up to you how you want your filenames to be structured, but we definitely recommend consistency. If you chose Artist—Track Title for all the songs you ripped from your CDs (see Chapter 4), it's probably a good idea to use the same format for songs you obtained from other sources.

NOTE *When you make changes to filenames and/or ID3 tags, your Musicmatch Library will change accordingly. Thus, songs might not appear in the same place as before. But now you should have a much easier time finding them, as they'll be named and tagged in a logical and consistent manner.*

You may also have noticed the Tag From Filename option. You can use this if the song's filename is "properly" formatted—meaning it has a hyphen (which Musicmatch dubs the Tag Separator) between the artist name, track title, and so on—and contains accurate information. Of course, as we discussed previously, this is rarely the case, so you probably won't want to use Tag From Filename very often—if it all. (We've never used it, not once.) Usually you're much better off using Lookup Tags.

Recording NPR and Other Internet Radio Shows

One of the Internet's most magical capabilities—and, we think, best-kept secrets—is streaming audio. Imagine listening to a beloved radio station from your old hometown, tuning into London's BBC for the latest European news, or enjoying around-the-clock sports coverage on the ESPN Radio Network. Imagine listening to your favorite NPR shows on your schedule instead of theirs.

Just as the Internet gives you access to information from around the world, so does it open the door to a global network of radio stations. And with a terrific program called Replay Radio, you can record any Internet radio show as an MP3 file, and then load it into Musicmatch. There, you can listen at your leisure, burn the show to a CD, or copy it to your favorite portable player for on-the-go listening. First, let's take a quick look at what Internet radio is and how you can take advantage of it.

NOTE *Musicmatch, of course, has its own Internet radio capabilities, which are discussed in full detail in Chapter 8. In this chapter, we're looking more at Internet radio* shows, *like the kind you hear on NPR, and ways to record them.*

Understanding Internet Radio

The core concept behind Internet radio is not much different from that of ordinary radio. Traditionally, a station broadcasts a signal that travels through the airwaves on a particular frequency, and you tune in to that frequency with a device (a radio) that converts the signal into sound. With Internet radio, the signal travels through the Internet instead of the air, and you use your PC and special software to tune in to desired stations. This process is referred to as *streaming audio.*

Listening to streaming audio is not the same as downloading an MP3 file and listening to it on your PC. Rather, you're listening to the audio *as* it's being received, not after. Unlike a file download, streaming audio doesn't permanently store anything on your hard drive. Just think of streaming audio as radio that's delivered electronically and you should have a clear mental picture.

Replay Radio enters the picture as a means to record that streaming audio. If you're familiar with TiVo, the magical box that records television shows to a hard drive, you can think of Replay Radio as the Internet radio equivalent. It intercepts streaming audio and stores it on your PC's hard drive, conveniently converting the file to the MP3 format in the process.

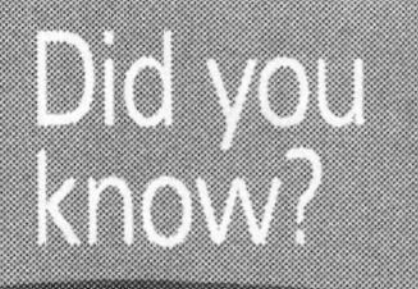

Internet Radio Sources

Internet radio comes from two main sources:

- **Actual radio stations** An increasing number of traditional radio stations have taken to simultaneous online broadcasting, meaning the same signal that's pushed into the airwaves is also available on the Internet. That means if you're out of range of a favorite station, or just want to listen to what's going on halfway across the country (or the world), you can easily tune in.
- **Internet-only stations** There are hundreds of radio stations that exist solely online, meaning they were created expressly for Internet listening. Some of these stations are supported by advertising, like their traditional radio counterparts, while others are produced by everyday users just like you.

It may surprise you to learn that both kinds of stations, tallied together, number in the thousands. That's great because it means you can probably find any kind of radio show you desire (music, talk, sports, and so on) at any time of the day or night.

We should also mention NPR.org, which is not a radio station in and of itself, but a site that broadcasts (make that *webcasts*) its original content. In other words, you can listen to any of NPR's programs right on your PC. And, we're happy to say, you can record them with Replay Radio.

The Importance of High-Speed Internet Access

Broadband (that is, cable or DSL) Internet service is the key to Internet radio happiness. While dial-up modem users can certainly tune in to web stations, they're likely to experience mediocre sound quality and frequent interruptions. Even at a low bit rate, streaming audio sends a lot of data to your PC. If you have broadband access, you should enjoy virtually flawless playback 99 percent of the time. But if you have a dial-up modem, it's quite likely that you'll experience interruptions—sometimes momentary, sometimes lengthy, always irksome. What's happening is that the audio stream isn't arriving at your PC fast enough to allow continuous playback. And that could lead to bad recordings when using Replay Radio.

Fortunately, you have nothing to lose by experimenting. Some stations may deliver more reliable playback than others, and you may encounter fewer interruptions if you're online when Internet traffic is lower, such as during weekdays. However, the fact remains that to make the most of what Internet radio has to offer, you need a broadband connection. Consider this the perfect excuse to take the plunge on cable or DSL service.

Getting Started with Replay Radio

To recap, Replay Radio is a software program that records streaming audio from the Internet. It doesn't matter if you use Musicmatch, Windows Media Player, or your web browser—Replay Radio can record regardless of the source. And it converts those recordings into MP3 files you can listen to in Musicmatch, burn to CD, or copy to a portable player.

Most radio stations stream their audio in just one format, usually Real or Windows Media. While Windows Media Player is already installed on all Windows-based PCs, you may want to download and install the free RealPlayer (www.real.com) to ensure compatibility with more stations.

To obtain Replay Radio, download it from Applian Technologies' web site (www.replay-radio.com). The trial version is full-featured but limits you to three-minute recordings. We say go ahead and pony up the $29.95 registration fee, as this is one program that's well worth owning.

When you first install the program, you'll see a Settings screen that looks like this:

Ignore this for now and click OK; you can always return to Settings later if you need to make changes. From there, you'll see the main Replay Radio screen, which is where you can configure automatic recordings (like setting a VCR) or start a recording manually.

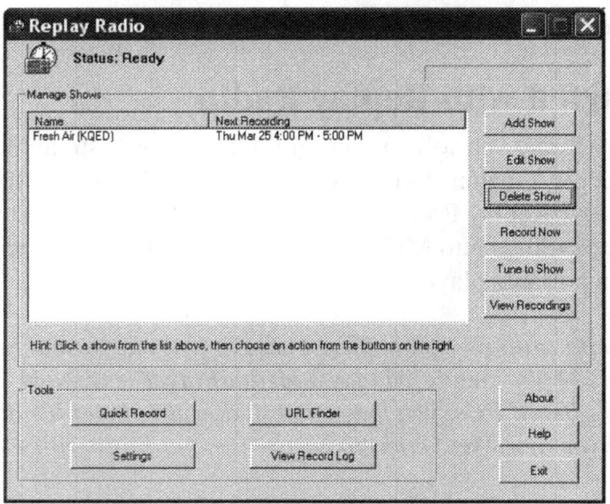

Automatic Recordings

A few pages back we likened Replay Radio to TiVo, the beloved set-top box that can automatically record shows at designated times, just like a VCR (but with a hard drive instead of tapes). Replay Radio works much the same way. For instance, suppose you want to record the NPR favorite *Fresh Air,* which airs every weekday. With just one simple setup procedure, you can configure Replay Radio to record every episode. Just leave your computer on and connected to the Internet, and the software handles the rest.

This would be a good time to point out that while Replay Radio is recording something, you can't listen to MP3s or CDs on your PC.

Here's a tiny sampling of the shows Replay Radio comes preprogrammed to record—you just tell it which ones you want:

- *All Things Considered*
- *Beatles Brunch*

- *Car Talk*
- *Fresh Air*
- *Jazz After Hours*
- *Prairie Home Companion*
- *Science Friday*
- *The O'Franken Factor*
- *Whad'Ya Know*

Let's walk through the steps of setting up an automatic recording of *Fresh Air*.

1. Click Add Show. The first time you do this, Replay Radio will offer to download an updated show list, which you should allow it to do. The download should take no more than a few seconds.
2. At the top of the window that appears next, click Pick A Show, then scroll down until you find *Fresh Air* in the list. Click to select it, and then click OK.

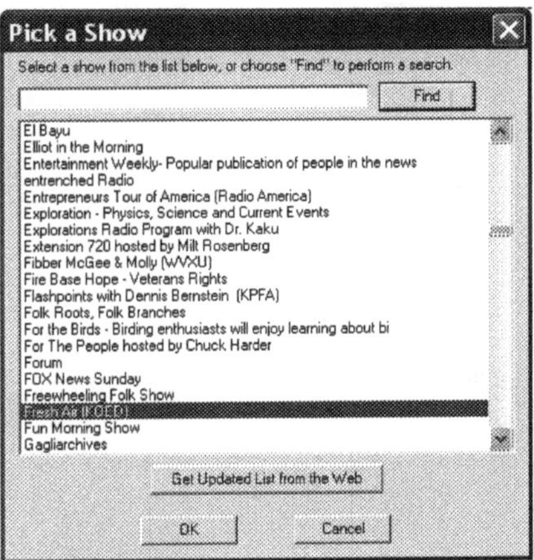

3. Next you'll see a screen that's chock full of options. For now, we recommend checking the checkbox marked Mute Sound While Recording, and then clicking OK. (We assume you don't want to listen to what's being recorded while it's being recorded.) You can return to this screen later to make further changes if desired. See the upcoming section "Recording Options" for an explanation of the various choices.

4. As Replay Radio's hint window now informs you, it's a good idea to test the connection to make sure the show's station tunes in okay on your PC. To do so, click the show to highlight it, and then click the Tune To Show button. After a moment or two, you should hear streaming audio from that particular station. If it sounds okay, you're all set.
5. You can minimize the Replay Radio window by clicking the minimize button in the top-right corner (a Replay Radio icon will appear in Windows' System Tray). Don't click Exit—that will shut down the program entirely, and no automatic recordings will occur.

By default, Replay Radio loads automatically when you start Windows. Thus, once you have a recording set up, you don't have to do anything except start your PC and leave it running (and online) during the time the show airs.

Recording Options As discussed in the previous section, there are lots of options you can modify when setting up an automatic recording. Let's take a look at the Enter Show To Record With Replay Radio window and the options therein.

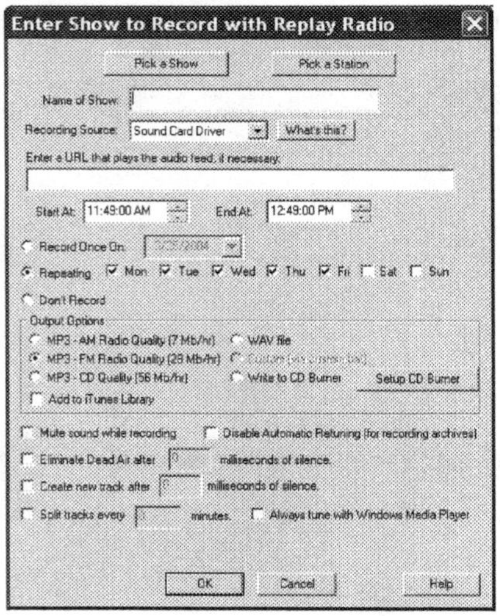

- **Output Options** This is where you select the recording quality—much like choosing between SP, LP, and EP on a VCR. As you can see, the first three choices are for MP3 recordings, which is usually what you want. We highly recommend using at least the FM Radio Quality setting, as storage space on your hard drive isn't much of an issue. A one-hour show will result in an MP3 that's roughly 28MB—the equivalent of roughly half a dozen songs. If you want the best possible audio, choose CD Quality.

- **Mute sound while recording** When selected, this option will mute your computer's audio while Replay Radio is recording a show—helpful if you're recording while doing other work. For what it's worth, you can always mute your speakers manually instead—it won't affect the recordings.
- **Split tracks every ___ minutes** This is one of Replay Radio's most valuable features. Suppose you record a one-hour show like *Fresh Air,* and then listen to, say, the first 45 minutes on a portable player like the Dell DJ. When you come back to the show at a later time and want to resume where you left off, there's no easy way to get there except by fast-forwarding (which can be anything but fast). However, if you split tracks every 15 minutes or so, you'll wind up with four separate MP3 files—not unlike tracks on a CD. Now you can go straight to the fourth file and enjoy the last 15 minutes of the show. When you enable this option, Replay Radio automatically names your files accordingly: "Fresh Air 01.mp3," "Fresh Air 02.mp3," and so on.

Manual Recordings

There may be times when you want to start a recording manually, like if a radio announcers says, "Stay tuned for our upcoming interview with Yanni" (Denny's dream come true). Better still, you can use it to record shows that are archived on various web sites. At NPR.org, for instance, you can download just about every episode of *Fresh Air* that has ever aired. Same goes for the site that hosts *This American Life.* Rick uses Replay Radio's Quick Record feature to collect a library of shows for anytime, anywhere listening. Here's how you can do the same.

Can you record Musicmatch Radio? You can, but keep in mind you'll just wind up with one long MP3 file filled with random music. What's more, even if you subscribe to Musicmatch MX (see Chapter 1), the quality won't be as good as if you purchased and downloaded the songs you recorded.

Let's assume you want to record an episode of *This American Life,* a terrific show that's alternately hilarious, offbeat, and thought-provoking. The show's web site, www.thislife.org, archives every episode. We're going to have you download one of their favorites (and ours as well).

Before you go any further, however, you must make sure to have the free RealPlayer installed on your PC, as *This American Life* is available only in the Real format. Visit www.real.com to download the player.

1. Head to the *This American Life* web site, and then click the Our Favorites link. Scroll down until your find either Superpowers or First Day. Notice the little blue/black RA icon that appears next to each show title. When you click it, the show will immediately (well, after a minute or two, anyway) start streaming into RealPlayer. *Don't click it yet!*
2. Start Replay Radio if it's not already running, and click the Quick Record button. You'll see a screen that looks just like this:

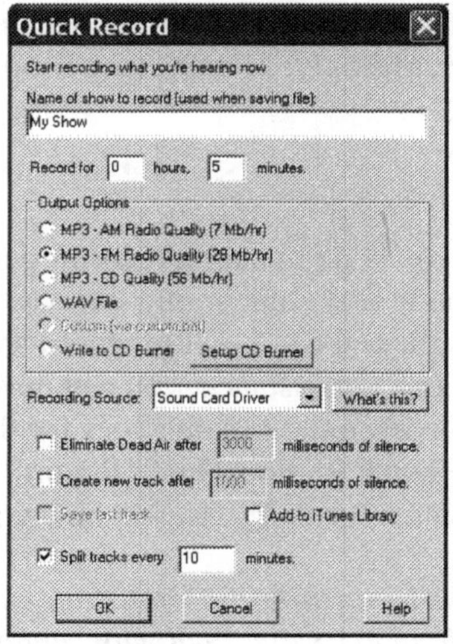

3. Type in the name of the show you're going to record (something like "TAL—Superpowers"), and then set the recording for 1 hour and 0 minutes.
4. In the Output Options section, choose a recording quality (see the earlier "Recording Options" section for details on that and track splitting, which you can also enable on this screen). We recommend FM Radio Quality.
5. When you click OK, Replay Radio will begin recording. Switch back to your web browser and click the RA icon next to the show title. That's it! The show will begin playing, and in an hour you'll have an MP3 of it.

Work the Internet to Find Songs You've Heard and Liked

A few years back, Rick discovered the dulcet voice of Lavay Smith, a modern-day swing-music singer who evokes comparisons to Billie Holliday, Ella Fitzgerald, and other jazz greats. He first encountered her while listening to a swing station on CyberRadio2000.com (a now-defunct Internet station) and immediately fell in love. An accompanying link enabled him to order one of her CDs. Even better, a quick visit to her web site revealed that she was performing near his hometown just three weeks hence (he ordered tickets online on the spot). This, friends, is why we love the Internet.

Here's a similar story. More recently, Rick and his wife were watching *Third Watch,* one of the most underrated shows on television. They both really liked a song that played near the end of the episode, but didn't know the name or artist. A quick Google search for "music of Third Watch" revealed a web page listing the songs from every episode. The artist: Nick Drake. The song: "Road." A few clicks later, they bought the song for 99 cents from Musicmatch Downloads. Talk about instant gratification!

NOTE *Although* This American Life *is usually broadcast on National Public Radio stations, it's not an NPR-sponsored show. Instead, it's paid for by Public Radio International—meaning it doesn't get any of the dough from those huge NPR fundraising drives. Plus, it costs them big bucks to make the show available in RealAudio format. Therefore, if you like the show and listen to it regularly, please consider making a donation, either directly to the show or to PRI. You can find details on the show's web site.*

Now that you've recorded a show, you're ready to add it to your Musicmatch Library for listening, burning, copying, and so on. See Chapter 4 for details.

Where to Find It

Web Site	Address	What's There
Ahead Software	www.nero.com	Nero 6 Ultra Edition (and FLAC plug-in).
Applian Technologies	www.replay-radio.com	Replay Radio
Etree.org	http://etree.org/mkw.html	mkwACT, an SHN-to-WAV converter
Internet Archive	www.archive.org/audio/etreelisting-browse.php	Free live-concert downloads in SHN format
Live Downloads	www.livedownloads.com	Live-concert downloads in MP3 and FLAC formats
Kazaa	www.kazaa.com	The Kazaa file-sharing program
Winamp	www.winamp.com	Winamp audio player (and FLAC and SHN plug-ins)

Part III

Play That Funky Music

Chapter 8 Playing Your Music

How to…

- Listen to your music library
- Build a basic playlist
- Change your library view
- Let Musicmatch's AutoDJ choose your tunes
- Play audio CDs
- Tap into Internet radio
- Listen to Musicmatch On Demand
- Improve the quality of your audio playback

"Lay down that boogie and play that funky music till you die." —Wild Cherry, band

"Oh oh, listen to the music." —The Doobie Brothers, band

In the first two parts of the book, we talked about just about everything related to digital music: ripping, choosing bit rates, burning, downloading, and sharing. That just about covers it, right?

What? You want to *listen* to your music? Well, perhaps that's not a completely unreasonable request. Actually, as you might guess from a product that includes "Jukebox" in its name, Musicmatch offers a wealth, a variety—dare we say, a *plethora*—of ways to listen to music. Not only can you play songs you've downloaded or ripped, you can also play audio CDs, stream playlists of music via the Internet, and (with Musicmatch 9.0 or later) stream any song from a library of over 600,000 tunes!

You can even exercise those DJ fantasies from your teen years, creating song lists you can send to others. In fact, there's so much you can do with playlists that we'll merely touch on them in this chapter and give them a spotlight all their own in Chapter 9.

Listening 101

If we had to hazard a guess, we'd imagine that by the time you've gotten this far into the book, you've listened to more than a few songs using Musicmatch already. Heck, even Rick figured out how to get tunes playing using his patented "click around the screen until something cool happens" method of learning new software.

Let's take a more targeted approach. First, you'll want to make sure that your music library is visible, as in Figure 8-1. If Musicmatch is showing a different view, left-click the View menu and choose Library from the pull-down menu to display your song library.

To start playing a song, you can either double-click it with the left mouse button, or click the song title to highlight it and then click the tiny *play* icon in the leftmost column, next to the selected song title. So why have two techniques that do essentially the same thing? Because they act differently once a song is playing. Once the music starts, double-clicking a song title will add that song to the end of the current playlist. Highlighting a song and clicking the icon in the left column,

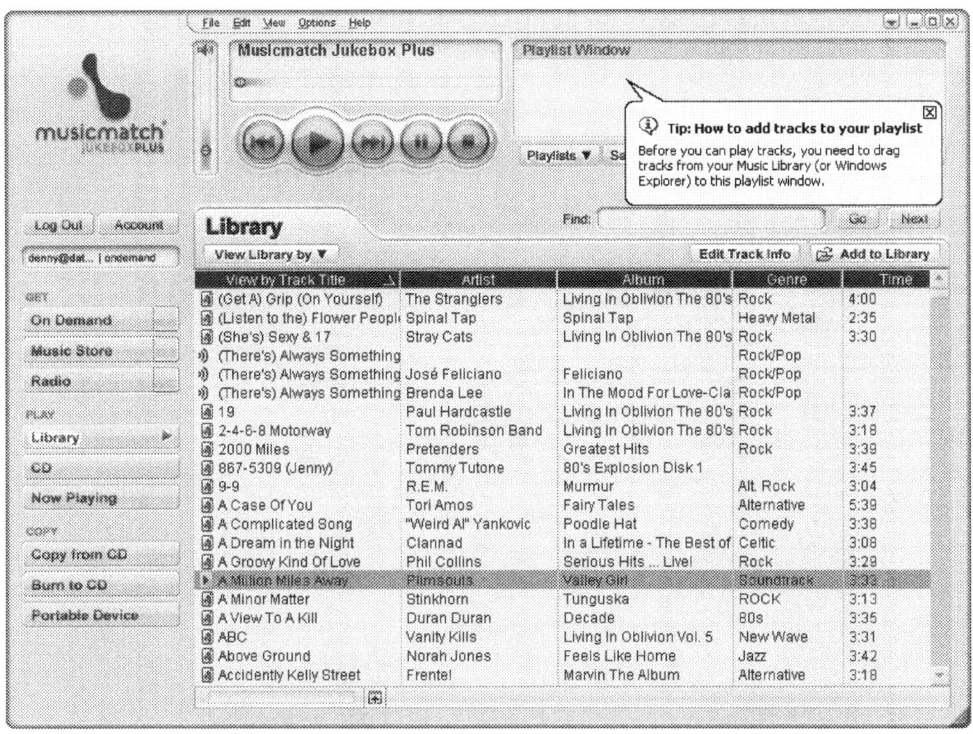

FIGURE 8-1 The Library view gives easy access to your music collection.

on the other hand, will cause the song to start playing immediately, and it won't add it to the playlist. So double-click if you want to add the song to the end of the current playlist, or use the play icon if you're seeking instant gratification.

We'll delve into the power of playlists in the next chapter, but a quick look is in order now. By default, the playlist appears at the top-right corner of the Musicmatch window. If your current Musicmatch display doesn't show the playlist, left-click the View pull-down menu and select Playlist Window, as shown in Figure 8-2. If the Library isn't currently displayed, enable it from the View menu as well.

What, you have no songs in your library? Skip back to Chapter 3 to see how to import existing MP3 and WMA songs on your hard drive, or to Chapter 4 to see how to add songs ripped from your CD collection.

Now you can build a lengthy playlist of songs. Add songs to the list by double-clicking them in the library view, or by holding down the left mouse button on the song title and dragging it up to the playlist window.

FIGURE 8-2 If it's currently hiding, the playlist is only a menu click away.

TIP *Want to drag and drop multiple songs at a time? Hold down your keyboard's CTRL key, and then select songs in the Library. You'll see that you can now highlight more than one song. When you're finished making your selections, release the CTRL key, click and* hold *the left mouse button on any of the highlighted songs, and then drag them to the Playlist. Another option is to select one song, and then hold down the SHIFT key and select another song further down the list. You'll see that all the songs in between become highlighted. (These CTRL and SHIFT file-selection methods work in all areas of Windows, not just Musicmatch.)*

You can re-order songs in the playlist by holding down the left mouse button and dragging them up and down through the list. When you have the playlist the way you like it, you can click the Save button below the playlist window if you think you'd like to listen to it again someday, or just click the Play arrow to start playback. You can jump directly to any track by double-clicking it in the playlist window, or use the next/previous track buttons to skip around the list.

TIP *See Chapter 3 for an overview of the playback controls, and the end of this chapter for some tips on fine-tuning your audio.*

Note that playlists can contain Musicmatch On Demand tracks in addition to songs stored on your hard drive. You can't, however, mix audio CD tracks with On Demand or Library tracks.

Play a Song by Double-Clicking a File Icon

Sometimes you may want to play a song that's not part of your Musicmatch library. For instance, you may want to check out a new song you've downloaded before adding it to the library, or play a song stored on a removable disc. Or perhaps your toddler is insisting on hearing The Wiggles' "Our Boat is Rocking on the Sea," but as much as you love him, you don't really want to find that song mixed in your random playlist along with Pink Floyd, Lou Reed, and Stravinsky.

No problem. You can set Musicmatch to play any song you double-click in any Windows folder. In fact, if you chose the default settings when installing Musicmatch, it will do this automatically. If you didn't, or if another program has "stolen" MP3 playback from Musicmatch, just follow these steps:

1. Choose Settings from the Options pull-down menu.
2. Click the General tab and select the file types you'd like to be able to play by double-clicking in the top section of the General Options window. If you select all of the boxes, Musicmatch will play any WMA, MP3, and WAV sounds, as well as audio CD songs and playlists, that you double-click.
3. If you want Musicmatch to always be the default player for the file types you've chosen, click "Reclaim media files without asking."
4. You can also have Musicmatch add songs that you double-click to the library and/or the current playlist. Just select the appropriate choices under the When Double Clicking Music Files listing on the General tab.
5. Once you've set everything to your liking, click the OK button and Windows will now use Musicmatch as the default player for the song formats you chose.

Organization, of Sorts

Playing songs is a snap, but *finding* them can be another matter. Sure, there's a handy dandy "Find" search button in the top-right corner of the Library window, but what if you can't remember the exact title of a song—just the artist or album name? Don't worry, Musicmatch's sorting options come to the rescue!

Musicmatch lets you list songs in your library using a variety of criteria. There are the obvious choices: sort by album, artist, or (the default) song name. However, you can also sort by more esoteric criteria: genre, song mood, preferences, or tempo. If you want to flash back to your high school years, sort by year. Or, if you're feeling techie, sort by bit rate or file type.

NOTE *With so many sorting options, it's easy to get confused and overwhelmed. We've had it happen that we make a slight change to the way we list our songs, only to discover we can no longer find a certain track, artist, or album. If you experience something similar, it's likely because your ID3 tags are out of whack. Remember, music is sorted based entirely on ID3 tags, so if you have songs with missing or incorrect tags, you may have a hard time finding them. When in doubt, look for the Miscellaneous category—and then use SuperTagging (see Chapter 7) to fix the tags for the songs you find in there.*

Just left-click the View Library By button near the top-left corner of the Library display and you'll be presented with a variety of sort options, as seen in Figure 8-3. Just choose the sort method of choice and the Library display will change to reflect that.

FIGURE 8-3 Musicmatch lets you view your library using a number of different criteria.

NOTE *By default, Tempo, Mood, and Preferences aren't defined for songs that you rip from CDs, and various other fields may be blank for these songs as well. If the fields you're sorting by are undefined, the songs will be filed under "miscellaneous." To set these fields, you'll need to edit the track tags, as outlined in Chapter 7.*

You can further refine your organization by using the Library's sorting capabilities. For instance, note that the songs in Figure 8-4 are organized by genre, and sorted by song name. This mixes songs from various albums and artists together.

You can change the sort order by left-clicking any of the column headers. For instance, in Figure 8-5, we've clicked the Album column, which re-sorts the information—you guessed it—by album.

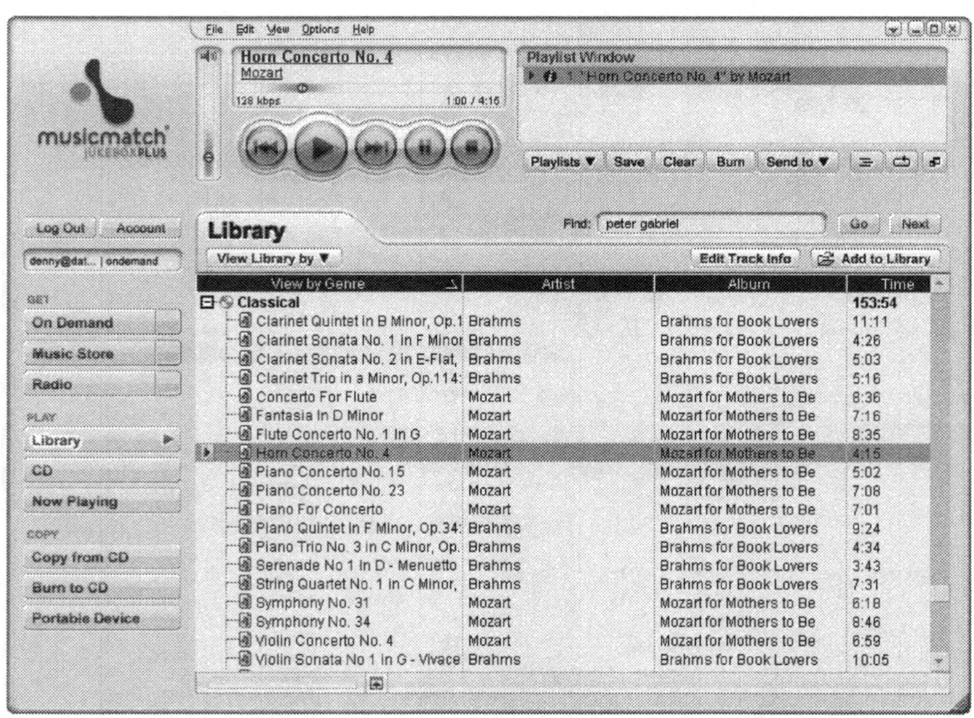

FIGURE 8-4 The default genre sorting will mix artists and albums.

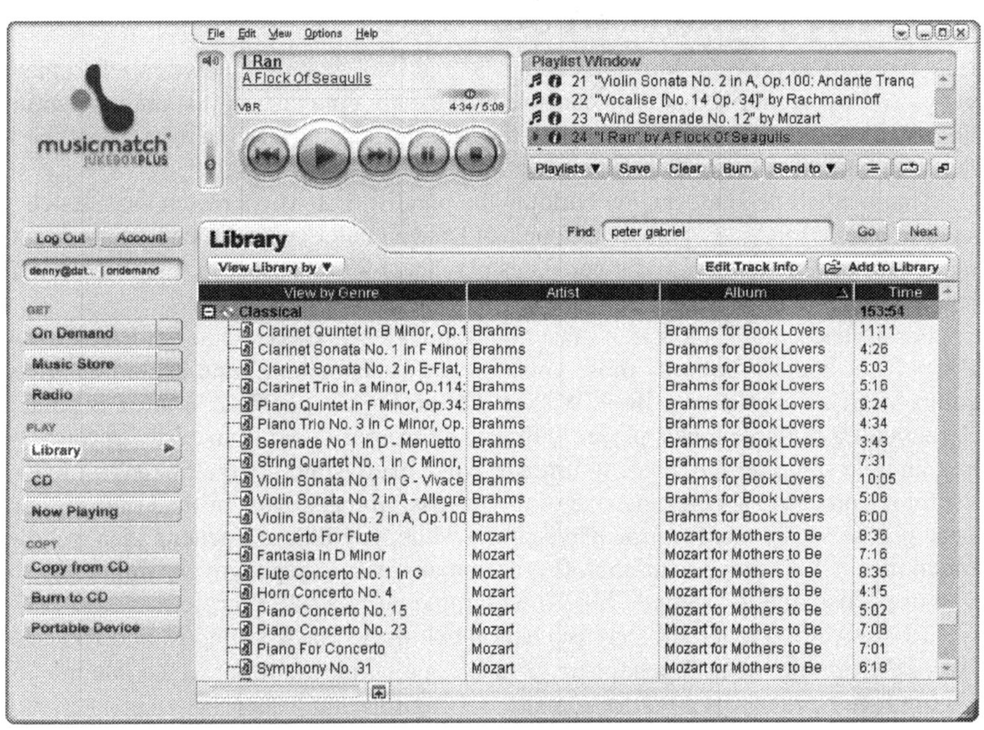

FIGURE 8-5 Sorting by album typically makes more sense than sorting by song title when you're adding multiple songs to your playlist.

TIP *You can play all the songs under a particular heading—such as a genre or artist name—by right-clicking the heading (rather than the songs below it) and choosing Play Now from the menu that pops up. All of the songs under that heading will be added to the current playlist.*

If you've ever tried to re-sort a large CD collection into alphabetical order, or tried to put together a mix tape for a friend, you'll marvel at the ease of finding albums and songs and creating playlists that Musicmatch offers. But what if you just want to listen to some music, without having to pick out every tune? Musicmatch has you covered there, too.

AutoDJ: The Element of Surprise

Like typical CD players, Musicmatch has a "random" feature that will shuffle-play songs in the current playlist. You can select an existing playlist, or just drag the entire library to the playlist window, and click the Shuffle Tracks button to the right of the Send To button (it looks like three horizontal lines, slightly offset).

That method depends on you building the playlist first. Musicmatch has a much smarter way to randomly grab tunes, one that lets you tailor your music to your current mood. It's called AutoDJ, and it generates playlists for you based on selected criteria and desired playback time.

For instance, you could specify that you want to listen to 90 minutes of Blues and Blues Rock songs—but only those you've rated as "excellent," and excluding any songs by Eric Clapton or T-Bone Walker. The ability to specify a duration is great if you have a portable music player with limited memory—you can easily generate, say, an hour of up-tempo music to listen to while exercising. It would be even more useful if you could specify the size of the playlist in megabytes instead of time, but once you've used portable music players for a while, you'll have a general idea of how much music your player can hold. (Figure on about one megabyte per minute if you use Musicmatch's default 128-Kbps sample rate for MP3 music.)

To use AutoDJ, click the Playlists button below the Playlist window and choose AutoDJ from the menu that pops up. You'll see a window similar to the one in Figure 8-6.

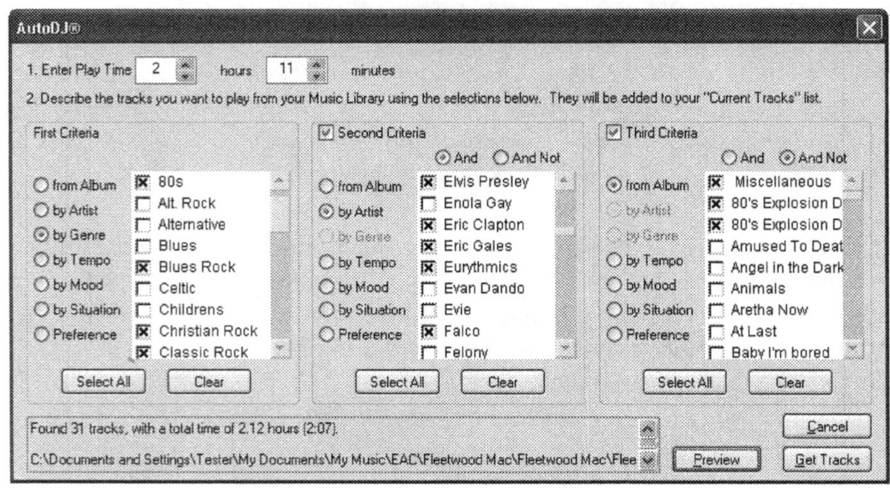

FIGURE 8-6 AutoDJ lets you create random playlists generated using up to three custom criteria.

Music for Moods

Sometimes when a mood hits, you think of, or want to hear, a particular song. Denny and Rick wrote down the first song in their collection that came to mind for a variety of emotions.

Denny: Hmm. Well, here's one for the psychologists in the crowd!

- Happy: "Cool Places" —Sparks
- Depressed: "Gloomy Sunday" —Billie Holiday
- Nostalgic: "Turning Japanese" —The Vapors
- Goofy: "Good Enough for Now" —Weird Al Yankovic
- Romantic: "Lovesong" —Tori Amos
- Bitter: "Thought I Knew You" —Matthew Sweet
- Hyper: "Shout" —The Isley Brothers
- Sleepy: "Falling" —Julee Cruise
- Fatherly: "Our Boat Is Rocking on the Sea" —The Wiggles

Rick:

- Happy: "We Like to Party" —Vengaboys
- Depressed: "Everybody Hurts" —R.E.M.
- Nostalgic: anything by Huey Lewis and the News
- Goofy: "Fat" —Weird Al Yankovic
- Romantic: "Lady in Red" —Chris de Burgh (I'm embarrassed)
- Bitter: "Love Stinks" —J. Geils
- Hyper: "What I Like About You" —Romantics
- Sleepy: I don't listen to music when I'm sleepy.
- Fatherly: "Old McDonald Goes Crazy" —Graham Clarke

You can choose just one criterion, such as a genre, artist, or album, or add one or two more to narrow the selection even further. Choose the criteria type, then select entries (which will vary depending on the type—group or album names, and so on) by clicking the boxes next to each entry you wish to include. If you want to add a second or third criterion, just check the box at the top of each column and repeat the process. Finally, click the Preview button to get a list of the songs that Musicmatch will choose, or the Get Tracks button to complete the AutoDJ process.

To really empower AutoDJ, use the Edit Track Info feature in the Library to add tempo, mood, situation, and preference information for your favorite songs. This will let you fine-tune the playlists—for instance, choosing down-tempo songs for mellow moments.

The song list created by AutoDJ is appended to the current playlist. If you currently have songs showing in the Playlist window and you want the playlist to contain just the AutoDJ songs, click the Clear button below the Playlist window before creating your AutoDJ song list.

Those Shiny Silver Discs: Playing CDs

As much as the practice seems like something you'd have done way back in the 20th century, there may be times that you actually want to…dare we say it…play actual CDs on your computer. Musicmatch includes basic CD player functionality, with the emphasis on *basic.*

Much of the flexibility that Musicmatch offers with digital music is lacking in the CD playback module. You can't reorder CD tracks using drag-and-drop, nor can you mix them with Internet radio or MP3/WMA tunes. About the only ability that Musicmatch's CD player module offers over a basic portable CD player is the ability to exclude tracks from the playlist.

If you've set Musicmatch as the default player for music CDs (see the sidebar "How to Play a Song by Double-Clicking a File Icon" earlier in this chapter for info on how to set Musicmatch's defaults), and if the Windows Autoplay feature is enabled, simply inserting an audio CD will cause Musicmatch to load and start playing your disc. Otherwise, you'll need to start the program manually and click the CD button in the Play section of the sidebar on the left side of the screen.

The main CD playback controls look and work just like those on a traditional CD player—see Chapter 3 for details on the various playback control buttons. To the right of the Eject button below the playlist you'll see two icons, as seen in

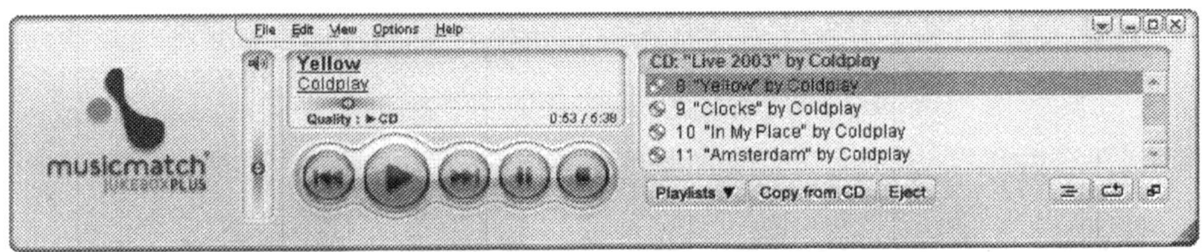

FIGURE 8-7 Musicmatch's CD playback window in action

Figure 8-7. The one with three horizontal lines activates shuffle play; the icon with the oval and the arrow sets the disc to repeat after it finishes playing.

You can tweak the CD playlist slightly by right-clicking a song title and choosing Remove From Playlist from the menu that pops up. Unfortunately, you can't save the altered playlist, so you must delete tracks you dislike from the playlist each time you insert the CD. Or better yet, click the Copy From CD button and rip the CD to MP3 or WMA format, which will let you do a lot more with the tunes. See Chapter 4 for full details on ripping.

Musicmatch's CD player does have one nice feature, if you have the program's CD Lookup enabled. It will show you the name of each track, album art, and the album name. Clicking the track title above the playback controls is supposed to take you to the "Now Playing" screen, with some information about the band—and, of course, easy access to more tracks from the artist, which you can purchase from the Musicmatch Music Store.

Internet Radio, the Free Variety

Musicmatch supports streaming music—that is, music that's transmitted (or "streamed") to your computer for instant playback via the Internet. Songs aren't stored permanently on your computer—it's like a modern version of listening to music on the radio.

Musicmatch offers a variety of impressive online music services, but before we delve into those, let's take a brief diversion to check out SHOUTcast. SHOUTcast is a public Internet protocol that lets just about anyone with a beefy server become a radio DJ. (You can download the server software yourself to create your own station, but with a standard consumer broadband connection you'll only have the bandwidth to serve music to a handful of listeners, and at a fairly low sound quality.) You can find SHOUTcast stations on hundreds of web sites, but the best place to start is at the www.shoutcast.com site, shown in Figure 8-8.

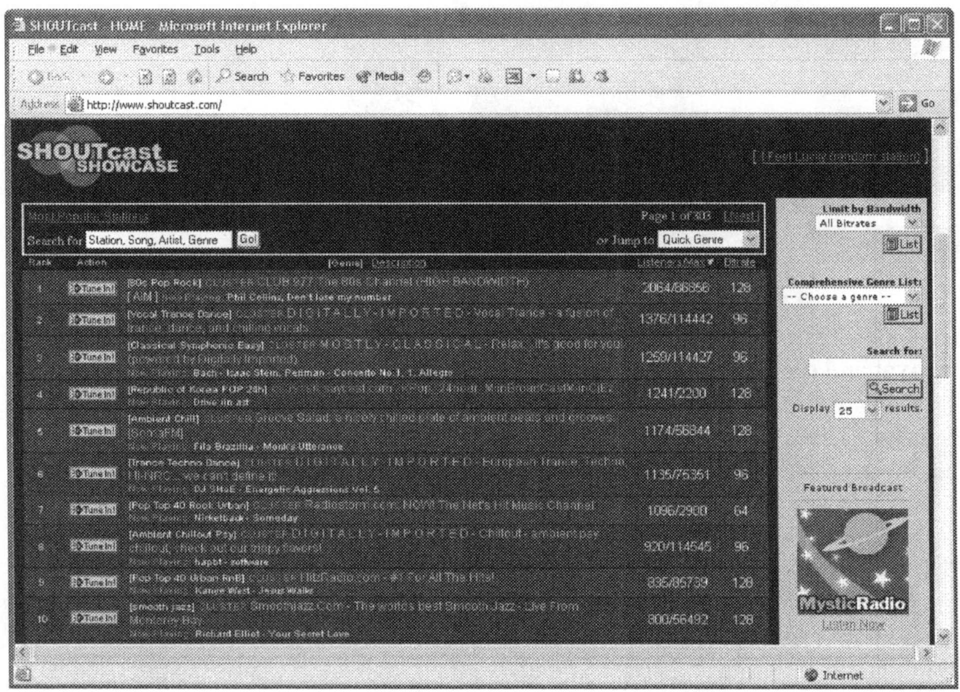

FIGURE 8-8 SHOUTcast.com is a good central hub for locating free Internet radio stations. Click any station to hear it played in Musicmatch.

To use Musicmatch to play SHOUTcast stations, just be sure that Musicmatch is set as the default player for SHOUTcast stations. (Click Options | Settings, select the General tab, and be sure SHOUTcast is checked.) Then you can listen to SHOUTcast stations by simply clicking the Play icon or the Tune In icon on the station's web page.

Just about any streaming radio service requires a broadband—cable or DSL—connection to afford good sound quality. Though some servers will play using a modem connection, the sound is sub-AM quality over a connection that slow.

SHOUTcast is much like the radio, and doesn't afford the playback control and flexibility of the various streaming services Musicmatch offers. But it's a great way to discover new music, or rediscover forgotten '80s tunes. Plus, you tend to find a much more interesting music selections than you'll hear on commercial radio stations.

Internet Radio, the Pay-to-Play Variety

Musicmatch's streaming music offerings have gradually grown in selection and versatility with each new release of the software. What started as a service not much different from SHOUTcast has now grown into what may be the most impressive online music listening service available today. The Musicmatch Radio service offers a variety of listening plans, the most impressive of which gives you instant access to over 600,000 songs!

Revamped with version 9.0, Musicmatch Radio is accessed by clicking the Radio and On Demand buttons in the command bar on the left side of the screen. You can try them out before making subscription decisions. The Radio section offers a limited number of stations for free, while the On Demand section lets non-subscribers sample 30-second clips of the songs in its library.

To use Musicmatch Radio, you'll need to set up a Musicmatch Downloads account, and then add the appropriate level of service. (For details on how to set up a Downloads account, see Chapter 6.) Log in to your account by clocking the Log In button on the left side of the Musicmatch window, then press the Account button and choose the service tier you'd like to subscribe to from the Services display that appears.

Just for the record, you have to be connected to the Internet in order to listen to Musicmatch Radio. This holds true not just for live streaming broadcasts, but also for the Musicmatch On Demand tracks you've added to your library.

Along with the freebie trial stations, Musicmatch Radio offers three tiers of service:

- **Musicmatch Radio Gold** This features Artist Match radio, which lets you choose an artist you enjoy and listen to tunes by that artist, as well as other artists who fall in the same musical vein. It also boosts the number of genre and era stations from the freebie version, and lets you play songs using a higher bit rate (CD-quality playback vs. low bandwidth). Prices range from $4.95/month (if paid monthly) to $2.95/month (if you pay for a year upfront).
- **Musicmatch Radio Platinum** Offers you all of the features of Musicmatch Gold, plus Artist Radio, which lets you listen to all of the available tunes from individual artists. Though you can't choose specific songs, Artist Radio allows unlimited song skipping, so you can use the Next Track feature to skip past songs you don't enjoy. The price ranges from $6.95/month (billed monthly) to $4.95/month (one year, paid upfront).

- **Musicmatch On Demand** This is the one to get since it offers all of the features of Musicmatch Radio Platinum, plus the ability to stream any of over 600,000 songs in the Musicmatch catalog whenever you want. Best of all, Musicmatch acts just as if you had all 600,000 songs right on your hard drive. You can add tunes to your library (where they're saved as links, not actual music files) and to playlists, where you can mix and match them with music stored locally on your PC. This service is a music fan's dream. Listen to a new album from a favorite artist—the entire album, not just 30-second clips—before you decide to buy it. Play favorite songs from your youth—songs with great nostalgia value, but which aren't worth the 99 cents you'd have to pay to own them outright. It's like having instant access to tens of thousands of CDs. The service costs $7.95/month if you pay for a year upfront, or $9.95/month if you prefer to pay monthly.

The original Musicmatch radio services were a nice audio diversion, but the On Demand service (which was introduced as this book was still being written) blew us away. The selection of songs that are just a few clicks away is mind-blowing. Musicmatch usually offers free trials of its services; we highly recommend giving On Demand a try. Even if you have to pay for it, $9.95 is a small price to pay for the ability to listen to thousands of albums every month, sample new bands, find new versions of beloved songs, and more. If you think about it, that's around 33 cents per day—not a bad deal at all, considering that most jukeboxes these days charge fifty cents for a single song.

TIP *Finally, a DJ with taste! Musicmatch can create custom streaming radio stations based on your personal listening preferences, or according to the songs in the current playlist. To create a custom radio station based on your song preferences, click the Jump To button in the top-left corner of the Radio window, select Stations, and then choose My Station. To create a station based on the current playlist (or on your entire music library), right-click a track in the current playlist (or in the Library) and select Create Radio Station From Playlist on the menu that appears.*

How to Play

To play a Musicmatch Radio station, click the Radio icon in the sidebar on the left side of the screen. You'll see a list of stations and popular artists, as shown in

Voices from the Community

The Doctor Is In…to Musicmatch

Dr. Seth Forman is the kind of pediatrician every parent wants for their kids: kind, open-minded, and willing to answer medical questions via instant message. The good doctor owns an Archos 20GB portable music player and uses Musicmatch to create playlists and copy songs to the device. We sat him down for a non-invasive Q&A.

Q: You're a pediatrician. What's your take on the whole "music heals" theory?

A: I think it helps. Music sets mood, which affects mindset, which, in my opinion, is a factor in patient recovery and healing. There have been multiple studies on imaging and hypnosis in kids getting procedures.

Q: Do you use Musicmatch on a daily basis or just for certain tasks?

A: I use Musicmatch daily. I love listening to jazz in my office between patients and while I'm doing paperwork. The AutoDJ function is awesome! It makes a mix that I can enjoy all day at the office, with music varying from Dave Matthews to John Coltrane. I also copy CDs into my computer to listen to later or load onto my MP3 player for the gym.

Some of my CDs are in a huge album, without markings other than the pictures on the label. Just plop the CD into your computer and presto-whammo, Musicmatch identifies it, shows you what the jacket looks like (so you can put it away), and lists all of the songs.

I also use the playlist function to make mixes. I have a mix for working out, a mix for a dance party for my five-year-old (plenty of cheesy disco), a "sophisticated" mix with jazz, Sinatra, Sting, etc., and even a mix for my crotchety uncle who only likes classic rock. I hook either my computer or MP3 player up to my stereo and play it either in the house or to my outside speakers for barbecues! AutoDJ also works great for parties when I hook up my laptop with a Y cable to my sound system.

Q: As the writers of this book, we have the ears of the Musicmatch bigwigs (not literally). If you could pass along any message to them, what would it be?

A: Please make an MP3 player with Musicmatch as the interface! It's so easy to use. You can find songs quickly. The pop-up tips are great. The CD lookup function is phenomenal. An AutoDJ on an MP3 player would ROCK! Add in a function so the player can broadcast to my car stereo and I would be in heaven!

> **Q: Your car breaks down on a deserted highway, but the CD player still works. What five albums would you want to have with you?**
>
> A: I guess I can't have my 20GB Archos, right? Tough question... If my kids are with me, then Avril Lavigne, *Let Go;* Frank Sinatra, *The Very Good Years;* and *Saturday Night Fever.* If my wife is with me, Bon Jovi, *Slippery When Wet,* and music from *Rocky* (she likes hair bands). If It's just me, I'd say Pink Floyd, *Dark Side of the Moon;* U2, *The Joshua Tree;* Van Halen, *5150;* and Jane's Addiction, *Ritual de Habitual.*

Figure 8-9. To choose a station, just click the station or artist name, then click the Play This Station button on the screen that appears next. If you want to play an Artist Radio station, you can use the search box in the top-right corner of the Radio display to search by album, artist, or song name.

FIGURE 8-9 Musicmatch Radio offers access a wide variety of genre, era, and artist stations.

To play On Demand tunes, click the On Demand button on the left-hand sidebar. You'll see a list of popular artists and albums. Choose one of these, or use the Search box to find songs, artists, or albums you're interested in. Once you select a group or album, you'll see a screen like that in Figure 8-10.

Click the Play icon in the track list to add the song to the current playlist. Clicking the Save icon in the track list will add the track to your Library. Songs added to your Library can be played at any time, as long as you're an active On Demand subscriber and you're connected to the Internet.

FIGURE 8-10 Musicmatch On Demand shines in action: You might want to listen to the Bay City Rollers again, but how likely are you to actually buy one of their albums nowadays?

Enhancing Your Listening Experience

We've covered how to get your music playing, but this book also aims to help you make it sound better. Musicmatch offers a number of features for fine-tuning your audio experience, such as a graphics equalizer and plug-ins, and for making sure that loud songs don't inadvertently blast you out of your seat by using volume leveling. See Chapter 12 for the full scoop on those useful features.

Let's revisit speakers for a moment. If you're listening to your Musicmatch tunes on monitor speakers or the tiny $20 set that came with your PC, you're missing out. You'll get the best audio experience with a good sound system from a company like Logitech or Klipsch. If you don't have the budget for a $150 set of computer speakers, try a set of decent headphones. Even the inexpensive Sennheiser PX100 headset (less than $50) offers astounding audio quality compared to inexpensive computer speakers. For more on making sure your system's audio is up to snuff, see Chapter 2.

To wrap up our listening party, let's take a look at a few shortcuts Musicmatch offers to simplify control during music playback.

The Small Player View

Musicmatch isn't just a big program in terms of capabilities; it's big in terms of the screen real-estate it takes up as well. Sure, you can remove modules such as Now Playing and the Library from the display to shrink the interface by turning off various displays using the View pull-down menu, but even the basic player window's fairly large. No worries, though: Musicmatch offers a compact view that's perfect for leaving on the screen while you're trying to get work done in another program.

The Small Player view, shown in Figure 8-11, offers just the basics: a volume control slider, basic playback controls, a progress meter, and the name of the currently playing song. It's tiny enough to shove in a corner of the screen, where it barely takes up any space at all.

To enable the Small Player view, choose Small Player from the View menu, press CTRL-PGDN while the Musicmatch window is selected, or click the down-arrow button in the top-right corner of the Musicmatch display. This display is most useful if you also enable the Always On Top feature (choose it from the View menu,

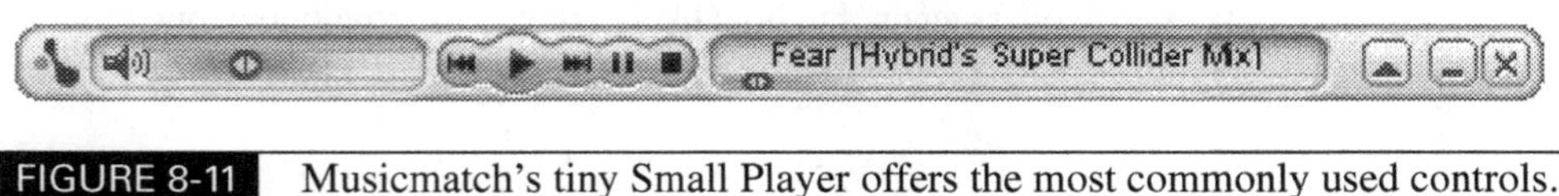

FIGURE 8-11 Musicmatch's tiny Small Player offers the most commonly used controls.

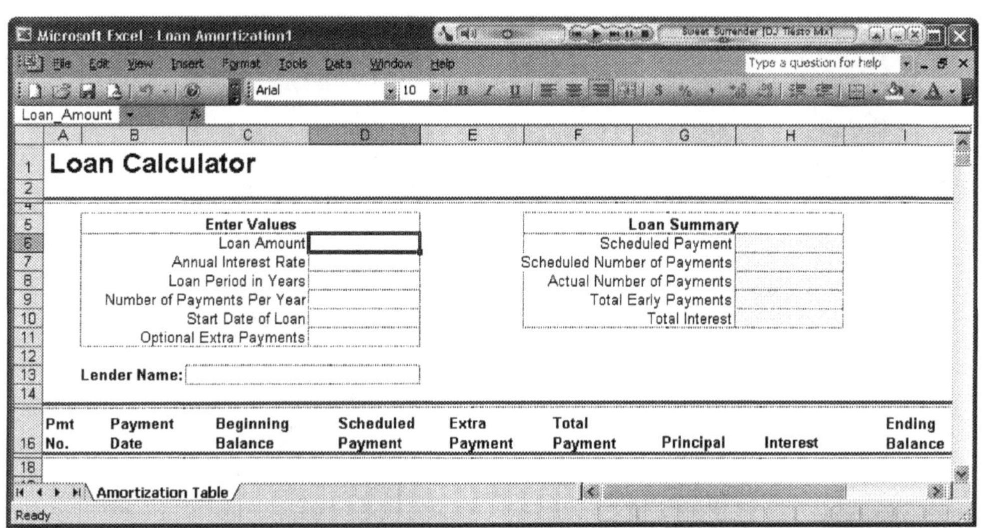

FIGURE 8-12 The Small Player view sharing space with the Excel title bar

or press CTRL-T). Then you can just use the mouse to move the player window on top of the title bar of whatever Windows program you're using. It should take up very little space. (See Figure 8-12.)

To return to the normal view, click the small up arrow near the right side of the Small Player view or press CTRL-PGUP.

Control Shortcuts

Left-click the Options menu and select the Player entry and you'll see a pull-down menu with a number of playback shortcuts, as illustrated in Figure 8-13.

Now, choosing these settings from the menu actually takes more clicks than just choosing their equivalents from the Player window's basic controls—why choose Options | Player | Increase Volume when you can just grab the Volume slider with the mouse and move it up? The real reason this menu is useful is that it lists a number of keyboard shortcuts that can give you quick control of Musicmatch's playback features. Learning these keypresses means you can make adjustments

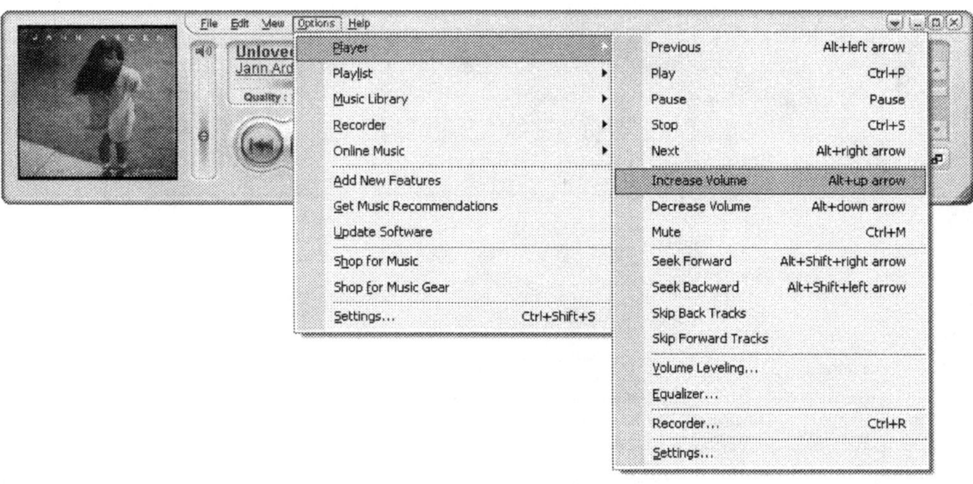

FIGURE 8-13 You can use the pull-down menus or keyboard shortcuts to change playback settings and navigate through songlists.

without reaching for the mouse. Note that Musicmatch's window must be active (click it or press ALT-TAB to activate it); these keypresses won't function if you're typing in a different program. Musicmatch's most useful keyboard shortcuts are presented in Table 8-1.

Play	CTRL-P
Pause	Pause
Stop	CTRL-S
Next Track	ALT-Right Arrow
Previous Track	ALT-Left Arrow
Skip Forward	ALT-SHIFT-Right Arrow
Skip Backward	ALT-SHIFT-Left Arrow
Volume Up	ALT-Up Arrow
Volume Down	ALT-Down Arrow
Mute	CTRL-M
AutoDJ	CTRL-D

TABLE 8-1 Useful Musicmatch Keyboard Shortcuts

Where to Find It

Web Site	Address	What's There
Klipsch	www.klipsch.com	Top-quality computer speakers
Logitech	www.logitech.com	More good computer speakers
Sennheiser	www.sennheiserusa.com	Our favorite PC headphones

Chapter 9

All About Playlists

How to...

- Understand playlists
- Create playlists
- Edit playlists
- Play playlists from the desktop
- Export playlist songs
- Share playlists with others

"Want to scare her off? Give her a mix tape on the second date." —Denny Atkin, college student at the time

"Now our children grow up prisoners, all their lives radio listeners." —R.E.M., band

The popularity of cassette tapes did much to release us from the "prison" of radio playlists way back in the hip '70s. With patience, a nice supply of albums or cassettes, and a cassette recorder, you could create a mix tape of your own design in just about an hour or so! Some of the hammier wannabe DJs in the crowd would even add their own voice-overs between tracks. Many an infatuated stereo buff expressed emotions by creating just the right mix tape: romantic songs to show those special feelings, rad New Wave tunes to show how cool you were, or 45 minutes of she-ran-off-with-my-truck-and-dog-too country to accentuate a breakup.

Then CD burners came along in the '90s and took a lot of the romance out of the process. No longer did creating a musical mix require long hours of trial and error, backing up the tape to just the right spot and simultaneously hitting Play and Record. Now you could just rip your songs, drag them into your CD burner program, and burn away. What used to take an hour now only took a few minutes—but at least the thought still went into the songs.

Welcome to the 21st century, where you don't even have to put the music on tape or CD. Just create a playlist in Musicmatch! Playlists are just what you'd expect from the name—a list of songs for Musicmatch to play. Musicmatch's AutoDJ feature (covered in Chapter 8) can even take the thought out of the "mix tape" process by creating playlists automatically. Tell Musicmatch you want an hour of mellow tunes—but no Tori Amos, thanks, because she's too depressing—and it'll automatically create your playlist for you. So, is romance dead?

Of course not! You still have full control over your playlists, and if you and the target of your affections subscribe to Musicmatch On Demand, you can spend even more time creating just the right mix of music than you did back in the cassette days. After all, even though you can create and e-mail a playlist with just a few clicks of the mouse, you now have over 600,000 songs to choose from, so there's a bit more decision-making than in the days when you'd just dig through your cassette pile.

Though sharing playlists is a lot of fun, you'll probably spend most of your time listening to playlists of your own creation. You can use playlists to gain instant access to entire albums, to create collections of music for certain moods, or to listen to "just the good songs" from an album you've ripped.

TIP *Have a portable player you like to take to the gym? Build a playlist containing nothing but high-energy workout songs.*

Top Five Things You Should Know about Playlists

1. A playlist contains no actual song files—it's literally nothing more than a list, not unlike one you'd jot down on a piece of paper. That's why you can create a near-infinite amount of them without worrying about running out of space. Try that with cassettes!
2. Overlap is allowed! Just because a song appears in one playlist doesn't mean it can't appear in another—or in a hundred others.
3. Accurate ID3 tags are essential if you want to generate playlists based on criteria such as tempo, mood, or genre. See Chapter 7 if you need a refresher in modifying or correcting ID3 tags for your songs.
4. The order in which songs appear in the playlist dictates the order in which they play. However, by enabling shuffle mode in Musicmatch or your portable player, you can randomize playback order. Thus, it doesn't permanently change the playlist itself, only the order in which songs are played.
5. It's easy to be confused by Musicmatch's Playlist Window, which is where currently playing songs appear—even if you weren't intending to create a playlist. Think of it as a temporary holding tank, like when a jukebox pulls 45s from the rack, then puts them back after they've been played. A playlist really only becomes a playlist when you perform the action of saving it.

Playlist Basics Revisited

We took a look at basic playlist creation back in Chapter 8. As a quick recap, here are the basics to using playlists:

1. First, be sure the Playlist window is showing—it's on the right side of Figure 9-1. If you don't see it, left-click the View pull-down menu and choose Playlist Window.
2. If there are already entries in the Playlist window and you want to start anew, click the Clear button below the song list. If you'd like to add more songs to the list that's there, just skip to step 3.
3. Now you can add songs to the playlist by double-clicking them in the Library window, dragging-and-dropping them from the Library window to the Playlist, or using the AutoDJ button to let Musicmatch build a playlist for you. (AutoDJ is covered in detail in Chapter 8.) You can also drag-and-drop songs from My Computer or Windows Explorer, as shown in Figure 9-2. This is handy for building playlists of songs that aren't in your library.

There are a few tricks you can use to quickly select multiple songs. For instance, you can use the usual Windows multiple-selection keys, SHIFT and CTRL, to select multiple songs. To select a sequence of songs, click the first song in a list, hold down SHIFT, and then click the last tune. Or hold down CTRL while clicking multiple songs that aren't in a sequence to select them all. Once you click the final song in the sequence, keep the left mouse button held down and drag the song to the Playlist window. All of the selected tunes will be added to the current playlist.

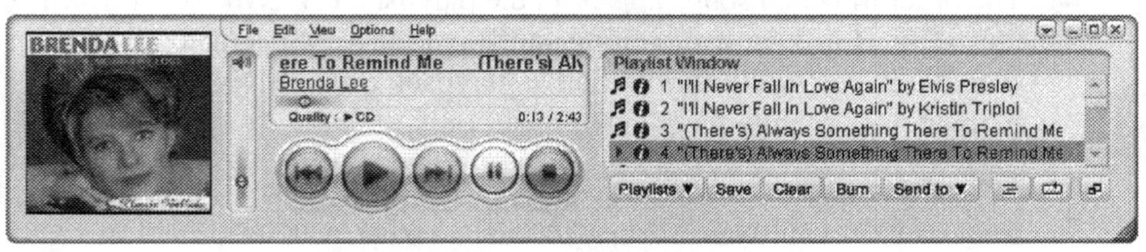

FIGURE 9-1 The Playlist view, on the right, shows your currently selected track list.

FIGURE 9-2 You can drag MP3, mp3PRO, WMA, and WAV file icons directly from Windows to Musicmatch's Playlist window.

You can also take advantage of the View Library By feature to easily create playlists from related groups of songs, such as all songs in a certain genre, off a particular album, or by a particular artist. As an example, we'll add all of the jazz songs in our library to the current playlist. Click the View Library By button and choose Genre as the sorting method, such as Genre. Now we scroll down to the Jazz heading and right-click it. You'll see the menu shown in Figure 9-3. Choose Add Tracks To Playlist Window.

Another option on the same menu is Add Tracks To Saved Playlists. This lets you add all the selected songs to an existing playlist. It would be more useful, alas, if you could also create a new playlist from the tracks, but to do that you'll need to add the tracks to the Playlist window and then click the Save button.

FIGURE 9-3 Clicking a section header in the Library lets you add all entries in that section with a single menu item.

If you subscribe to Musicmatch On Demand, you can create playlists of streaming On Demand songs, or even mix-and-match songs stored on your hard drive with streaming tunes. Just use the left mouse button to drag-and-drop any song from the On Demand window to the Playlist window. The only difference between playing a song from the On Demand service and one from your hard drive is that you need to be connected to the Internet (and of course, subscribed to On Demand) for the song to play. Otherwise, On Demand songs act just like songs on your drive—you can reorder them, delete them, and so on.

To access a previously saved playlist, just click the Playlists button below the Playlist window. A menu will pop down listing all of the playlists in the Musicmatch library. Select any item and it will replace the current playlist.

Editing Playlists

Once you've added a group of songs to your playlist, you may want to change their order, delete a few, or slip a few new songs in. Before we start, let's maximize the Playlist window so we can see the entire list. If you click the maximize icon in the lower-right corner of the playlist window, the display will change to look like that in Figure 9-4, showing a longer view of the current playlist.

To move a song up or down the playlist, click it and hold the left mouse button down, then simply drag the song up or down until it's in the right location, and release the mouse. When you drag a new song onto the playlist, you can deposit it between songs if you want to slip it somewhere into the middle of the current play order.

FIGURE 9-4 Expanding the Playlist window to see more songs simultaneously makes editing easier.

If you make any changes to an existing playlist, remember to click the Save button if you want to make those changes permanent. Otherwise, they'll be lost when you shut down Musicmatch. You can also give the changed playlist a new name, thereby keeping the original intact.

To delete a song (or a group of songs) from a playlist, use the mouse to select the songs in the playlist and then press the DELETE key on your keyboard, or click the right mouse button and choose Remove From Playlist from the menu, as shown in Figure 9-5. Note that songs removed from the playlist aren't erased from your Library or from your computer.

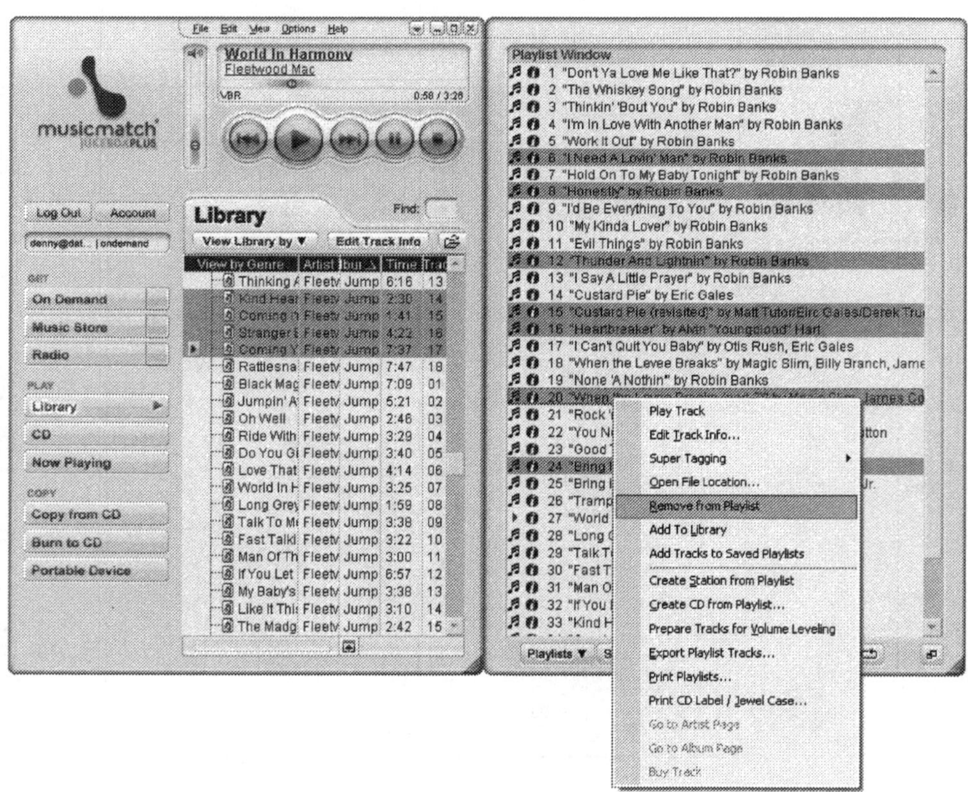

FIGURE 9-5 Click the right mouse button and choose Remove From Playlist to remove songs from the current play order.

How to ... Use Playlists Created by Other Programs

Musicmatch's Playlists are stored as standard playlist files in the popular M3U format. These files include the full directory information for each song in the playlist, including the drive letter. Thus, you should be able to copy playlists to other computers or even external hard drives, so long as the file structure for the songs themselves remains intact. However, you can't, say, copy these files to a memory card for use on a PDA, or over a network for use on another computer, because the M3U file contains *too much* information about the songs' locations—information that probably won't be correct once you copy the songs and playlist: C:\Program Files\MUSICMATCH\MUSICMATCH Jukebox\Playlist\Default\

What you can do, however, is use playlists created by other programs with Musicmatch by double-clicking them in Windows, or even create a copy of Musicmatch's playlists on your Windows desktop so that you can instantly access a favorite playlist.

To launch playlists from Windows, you'll need to make sure that Musicmatch is the default player for M3U files. Click the Options menu and choose Settings, then be sure that the box next to M3U Files is checked. Click the OK button to exit the Settings window.

Now you need to locate your playlists. You can use the Search feature in Windows to locate all the M3U files on your computer by clicking the Windows Start button, choosing Search, selecting All Files And Folders, entering ***.M3U** as the file to search for, and selecting All Drives. Then right-click any file in the search results list that you'd like to copy to your desktop and hold down the button, drag it to your Windows desktop, then release the mouse button and choose Copy Here from the menu that pops up.

You can also use My Computer or Windows Explorer to navigate directly to Musicmatch's playlist files, which (assuming you didn't choose a custom installation directory for Musicmatch) are stored in the directory C:\Program Files\Musicmatch\Musicmatch Jukebox\Playlist\Default. From there, you can follow the procedure in the preceding paragraph to copy M3U files to your desktop.

Now just double-click an M3U file on your Windows desktop and Musicmatch will load and start playing your playlist!

Exporting Playlist Songs

There's another handy use for playlists besides the obvious one of playing music. Musicmatch lets you export all of the songs in a playlist to another drive or directory. This can be handy if, say, there's a group of songs that you want to copy to a memory card for playback on an MP3 player or PDA that Musicmatch doesn't directly support. The playlist can be used to choose the songs you want to export. Ironically, when Musicmatch does a playlist track export, it doesn't actually export a playlist file, just the songs in it. So you'll get the songs, but not any customization you've done to the playback order.

To export a playlist, first be sure it's loaded in the Playlist window, then click the File pull-down menu and choose Export Playlist Tracks, as seen in Figure 9-6.

The Export Playlist Tracks window, shown in Figure 9-7, will appear. Use the Select Destination Folder window to navigate to the directory where you want to store your files; the Contents Of Folder window will show you the files in the currently selected directory. In the example shown, E: is actually a Memory Stick card from a Sony CLIÉ PDA, inserted in a USB memory card drive. At the top of the window, you'll see two choices for the export format. The Convert To WAV option probably won't see much use—it's most useful if you plan to use a program besides Musicmatch to burn the song to CD, or to use a sound editor to modify the files. Choosing Copy As Is will copy the files in their current MP3 or WMA format.

Click the Start button to begin the export process. When it's complete, the destination directory will contain a copy of every song in the current playlist, as well as the M3U playlist file.

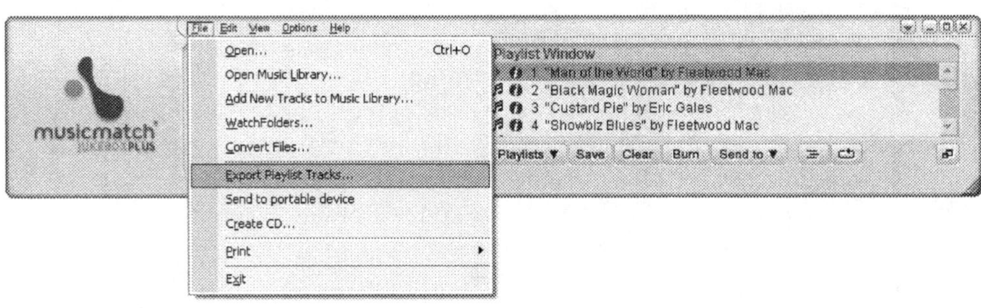

FIGURE 9-6 Exporting the current playlist to another directory

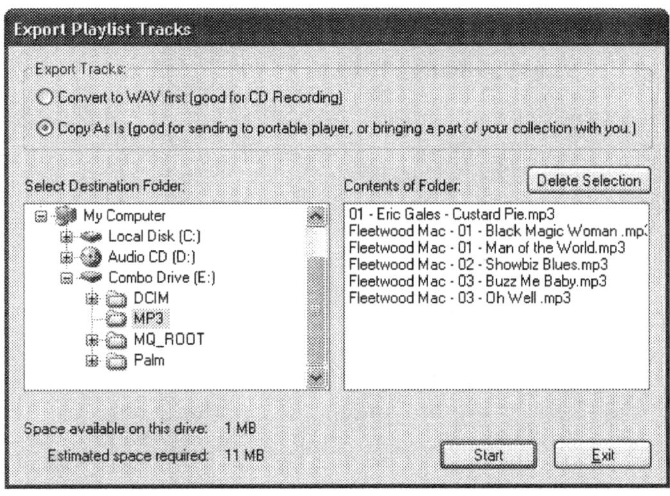

FIGURE 9-7 Choose the directory where you'd like to copy the song files.

If you're listening to music, click the Stop button before you export your playlist; Musicmatch won't export songs while it's playing.

Playlists… of Doom!

When Denny and Rick were discussing this chapter, the immediate topic that came to mind was "ultimate mix tapes." But they figured they'd save those for Chapter 10, and instead talk about the worst playlists ever, the mix tapes from the pits of Hades. Yes, these are the songs we hope to never, ever hear again.

Denny: These are the songs that send me leaping for the station button in my car, or which make me start humming a different tune loudly despite the stares of those around me when I hear them in public. Please, stop the madness, and never, ever play these songs again.

- "I Will Always Love You" —Whitney Houston
- "Solid as a Rock" —Ashford and Simpson
- "Anticipation" —Carly Simon

- "We Built This City (on Rock and Roll)" —Starship
- "Elvira" —The Oak Ridge Boys
- "Achy Breaky Heart" —Billy Ray Cyrus
- "I Got Friends in Low Places" —Garth Brooks
- "All My Rowdy Friends (Have Settled Down)" —Hank Williams Jr.
- "Mickey" —Toni Basil

Rick: Wow, that's a tough list to compete with, though I must admit to having liked that Starship tune in my youth. But "Achy Breaky Heart" is without a doubt the song I loathe the most—I think the planet would be better off without it. Here are the other tunes that are high on my Ick Scale:

- "That's What Friends Are For" —Dionne Warwick
- "Don't Worry, Be Happy" —Bobby McFerrin
- "Losing My Religion" —R.E.M.
- The entire Milli Vanilli library
- Everything that comes out of Britney Spears' mouth

Sharing the Playlist Joy

The most recent releases of Musicmatch let Musicmatch On Demand subscribers play virtual DJ for their friends—and save postage on mailing mix CDs—by sending playlists via e-mail. Best of all, the playlist recipients don't have to be On Demand subscribers, they just need to have Musicmatch installed. They can listen to the first 20 tracks in the playlist three times for free. Of course, if they're On Demand subscribers, they can hear the entire playlist with no replay limitations.

TIP *If you're not a subscriber to Musicmatch On Demand, you can still send playlists to a friend. But the friend will only be able to hear 30-second samples of each song on the playlist.*

To send a playlist to your friends, add a list of songs to the Playlist window as outlined earlier in this chapter, or click the Playlists button to load an existing playlist. Now click the Send To button below the playlist and choose A Friend (Email Track List). The display will change to look something like Figure 9-8.

As you fill in the fields, keep in mind that the Playlist name will be used as the e-mail message subject, so don't get too creative with it or your recipient may decide not to open an unexpected message from a Musicmatch address. You can send your playlist to multiple friends. Just enter each address one-by-one in the Add Recipients text box, then click the + button to the right of the box after each entry. Once you have your recipient list complete, click the Send Playlist button near the bottom-right corner of the screen.

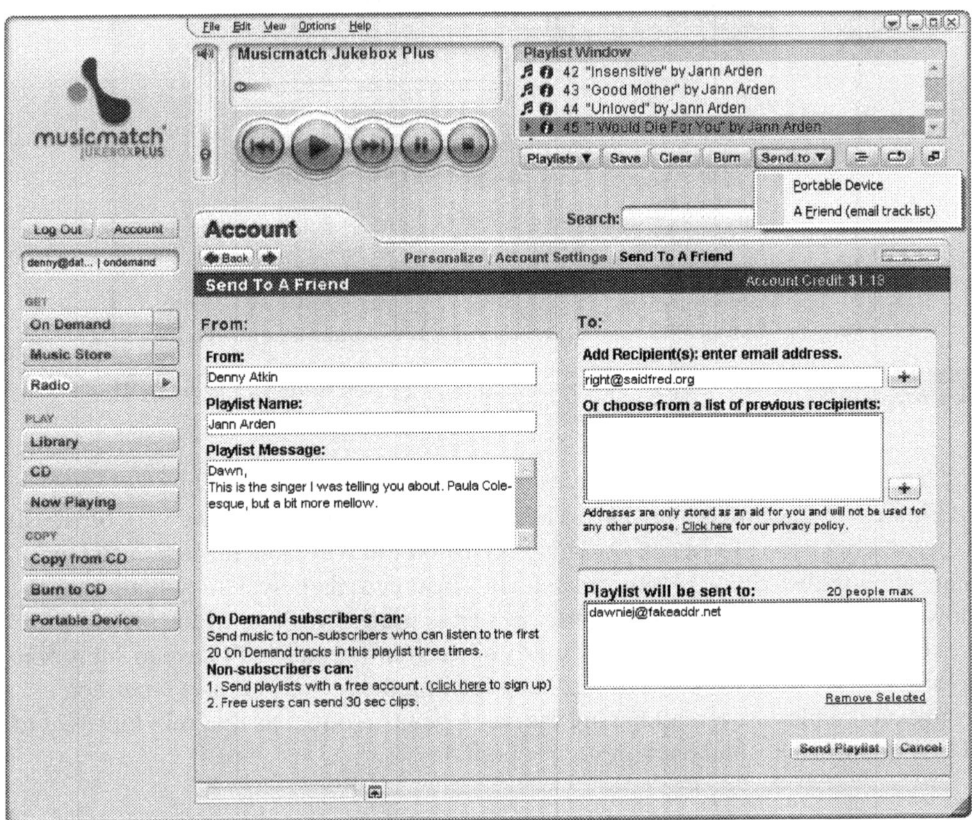

FIGURE 9-8 You can include a note when sending a message to a friend.

9

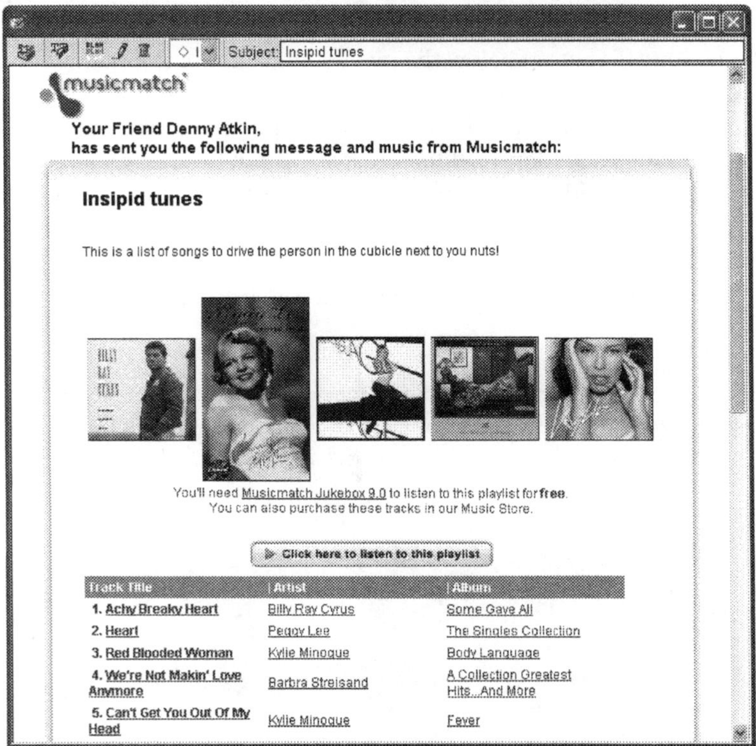

FIGURE 9-9 Your friend will get an e-mail with a Click Here To Listen To This Playlist button and a list of the songs in your custom playlist.

The e-mail your playlist recipients will get will look something like the message in Figure 9-9. Assuming they have Musicmatch installed, clicking the very obviously labeled Click Here To Listen To This Playlist button will launch Musicmatch and start playing the songs. If Musicmatch isn't installed, their system will attempt to download a file called mmzNav.mmz, which is useless without Musicmatch.

It's a pretty neat feature—particularly since your friends don't have to subscribe to any pay services, so you can just keep feeding them free playlists—but don't count on the playlist e-mail having the same positive effect as that mix tape tied to a box of chocolates did back in your school days…

Chapter 10

From PC to CD: Burn, Baby, Burn!

How to…

- Burn a quick CD with Musicmatch
- Distinguish between audio CDs and MP3 CDs
- Determine if your PC has a CD burner
- Buy a new CD burner
- Choose the right kind of blank media
- Modify burn options
- Save burn projects
- Print CD labels
- Print jewel-case inserts

"When I hear music, I fear no danger. I am invulnerable. I see no foe. I am related to the earliest times, and to the latest." —Henry David Thoreau

So far, we've spent most of our time talking about how to get music *into* your PC: ripping CDs, buying songs from Musicmatch Downloads, connecting to Internet radio, and so on. It's time to move on to getting music *out* of your PC: namely, copying it to CD for anytime, anywhere listening. (That kind of listening can also be accomplished with a portable audio player, as discussed in Chapter 11—the *other* chapter on getting music out of your PC.)

Let's take a look at this process of *burning* CDs—how to do it, why to do it, and what you need to get it done. We'll also teach you how to choose the right kind of blank media, print custom CD labels and jewel-case inserts, and burn high-capacity MP3 CDs.

Burning Your First CD: A Quick-Start Guide

Pressed for time? No worries, we've got you covered. Let's get you burning your first CD right now, then you can come back and pore over the fascinating details when you're not so busy. We're going to assume your computer has a CD-RW drive (or even a DVD burner, which can also burn CDs) and you have at least one blank CD (we recommend using CD-R media for this exercise, but you can also use CD-RW if you think you'll want to re-use the disc for something else). When you're done, you'll have a CD you can play in just about any player on the planet.

NOTE *Most older CD players can't read CD-RW media, so you may want to stick with CD-R.*

1. Start Musicmatch.
2. Open an existing playlist, or create one containing the songs you want to copy to the CD. (See Chapter 8 if you need a playlist refresher.)

TIP *Want to create a random "mix tape" CD from your library? Use Musicmatch's AutoDJ feature to create a 70-minute playlist.*

3. Insert a blank CD into your computer's CD-RW drive. If you have Windows XP and a window pops up asking what you'd like to do with the disc, click Cancel.
4. In Musicmatch's Playlist window, click the Burn button. This will open the Musicmatch Burner Plus window, where you can make on-the-fly changes to song order and modify burn options if desired.

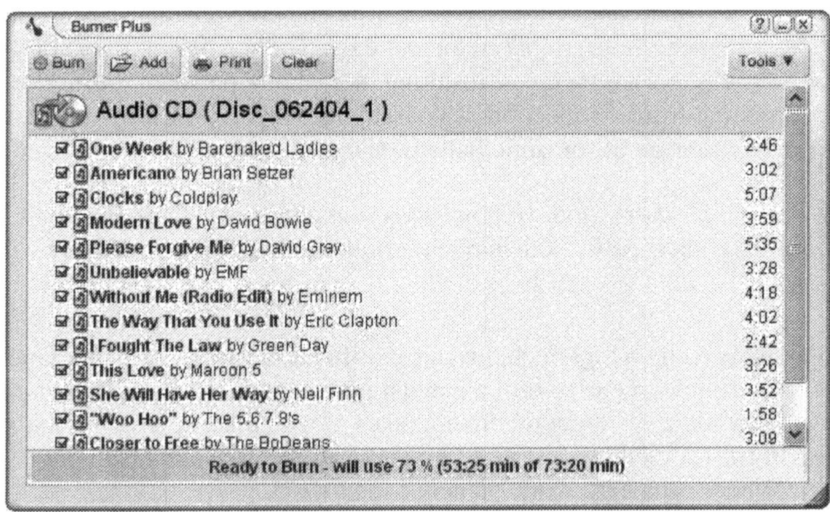

5. Make sure the icon indicating audio CD is selected (it's the one with the CD and the musical notes), then click the Burn button. (Note: In Musicmatch 9.0, there are no such icons—you must select audio CD by clicking Tools | Disc | Change Type.)
6. You can monitor the burn process in the window; when it's done, the disc will automatically eject from the PC. If you want to test it out, close the CD-RW drive again—in a moment, the disc should start playing in Musicmatch.

That's all there is to it! Pretty easy, huh? Of course, we didn't cover some of the important details, like what kind of blank media to choose, how to tell how much music you can fit on a disc, and the all-important MP3 CD option. In the sections to come, we'll delve into the finer details of burning your own CDs.

Why Burn CDs?

There are two main reasons you'd want to burn a CD with Musicmatch. First, suppose you purchase an album from Musicmatch Downloads. We don't know about you, but we're just old-fashioned enough to want it on CD, both for safekeeping and for easy playback in our car stereos. If you're like us, you like to get something tangible when you plunk down your hard-earned cash.

The other reason to burn CDs is to keep alive the ever-popular idea of the "mix tape." You remember those, right? In the old days, you'd painstakingly copy songs from LPs and 45s to cassette tapes, resulting in a wholly personal music mix. This could be anything from a collection of your favorite driving-with-the-top-down tunes to an assemblage of romantic ballads designed to woo your significant other.

If you miss those days, you owe it to yourself to read Nick Hornby's classic novel, High Fidelity. *The movie version starring John Cusack is nearly as good.*

A playlist is really a high-tech, instant-gratification version of a mix tape. And because it's a simple matter to turn a playlist into an audio CD, you can crank out your legendary mixes in about the time it takes to read this paragraph. That's great, you say, but isn't something lost when you take all the time and effort out of the equation? Where's the hard work? Where's the *love?*

Hey, call us cold and callous, but we've got much better uses for our time than spending hours making a mix tape. And if you think there's no love without painstaking manual labor, you can always print up CD labels, jewel case inserts, and all that stuff. That adds plenty of time to the process, believe us. (You'll find out later in this chapter.)

The Two Kinds of CDs You Can Burn

It may surprise you to learn that Musicmatch can burn two decidedly different kinds of CDs:

- **Audio CDs** These are "standard" music CDs, akin to the kind you used to buy at your favorite record store. Er, CD store. Whatever. They usually hold about 70 minutes' worth of music, and they're almost universally compatible: they work in computers, car stereos, home stereos, portable CD players, and even most DVD players.
- **MP3 CDs** MP3 CDs are exactly that: CDs filled with music in MP3 format. For all intents and purposes, it's like copying MP3 files from your PC to a blank CD. The benefit here is obvious: because MP3s are so highly compressed (see Chapter 1), you can fit a ton of them on a CD. In fact, a single disc can hold upwards of 150 MP3s, assuming they're encoded at a 128-kbps bit rate. You could put every one of your Beatles albums on one CD, or create the ultimate mix tape with ten hours' worth of music instead of just one. The only problem? While nearly any computer can play MP3 CDs, not many car stereos can. Fortunately, an increasing number of portable players support MP3 CDs, and car makers are slowly starting to add the capability to their stereos.
- **Data CDs** Hey, didn't we say there were *two* kinds of CDs Musicmatch could burn? This kinda looks like a third one. As it happens, Musicmatch can also burn data CDs. Why you'd want to use a music manager to burn a data CD is beyond us, but the capability is there nevertheless. In this chapter, we look exclusively at burning music CDs.

Needless to say, you'll want to give some thought beforehand to the kind of CD you want to burn, and make sure to choose the right option in Musicmatch. We'll guide you through it later in the chapter.

Our Ultimate Mix Tapes

Back in the day, Rick was known far and wide for his incomparable mix tapes. Okay, maybe not far *and* wide, but far, anyway. Nowadays he still likes to dabble with mixes, a task made much easier with Musicmatch's playlists. Denny, meanwhile, generally likes to slap together a batch of John Denver and Dan Fogerty tunes and call it a mix. Anyway, here's a list of the songs we'd put on our ultimate mix tape—er, CD.

Rick: I have to admit, the very notion of mixing together an audio CD seems silly to me now that I can carry my entire music collection in my Dell DJ. Why bother with just 15–20 songs when I can have 5000? That said, I sometimes put together mixes for my wife to listen to in her car, and once in a while I'll pull together a bunch of new tunes and pop 'em on a CD. (Sometimes it's just easier to slide a CD into the stereo than mess with the DJ.) So, here's the mix I'd make for some serious jammin':

- "Start the Commotion" —Wiseguys
- "This Love" —Maroon 5
- "One Week" —Barenaked Ladies
- "Without Me" —Eminem
- "Americano" —Brian Setzer
- "Clocks" —Coldplay
- "Please Forgive Me" —David Gray
- "Modern Love" —David Bowie
- "I Melt with You" —Modern English
- "Unbelievable" —EMF
- "The Way That You Use It" —Eric Clapton
- "Stacy's Mom" —Fountains of Wayne
- "I Fought the Law" —Green Day
- "She Will Have Her Way" —Neil Finn

Denny: Wow. Looking at Rick's song list (Eminem with Clapton?) makes me wonder what other bizarre mixes he puts together. It makes me imagine a typical meal in the Broida household: a Sushi appetizer; a main course consisting of filet mignon, pork and beans, basmati rice, bangers & mash, and cornbread—all wrapped up by crème brulee topped with Hershey's syrup. Me, I tend to think "themes" when I put together a mix CD. Here's a recent mix I put together of acoustic, unplugged versions of some favorite songs.

- "Perfect Memory" —Remy Zero
- "Iris" —Goo Goo Dolls
- "Winona" —Matthew Sweet
- "Down About It" —Lemonheads
- "Just Like Heaven" —The Cure
- "Walk on the Ocean" —Toad the Wet Sprocket
- "Lightning Crashes" —Live
- "Shine" —Collective Soul
- "Plush" —Stone Temple Pilots
- "Creep" —Radiohead
- "One" —R.E.M. with U2
- "Landslide" —Fleetwood Mac
- "Time of Your Life" —Green Day

What about WMA CDs?

At this point you may be thinking, "Hey, those MP3 CDs sound pretty great, but I have a lot of WMA files—including those I purchased from Musicmatch Downloads. Can't I make WMA CDs?"

That's a really good question, and unfortunately the answer is not positive. For starters, no, Musicmatch doesn't enable you to burn WMA CDs. Furthermore, it won't do on-the-fly conversions of WMA files to MP3 format (even though it can burn WMA files onto standard audio CDs). Finally, even if you could create WMA CDs with Musicmatch (as you can with some other programs), you wouldn't be able to play those CDs in many places other than computers. Very few car stereos, portable players, and DVD players support WMA CDs. Microsoft is trying to change that, but progress has been slow—probably because it costs manufacturers a fair chunk of money to add WMA support to their CD players, while adding MP3 support is relatively cheap.

So, what's the solution if you have a bunch of Musicmatch Downloads and/or WMA files you want to turn into MP3 CDs? Actually, there are different steps you need to take for each:

- **Musicmatch Downloads** As discussed in Chapters 6 and 7, it's possible to turn songs and albums purchased from Musicmatch Downloads (and other online services) into MP3 files. Just burn them to CD (audio CD, that is), and then rip them in MP3 format. This is something of a hassle, no doubt, and it creates something of an organizational challenge, as you inevitably wind up with two copies of each song—one in the original WMA format, another in MP3—in your Musicmatch Library. The sound quality suffers ever so slightly, but this trick gets the job done.
- **Other WMA files** If you've ripped a bunch of your own CDs using the WMA format and now want to create an MP3 CD, you'll have to convert the files using a third-party utility. Why can't you do the same thing with songs you purchased and downloaded? Because they're protected with Digital Rights Management (DRM), and therefore can't be legally converted (hence the burn-and-rip method). But unsecured WMAs, the kind you created when you ripped your CDs, are easy to convert to MP3. Try a program like AVOne All to MP3 Converter (www.rm-mp3.com), which performs "batch" conversions (meaning it can do multiple files at a time) and lets you choose your preferred bit rate (see Figure 10-1). It's $19. We recommend avoiding the freebie converters you'll find floating around out there, as they often add spyware to your PC.

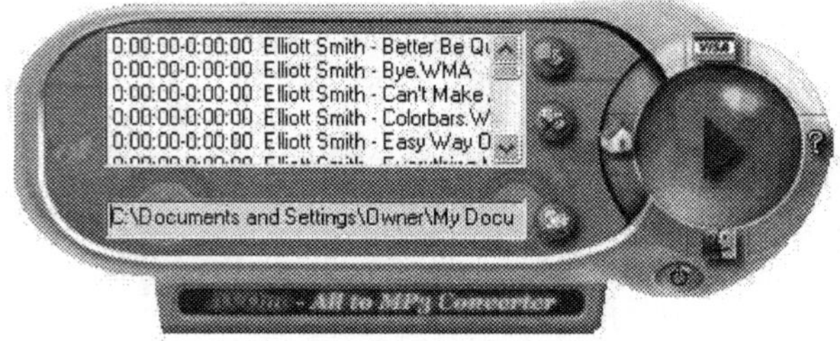

FIGURE 10-1 A utility like AVOne All to MP3 Converter quickly and easily converts unsecured WMAs to MP3s—ideal if you want to burn MP3 CDs.

Did you know?

You Can Play CDs in Most DVD Players

It's a little-known fact (okay, maybe a *lesser*-known fact) that most set-top and portable DVD players can also play audio CDs—the kind you buy from stores and burn with Musicmatch. Newer models go even further, enabling you to play MP3 CDs as well. How can you tell if your player supports them? It's not enough if the documentation says it plays CD-R/CD-RW discs—that usually refers to audio CDs burned with a program like Musicmatch. No, you need to look for a reference to MP3. If it's not mentioned anywhere, the player probably doesn't support MP3 CDs.

The Right Equipment: Hardware and Media

Now that you know what you're going to create, let's take a look at the tools you need to create it. Specifically, you need a drive that can burn CDs, and you need some blank media. In the following sections, we'll teach you to identify CD burners, add one to your PC (if necessary), and choose the right kind of media for optimal audio- and MP3-CD creation.

All about Burners

There's a very good chance you already have a CD burner in your PC or notebook. While it's hard to gauge a percentage, we'd say the majority of computers made in the last couple of years came with a CD burner—also known as a CD-RW drive. Not sure if yours did? Look for this logo stamped on the front of the drive:

COMPACT disc DIGITAL AUDIO ReWritable

If your computer is a few years old but has a CD-RW drive, it's probably a relatively slow model. Consider replacing it with a faster drive, particularly if you plan to burn a lot of CDs. It can mean the difference between a burn session that takes, say, five minutes and one that takes 15 minutes.

If your computer has only a standard CD-ROM drive or perhaps a DVD-ROM drive, you'll need to install a CD burner. It shouldn't cost you more than about $40 for an internal model, though you may want to consider an external drive if you have a notebook or don't have the time or acumen to monkey around inside your PC. (For what it's worth, installing a CD-RW drive is perhaps the most painless computer upgrade you can perform, especially if you get one that has good installation instructions.)

Looking for good deals on drives? Try the Computer Geeks Discount Outlet (www.compgeeks.com). There you can scoop up deals on refurbished and off-brand drives (which usually work just as well as their pricier name-brand counterparts).

TIP *If you're going to buy a new drive anyway, consider getting a DVD burner. You'll pay upwards of $100 for an internal model, but consider the advantages: in addition to burning CDs, you'll be able to watch and burn DVDs. Yep, that's right: DVD burners can also burn CDs. Such a deal!*

What Do the Numbers Mean?

As you shop for a CD (or DVD) burner, you'll encounter a lot of numbers that look like this: 40x24x40 and 52x32x52. No, they aren't the drive's measurements (hubba-hubba!)—they're speed ratings. Specifically, they refer to the drive's CD-ROM read speed, CD-RW rewrite speed, and CD-RW write speed, respectively.

How important are these numbers? Where CD burning is concerned, not very. Put simply, all the latest drives are fast enough—they've reached their maximum performance levels. A drive that can write CDs at, say, 52x offers little real-world advantage over one that writes at 40x. What's more, not all blank CDs can record at those speeds—some are limited to 24x or 32x. In other words, don't let the numbers play too big a role in your purchase decision. Buy what you can afford, and look for a halfway decent warranty (at least one year). You'll do fine.

Choosing the Right Blank Media

There's a bit more to buying blank CDs than you might think. Sure, you can walk into your local office-supply store and walk out with a ten-pack, simple as that. But you may want to consider a few other options first:

- **Type** Do you want CD-R or CD-RW media? The former are write-once discs, meaning after you burn your songs on one, you can't burn anything else to it. A CD-RW disc, meanwhile, is rewritable—just like the floppy disks of yesteryear. In most cases, we recommend using CD-R media, which are very inexpensive compared to CD-RWs. Plus, CD-Rs tend to be more widely compatible with audio CD players than CD-RWs, so use the latter for backing up data and other computer-oriented tasks. On the other hand, CD-RWs are ideal for material you plan to listen to only once—like, say, NPR shows you've recorded with Replay Radio (see Chapter 7)—as long as you play them back on players that can handle CD-RW discs.

- **Quantity** The more CDs you buy, the less expensive they are. We recommend perusing your Sunday paper (specifically, the ads) for deals on 25-, 50-, and even 100-CD spindles. A quick look at the latest CompUSA ad, for instance, revealed a 50-pack of Sony CD-R media for just $19.99. But even that's a bit steep—our local Staples had a 50-pack of "house brand" discs for $10.94. Look for rebate deals and you may find yourself with a stack of blanks that cost you absolutely zip.

TIP *If you're planning to play CDs in a car stereo or older CD player, you might want to make sure that CD-Rs will play properly before spending money on 100 of them. Buy a three-pack first and test compatibility with the various players you plan to use.*

- **Speed** Just as CD burners have their own speed ratings, so do blank CDs. If you have a drive that can burn at, say, 40x speed, but the media is rated at only 24x, you're not taking full advantage of your drive's performance capabilities. Not all blank discs are engineered for high-speed burning, so check the speed rating of the media before you buy.

TIP *There's no advantage to buying, say, 48x blank CDs if your drive tops out at 24x. Although the blanks will work, they'll be limited by the maximum speed of your CD burner.*

- **Capacity** Most blank CDs can hold up to 700MB' worth of data, or 80 minutes of uncompressed audio (which is what you get when you burn an audio CD with Musicmatch). In the old days, CDs were limited to 650MB and 70 minutes of audio—but we haven't seen that kind of media in years.
- **Cases** If you buy one of the aforementioned CD-R spindles, all you get are the discs. This is fine if you plan to store them in one of those CD-sleeve cases, but not if you want to keep them on a shelf or in a storage tower. Fortunately, you can also buy CD jewel cases in bulk. At that point, does it make sense to buy smaller quantities of blank CDs that come with their own cases? Usually, it's still cheaper to buy both items separately.
- **Printability** No, we're not sure printability is a word, but our word processor's spell checker didn't flag it, so let's assume it's okay. Some of the newer inkjet printers can print right on blank CDs, making it decidedly easier to label your media. Of course, you need special media that supports this kind of inkjet printing. Look for white- or silver-surface CD-Rs from Maxell, Memorex, Verbatim, and other manufacturers.

- **Coolness** We'd be remiss if we didn't mention the coolest-looking blank CDs of all time: Verbatim's Digital Vinyl. The top side of each disc looks exactly like a 45-rpm record of yesteryear. This grayscale photo doesn't really do them justice—but trust us when we say they're the ultimate blank media.

Burning CDs with Musicmatch

Okay, you've got the drive, the blank CDs, and a yearn to burn. It's time to put Musicmatch to work turning those downloads and playlists into CDs. You already got an overview in the section "Burning Your First CD: A Quick-Start Guide" at the beginning of this chapter. Now, let's look more closely at the process and some of the important options that are part of it.

Actually, the first few steps are the same:

1. Start Musicmatch.
2. Open an existing playlist, or create one containing the songs you want to copy to the CD. (See Chapter 9 if you need a playlist refresher.) If you create a new playlist, be sure to save it so you can easily make additional copies of this CD.

Want to create a random "mix tape" from your library? Use Musicmatch's AutoDJ feature to create an 80-minute playlist.

3. Insert a blank CD into your computer's CD-RW drive. If you have Windows XP and a window pops up asking what you'd like to do with the disc, click Cancel.
4. In Musicmatch's Playlist window, click the Burn button. This will open the Musicmatch Burner Plus window, where you can make on-the-fly changes to the song order and modify burn options if desired.

Want to make the Burner Plus window larger so you can see more songs? Move your mouse to the lower-right corner of the window. When the cursor changes to a bi-directional arrow, click and hold the left mouse button, drag down and to the right, and then release the button when the window has been resized to your liking. Reverse the process to make the window smaller.

Modifying Burn Options

With the Burner Plus window open and your desired songs listed (they should have been imported directly from your playlist), you can pretty much click Burn and be on your way. However, Burner Plus affords you all sorts of options, and you should make yourself familiar with some of them.

If you have an older version of Musicmatch, one prior to 9.0, you'll find that the Burner Plus window has changed. Fortunately, all the same options are there—they're just presented differently. In Musicmatch 8.0, for instance, you access Burner Plus options by clicking the Options button. In version 9.0, you click Tools. Why the change? Beats us. We think "options" is a bit more accurate.

Let's go down the list of options that appear when you click the Tools button (see Figure 10-2).

If you right-click anywhere in the upper portion of the Burner Plus window, you'll get the same list of options as if you clicked Tools (or, in the case of pre-9.0 versions of Musicmatch, Options).

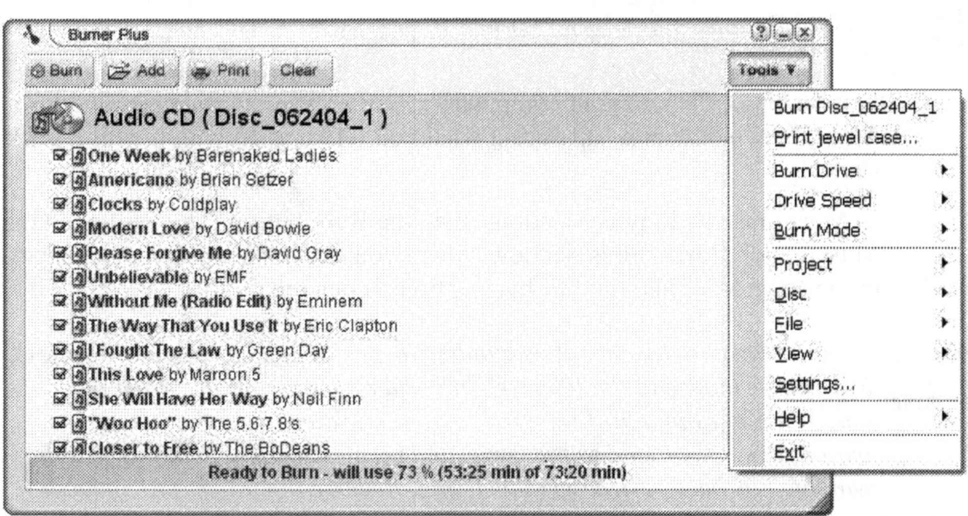

FIGURE 10-2 Click the Tools button (or the Options button in pre-9.0 versions of Musicmatch) to access these burn options.

- **Burn Disc_062404_1** By default, Musicmatch assigns a seemingly random label (it's actually the date) to blank CDs. You can change the disc label if you wish (see "Disc" a few bullet points down), but this option is the menu equivalent of clicking Burn. In other words, it starts the Burn process. Why go about it this way? We have no idea. None. But it's there if you want it.
- **Print jewel case** This takes you to the Print CD Insert menu, where you can print CD labels and jewel case inserts. It's a pretty cool feature, one we'll discuss later in the chapter.
- **Burn Drive** This fly-out submenu lets you select which drive to burn to (usually the one with the blank CD in it, natch). If you have more than one burner in your system—say, a CD-RW drive and a DVD+RW drive—you'll want to make sure the correct one is selected. Musicmatch is usually pretty smart about figuring out which drive to use—and if it gets it wrong, you won't be able to start the burn process, so no harm done.

- **Drive Speed** You may have a choice here, you may not. It depends on your drive. Whatever the case, choose the fastest available speed—unless you're using slower media, in which case you should choose whatever speed matches (see the earlier section "Choosing the Right Blank Media" if you have no idea what we're talking about).
- **Burn Mode** The first time you burn a CD with Musicmatch, you may want to set this to Test so the program can gauge your CD burner's speed. In most cases, though, you can leave it set to Write.
- **Project** Want to save this CD project for later use? If so, click Project | Save, and then choose a name for it. (To open a past project, click Project | Open.) How is this different from launching Burner Plus with an already-saved playlist? When you save a CD project, you save all the settings along with it—the settings you're learning to modify right here in this very section. How's that for merge!
- **Disc** Within this menu, you'll find a number of submenus and options. For instance, you can add more discs to the Burner Plus window, effectively queuing them up if you want to do a lot of burns all at once. The Change Type option lets you choose between audio and MP3 CDs (you'll see a Data option listed as well, but as we've already noted, why bother?). Most of the other choices here are self-explanatory (including Rename, used to change that cryptic CD label), with one exception: SmartSplit. See the upcoming sidebar "When to Use SmartSplit" for details.
- **File** Within the File menu you'll find several options. The first one is Add, which enables you to add songs to the burn queue. This can come in handy if you have songs stored on your hard drive that aren't part of your Musicmatch Library or that you want to tack on to the playlist you initially copied to the burn queue. To remove a song from the queue, click it once to highlight it, and then click Tools (or Options) | File | Remove. You can also use the File menu to launch Windows Explorer, helpful for dragging and dropping song files to the burn queue.
- **View** The View menu has two options: Details, which, when selected, displays information about any selected track; and Always On Top, which is selected by default and keeps the Burner Plus window on top of other windows until you minimize or close it. Why keep it on top? To simplify dragging and dropping files from your Musicmatch Library or, say, Windows Explorer.

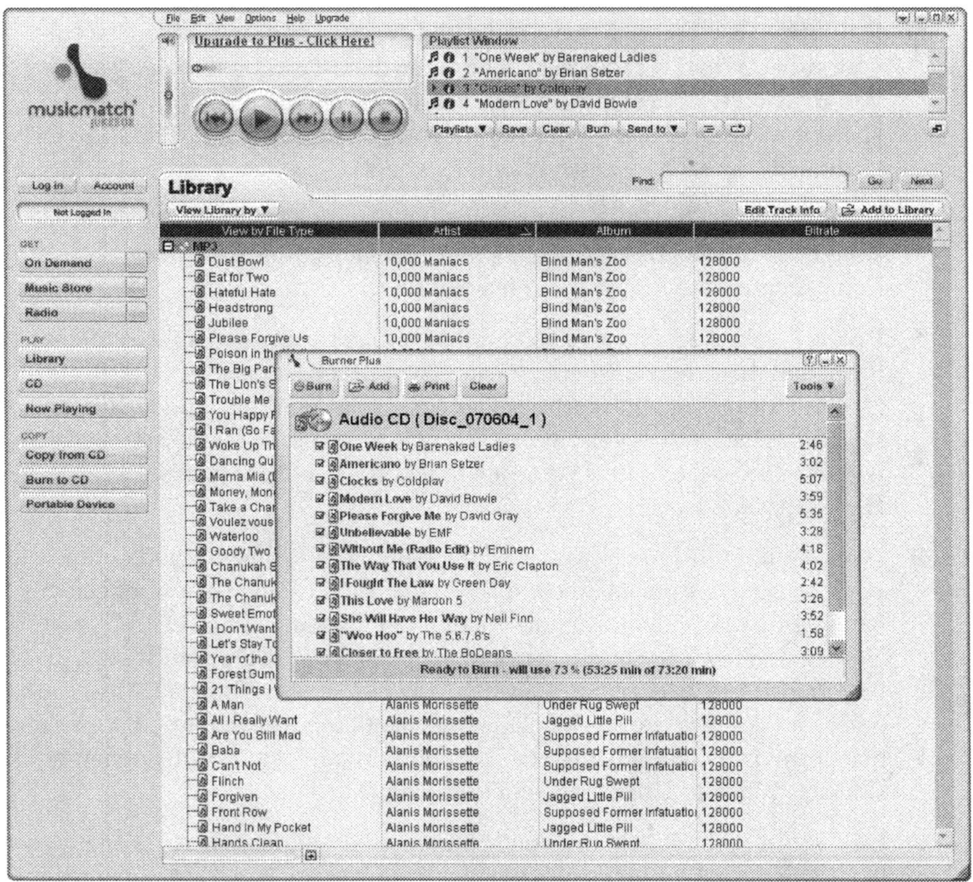

- **Settings** Finally, we come to Settings, which opens up a multitabbed window packed with, well, settings. There are so many that we're going to give them their own section. And here it comes…

Burner Plus Settings

Burner Plus is kind of like a mini-program that operates independently of Musicmatch—hence it has its very own settings. In fact, the Settings window is accessible only from within Burner Plus. To get to it, click Tools (or Options, if you have an older version of Musicmatch), then Settings. This is what you'll see:

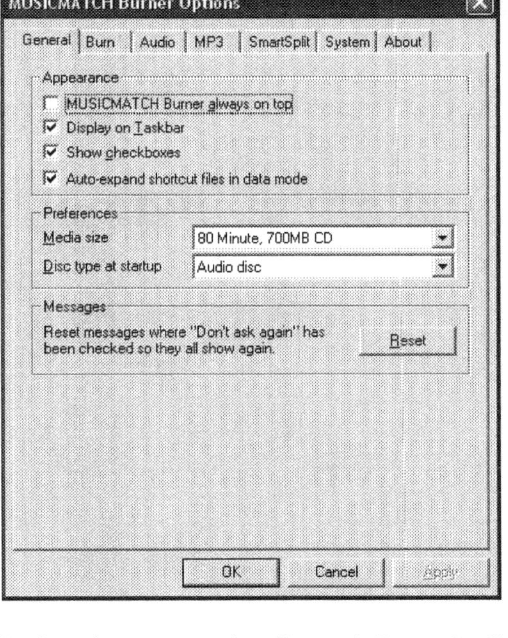

As you can see, Settings has seven tabs: General, Burn, Audio, MP3, SmartSplit, System, and About. The latter merely displays version information about Musicmatch, so we can pretty much ignore that one. As for the rest, let's take a look at some of their functions.

NOTE *This stuff is really only for advanced users. In most cases, you can operate Burner Plus without ever changing—or even looking at—these settings. And we're not going to cover every single setting in every single tab, as many of them are self-explanatory and some just aren't relevant for 99.9% of the CD-burning population.*

General Many of the options listed here (and in other tabs) are self-explanatory. The key items to look at are Media Size (in most cases you'll want "80 Minute, 700MB CD," but if you have older, 650MB discs or perhaps even one of those business-card CDs, you can select it here) and Disc Type At Startup. The latter determines what kind of CD you're going to burn: audio, MP3, or data. This isn't a permanent choice—it merely dictates the default setting for disc type.

Burn The Burn tab is where you specify the default drive and burn speed. As we noted earlier, if you have more than one optical drive in your PC, Musicmatch may inadvertently select the wrong one. Here's the place to choose the drive you want to use for burning, and to set the desired speed (usually the maximum, but you can drop it down if you have "slow" blank media).

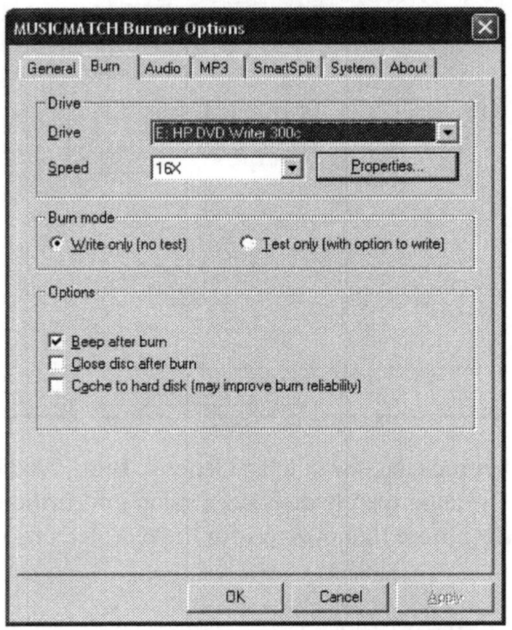

TIP

If you encounter problems burning CDs—for instance, you get an error message or the disc ejects prematurely—you may want to choose a slower burn speed. More often than not, that fixes the problem. But this is another point in favor of using CD-RWs, at least for your first few burns. If an error occurs, you can erase the CD and try again. But a CD-R with an error is a coaster.

Audio The Audio tab contains options related to burning audio CDs (as opposed to MP3 CDs, which are represented in the next tab). A few of these are pretty important, so let's take a closer look:

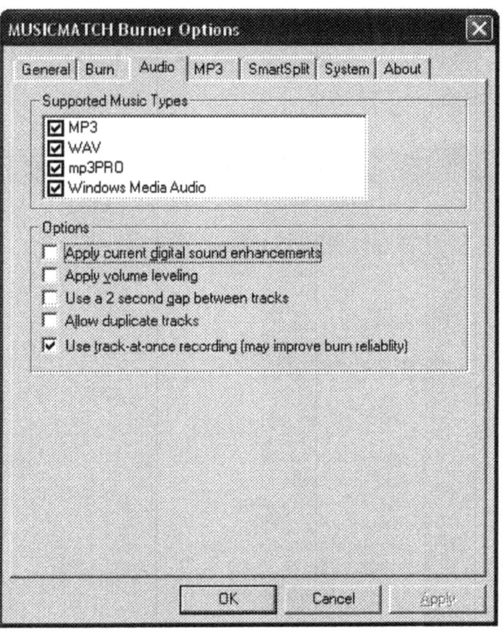

- **Apply current digital sound enhancements** As you learned in Chapter 8, music you play in Musicmatch can be enhanced through the use of digital-effects (or DFX) plug-ins. If this option is selected, any applied enhancements will be included on the burned CD, although it'll take a little longer, since Musicmatch will have to process the audio on its way to the disc.
- **Apply volume leveling** Also discussed in Chapter 8, volume leveling is a handy tool for keeping volume levels consistent in your songs. Without it, you may wind up adjusting the volume from one track to the next—and that's mighty annoying. If you haven't already applied volume leveling to your songs, select this option and Burner Plus will take care of it.
- **Use a 2 second gap between tracks** Most commercial audio CDs have two seconds of silence between each track. If you want Burner Plus to insert a similar gap between tracks, select this option. For the record, most ripped and downloaded songs already have at least one second of silence at the end, so this may be a superfluous step. We don't use it, and we've never encountered a situation where one track started playing "too quickly" after the previous one.
- **Allow duplicate tracks** By default, Burner Plus won't burn a CD containing two or more identical tracks. If you want it to for some reason, check this checkbox.

MP3 We love MP3 CDs, because they hold roughly ten times as much music as standard audio CDs. The MP3 tab contains some decidedly useful options, including the following.

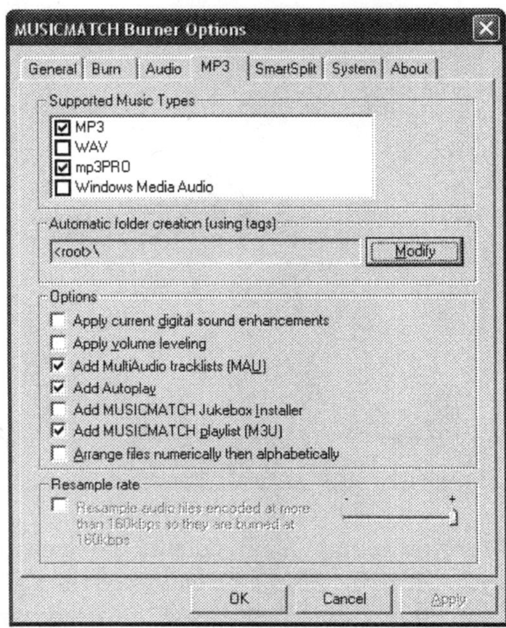

- **Apply current digital sound enhancements** See the previous section, "Audio."
- **Apply volume leveling** See the previous section, "Audio."
- **Add Autoplay** If you want this MP3 CD to automatically start playing when you load it in a PC or notebook, select this option. (Note that the computer's CD drive must also be set to Autoplay.)
- **Add MUSICMATCH Jukebox Installer** Because there's so much room available on MP3 CDs, Burner Plus can actually add a copy of Musicmatch Jukebox to the disc. The idea here is that if you give the MP3 CD to a friend or just want to play your tunes on a foreign PC, your beloved Musicmatch will be at the ready.

- **Automatic folder creation (using tags)** Just as Musicmatch can organize songs on your hard drive based on their ID3 tags, so can Burner Plus organize them on MP3 CDs. Click Modify, select the tag(s) you want to use for the folder structure, and then click Add. If you don't use this option, you'll wind up with one giant song folder that's organized alphabetically—fine if you just want to shuffle-play your tunes, but a nightmare if you want to play, say, all the songs by a particular artist.

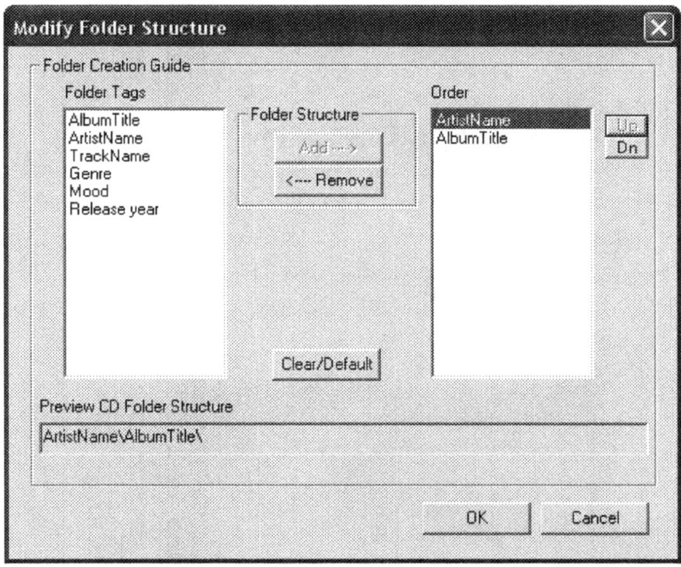

SmartSplit See the "When to Use SmartSplit" sidebar later in the chapter for an explanation of this feature and its corresponding options.

System In the System tab, you can adjust things like cache size, temp-file storage location, and burn priority relative to other system tasks. Our advice: leave these settings alone unless you have a very specific reason for changing them.

And, Finally, Burning a CD

Man, Musicmatch has a lot of burn options, doesn't it? Kinda makes you wish you could just pop in a blank CD, add your songs to the queue, and click the Burn button, sort of like popping in a blank cassette and hitting record. Well, as we discussed way back in "Burning Your First CD: A Quick-Start Guide," you can usually do exactly that. The only really important variable is choosing between audio CD and MP3 CD.

When to Use SmartSplit

Let's say you've got more songs in your playlist than will fit on a single audio CD. (That's usually not a problem for MP3 CDs, which can hold well over 100 tunes, but the same rules apply.) Musicmatch's SmartSplit option will divide them up over as many CDs as necessary, prompting you to insert one blank after another until the entire playlist has been burned. This is a decidedly handy option if you're trying to burn a large number of MP3s to disc, as with, say, an audiobook. However, SmartSplit cannot split individual files that are too large to fit on one audio CD. For that you'd need a third-party utility like GoldWave (www.goldwave.com).

You can modify SmartSplit options in Burner Plus by clicking Tools (or Options, depending on your version of Musicmatch) | Settings, and then clicking the SmartSplit tab. For the most part, you'll want to leave these settings alone. The one option to pay close attention to is Do Not Allow Folder Contents To Be Split Between Disks. When selected, it will keep folders together on the same CD—helpful if you want to keep specific artists or albums from being split across multiple CDs.

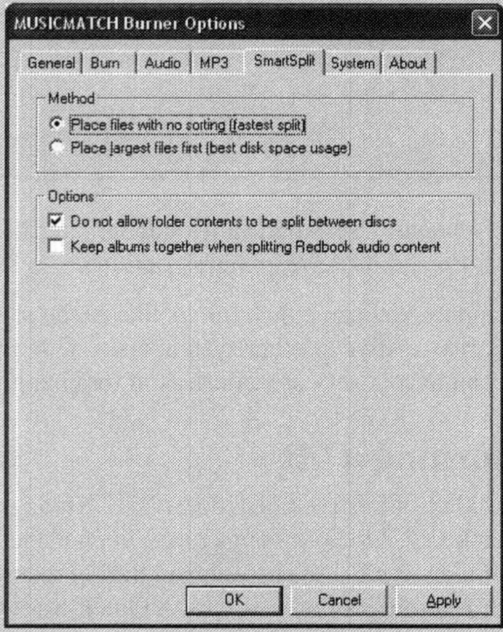

Anyway, the bottom line is, once you've added your songs and tweaked the options, all that's left is to click the Burn button and go get a cup of coffee. The time it will take Musicmatch to burn the CD depends on the speed of your computer, CD burner, and media.

When it's done, you may want to print a label for the CD and possibly the jewel case as well. To find out how, skip ahead to "Making Labels." In the meantime, there's one last CD-burning topic we need to address—the very annoying matter of digital rights management (DRM).

DRM Limitations for Burning Downloaded Songs

When you purchase songs from Musicmatch Downloads, there's a DRM limitation built into each WMA file that limits how many times it can be burned to a CD. Actually, it's a pretty minor restriction: You can burn a particular playlist (say, an album with songs in the original order, or a custom mix CD) only five times,

Why Musicmatch Offers Free MP3 Encoding

Eliot Van Buskirk is not only this book's whip-smart tech editor, he's also Section Editor, Technology, at CNET's MP3.com and the author of Burning Down the House: Ripping, Recording, Remixing, and More! Here he sheds some light into the little-known secret behind Musicmatch's free MP3 encoding capabilities.

You may have noticed that Microsoft's Windows Media Player and other programs charge you extra (either up front or after the fact) for the right to encode MP3s, while the free version of Musicmatch lets you make as many MP3s as you want. There's a very good reason for this. While the MP3 format sort of feels free, it's not—it's copyrighted code that's owned by its inventor, Fraunhofer Gesellschaft—a German engineering company. Thomson Multimedia administers licensing for the MP3 codec worldwide, due to a deal with Fraunhofer, which would rather concentrate on engineering things. Thomson normally charges developers for hardware or software that plays or creates MP3s. As it turns out, Thomson Multimedia also owns a large chunk of Musicmatch. There's not a lot of margin in charging yourself money, so I'm fairly certain Musicmatch gets to include the encoder part for free—which is why, my friends, you can use it to encode MP3s without paying a dime.

though there's no limit to how many times an individual song can be burned to disc—as long as you vary the playlists it's used in.

The other workaround is one we've discussed many times already: burn the songs or album to an audio CD, then rip them back to your PC in MP3 format. Presto: no more DRM.

NOTE *The purpose of DRM is to keep you from illegally distributing commercial songs. While we think you should have the right to do just about anything you want with music you've bought and paid for (short of making money from it), we also think artists deserve to be paid for their work. In other words, please don't pirate music.*

Making Labels

As far as Rick is concerned, an audio CD is not an audio CD unless it has a label. There's just something, well, *messy* about a pile of unlabeled CDs, which is what you're likely to wind up with after spending some time with Burner Plus. Fortunately, Musicmatch makes it quite easy to create and print both CD labels and jewel-case inserts.

NOTE *In case you're unfamiliar with the term, a jewel case is the standard plastic holder that store-bought CDs come in. You know, the kind with the lid that always cracks down the middle or loses one of its little pivot arms. Why they haven't invented stronger cases after all these years is beyond us.*

Before you can get started, however, you'll need a few things:

- A CD labeling kit
- CD and jewel-case labels
- An inkjet printer (if you want color labels)
- Musicmatch Jukebox Plus (the Basic version lets you get as far as setting up your label for printing, but when you actually click Print, you'll see a message saying you have to upgrade—see Chapter 1 for information on upgrading to Musicmatch Plus)

TIP *They cost a little more, but we highly recommend labels with glossy finishes. They look much more professional than basic paper labels, and generally do a better job of covering whatever printing is already on the blank CDs.*

A CD labeling kit usually includes a tool that enables you to apply labels to your CDs with near-perfect precision, plus a batch of labels to get you started. Some also include label-printing software, which you can certainly use in lieu of Musicmatch if you prefer. But Musicmatch does a pretty good job with audio CDs, so we recommend giving it a try.

CAUTION *Make sure you apply your label only after you've finished burning the CD. Otherwise, well, the results might not be pretty.*

You can find CD labeling kits (see Figure 10-3 for an example) at most computer and office-supply stores. But before you pick one at random, check to make sure Musicmatch "supports" it. Specifically, make sure the labels that are included with the kit are listed among the layouts Musicmatch recognizes. That way, Musicmatch will know exactly where to print when you feed the labels into your printer. If you use labels that aren't on the list, you'll have to fiddle with some rather imprecise "nudge" settings to get accurate printing.

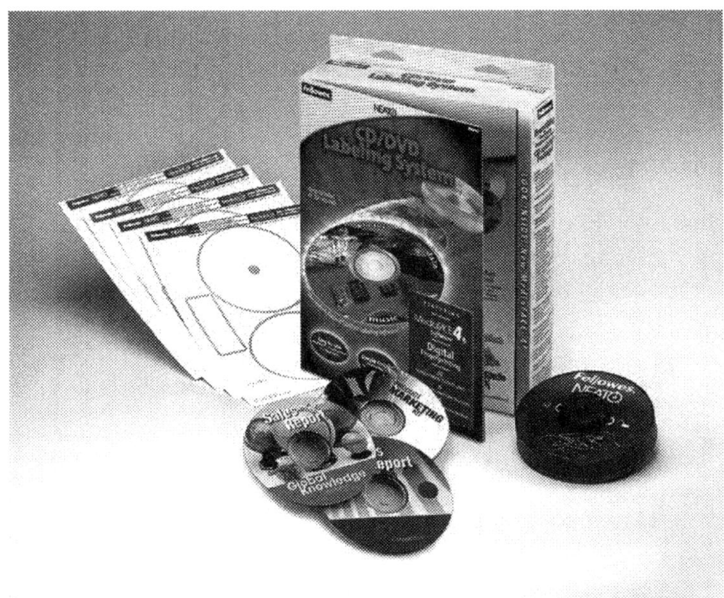

FIGURE 10-3 The Neato CD Labeler Kit comes with a label applicator, a bunch of sample labels, and label-creation software. It sells for about $20.

How can you find out what label brands and varieties are on Musicmatch's layout list? For starters, you can examine this screenshot:

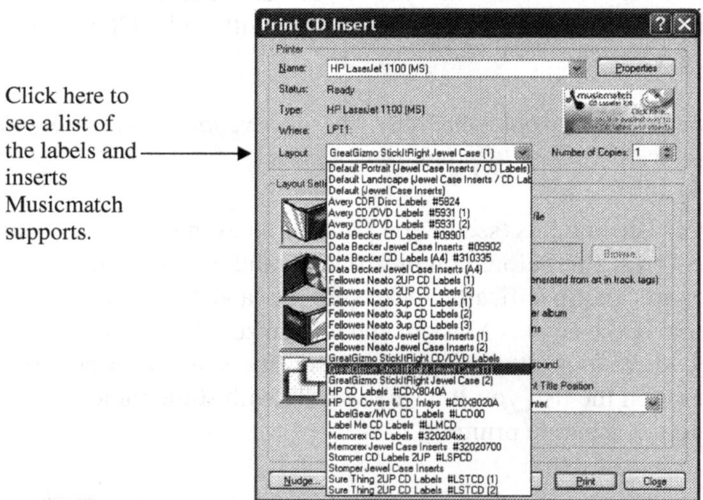

To see the list up close and personal, you'll need to open Musicmatch's Print CD Insert utility—something you're going to do eventually anyway. There are two ways to go about this:

- If you still have Burner Plus running, click the Print button.
- In Musicmatch, open the playlist that contains the appropriate album or songs, then click File | Print | Print CD Label / Jewel Case. You can also click Options | Playlist | Print CD Label / Jewel Case.

Click the Layout field to see the complete list of labels and inserts Musicmatch supports. Now you'll know which kit—or at least which labels—to buy.

TIP *If you buy a labeling kit from, say, Neato, you needn't necessarily buy Neato labels when you use up the samples that came with the kit. The applicator should be compatible with just about any label on the planet, so feel free to choose whatever label color, finish, or price you like best—as long as the label brand and number are on Musicmatch's Layout list.*

Now that you've loaded the Print CD Insert utility and selected a layout, you're halfway to printing a label or insert. The second half awaits you in the following two sections.

Printing CD Labels

Now that you have the Print CD Insert utility open, you need to select a layout that matches the kind of labels you have. As you can see when you click the Layout field, the list of choices includes both CD labels and jewel-case inserts. We'll get to the latter a bit later. For now, select the appropriate CD label and let's get started. (As you may notice, the layout you choose determines the options that appear in the main portion of the Print CD Insert window. That's because there are different options associated with printing a CD label than with printing jewel-case inserts.)

CAUTION *There's a school of thought that says you shouldn't apply adhesive labels to CDs, as they can "unbalance" the discs and lead to playback and longevity problems. We've never experienced any such problems, but one thing is for certain: you should never try to apply labels manually, without an applicator. That said, you can avoid any such problems if you have an inkjet printer that can print directly onto the label side of blank CDs (see "Choosing the Right Blank Media" earlier in this chapter for more details). However, usually that process requires special software, so you probably won't be able to print from Musicmatch.*

The next step in designing a CD label is deciding whether to include a photo or image of some kind. If the CD in question is a mix, there's probably no single picture that's appropriate, though obviously you could use just about anything: a photo of one of the artists, a picture of your dog, or whatever. But you may just want to skip the photo altogether, in which case you should select the option marked Create CD Label With Blank Background. You'll still be able to print track names on the label.

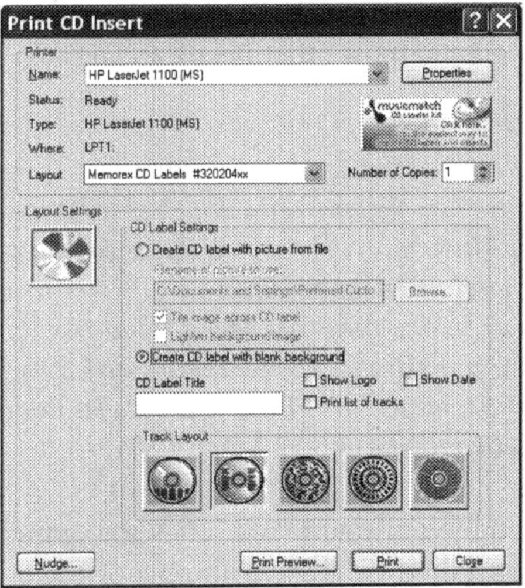

Finding Artist Art on the Web

Let's say you want to nab a photo of Natalie Imbruglia for your CD label. It's easy—all you need is an Internet connection. (This how-to falls under the beloved category, "Google: Is There Anything It Can't Do?")

1. Fire up your web browser, head to Google.com, then do a search for the singer.
2. Once Google presents the results, click the Images link.
3. Find a photo you like (ideally, it should be something square, at least 400×400 pixels or 50K—any smaller and it won't look too sharp when you print it), click it, and then click the See Full-Size Image link.
4. When the photo appears in your browser, right-click it, then choose Save Picture As. Store it in a folder where you'll be able to find it easily (we recommend My Documents), and then head back to Musicmatch.

Let's assume, however, that the CD you burned was an entire album—say, Natalie Imbruglia's *Left of the Middle*. Wouldn't it be nice to have a picture of the lovely singer on the CD label? Well, we've got good news and bad news. The bad news is that Musicmatch can't just paste in the album art it automatically downloaded when you purchased the album onto the cover—though oddly enough, it can when you print an insert for the jewel-case. The good news is that you can easily find a photo of Ms. Imbruglia (and most other bands and artists) on the Web and use it on your label.

TIP *Actually, you can use Musicmatch's album art—you just have to perform a few steps before you get started with Print CD Insert. Start playing the desired song in Musicmatch, right-click the art image that appears in the top-left corner, and then choose Edit | Copy Art To Clipboard. Now fire up your preferred graphics program (even Windows Paint will do), choose Edit | Paste, and presto: there's the album art! Save it as a JPEG, then head back to Musicmatch and Print CD Insert. Load the newly saved JPEG as described next.*

If you do have a picture you want to use, click the option marked Create CD Label With Picture From File. You'll see a number of options appear just below it:

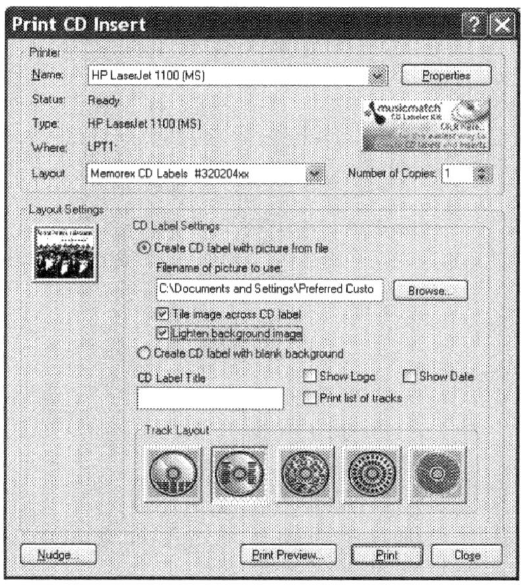

- **Filename of picture to use** Click Browse to navigate your hard drive and find the picture you want to include on the label. The picture must be in either BMP or JPEG format.
- **Tile image across CD label** This is mostly a matter of personal preference. If checked, this option will make your photo smaller and tile it across the label.
- **Lighten background image** If you plan to print track names on the label, check this option to make your photo lighter. Otherwise, you may have a hard time reading the track names.

Now let's take a look at some of the other options available in the CD Label Settings section:

- **Show Logo** When checked, this will add the Musicmatch logo to your label. Bleh! Who wants that?
- **Show Date** This is pretty self-explanatory—check it to include the date your label (and, ostensibly, your CD) was created.
- **CD Label Title** Use this field to include the name of the artist and/or album, or whatever name you want for the CD (such as "Rick's Mix"). Leave it blank if you don't want a title on the label.

- **Print List of Tracks** Again, this is largely a matter of personal preference. If you're going to go on to the next step of printing a jewel-case insert, you may not want to bother printing the track names on the CD label. They just take up space and block out whatever picture you've selected. If you do check this option, you'll want to move on to the final step:
- **Track Layout** Musicmatch offers a choice of five layouts for your CD label (not to be confused with the Layout menu used to select the CD label brand). Click one to select it, and then click Print Preview to see exactly how the label will look.

You can (and should) click Print Preview at any time while fiddling with label options. It's very helpful in determining how different options affect the appearance of the label.

Once you've set all the options to your liking, put a label sheet in your printer, click Print, and you're on your way!

Printing Jewel-Case Inserts

Printing jewel-case inserts is a bit more involved than printing CD labels, mostly because you've got three different items to print: the front cover, the inside front cover, and the back cover. When you select a jewel-case insert from the Layout field, you'll see that several additional icons appear in the Layout Settings area below.

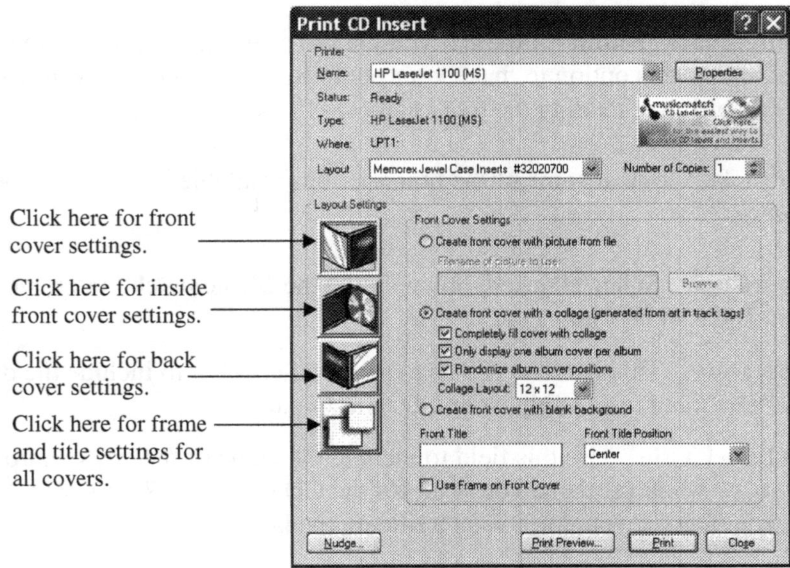

When you click any of these icons, you'll see various options appear in the section to the right. Many of them are the same as—or at least similar to—the options explained in the earlier "Printing CD Labels" section. Others are pretty self-explanatory. Therefore, we're not going to go into exhaustive detail on all of them. But we are going to give you some help with one: Front Cover Settings (the top icon in the Layout Settings section).

Specifically, notice the option marked Create Front Cover With A Collage (Generated From Art In Track Tags). This is a really cool way to make use of the album art that Musicmatch downloads when you use the Edit Track Tags feature (see Chapter 7), and it saves you from having to go out and find your own art for the jewel-case front cover. We could explain most of the options here in detail, but we think it's more fun to experiment. Try one or two of the suboptions, and then click Print Preview to see how the cover will look. Here's an example:

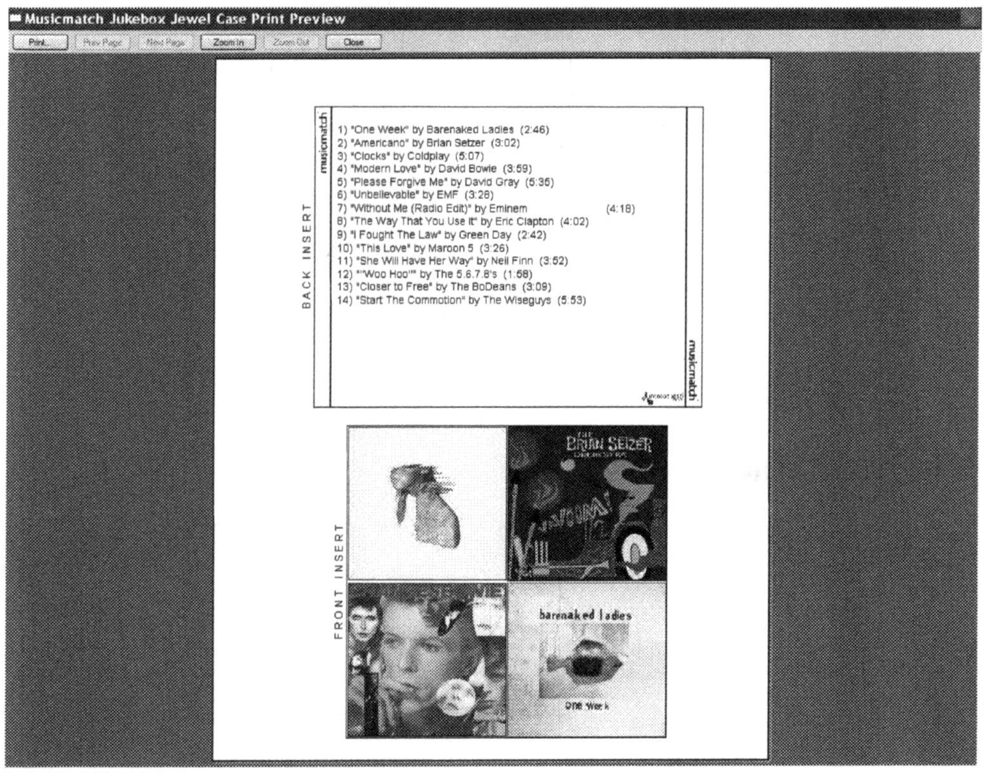

Cool as we think this art-collage feature is, we found it to be a bit buggy. For instance, sometimes it would duplicate album covers, even though we'd checked the option marked Only Display One Album Cover Per Album. And the Collage Layout option didn't always produce the selected number of album covers.

Finally, if you want to add a frame to any of your covers, check the appropriately labeled box near the bottom of the window, and then click the bottom icon in Layout Settings. From there you'll be able to choose from a handful of spiffy-looking frames or even download additional ones.

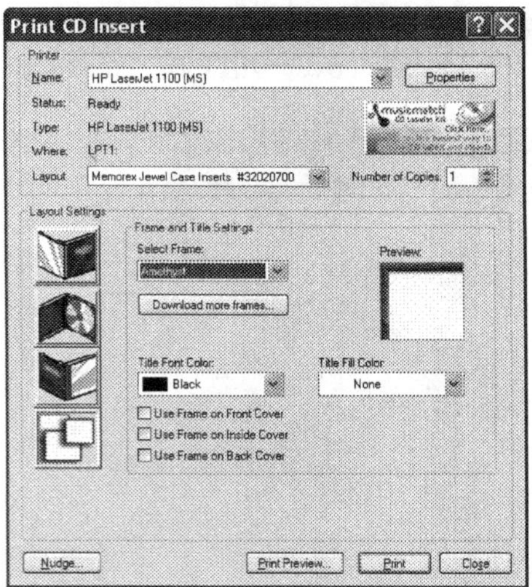

Where to Find It

Web Site	Address	What's There
Neato	www.neato.com	Neato CD Labeler Kit
Verbatim	www.verbatim.com	Digital Vinyl blank CDs

Chapter 11 Working with Portable Players

How to...

- Choose a portable audio player
- Make sure your player is compatible with Musicmatch
- Install portable player plug-ins
- Work with PDAs
- Copy songs to your portable player
- Create playlists on your player
- Modify Portable Device Manager settings
- Troubleshoot songs that won't play
- Synchronize your player with your song library
- Copy audiobooks to your portable player
- Resample songs to fit better on your player

"What besides music is so personal and yet so communal?" —Rick Broida, co-author of this book

It's one of those timeless questions: which came first, the MP3 or the MP3 player? Okay, so it's not exactly the chicken and the egg—we happen to know for a fact that the MP3 came first (see Chapter 7 if you'd like to learn the history). But it was the arrival of the MP3 player that ushered in a new era of music portability, which many would say culminated with Apple's now-legendary iPod.

In this chapter, we're going to teach you to use Musicmatch with portable players and introduce you to some of our favorite models (in case you don't own one yet or you're thinking of upgrading). You can use the program to copy not only your music library (or portions of it), but also your playlists. At the same time, we'll teach you a few nifty tricks, like how to squeeze more music into a portable player that doesn't have a lot of storage space, and how to synchronize the player with Musicmatch so that new songs are automatically transferred.

It's time to liberate your music from your PC and let it roam where you want to, all around the world (sorry for the cheap B-52s paraphrasing, but we couldn't think of another song that had to do with roaming).

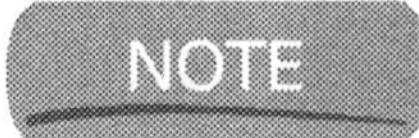

This chapter focuses entirely on Musicmatch 9.0. If you have an earlier version, we highly recommend upgrading, as the Portable Device Manager used to access portable players is much improved in 9.0.

Choosing a Portable Player

In the market for a portable player? We can help you pick one, but there's a crucial bit of information you need first: Musicmatch doesn't support all the players that are out there. (By "support" we mean able to interface with a player for copying songs and playlists.) It works with quite a large number of them (about 50 as of press time), including most of the really popular models, and the company continues to add support for new players as they come out—but there are still a few that aren't on the list. If you really want to leverage Musicmatch to the fullest, choose a player that works with it directly. You can find a list of them by visiting the Musicmatch web site, clicking the Plug-ins link at the bottom of the home page, and then clicking the Portable MP3 Players link (see Figure 11-1). We'll talk more about these plug-ins (and players that don't need them) in the "Configuring Musicmatch to Work with Your Player" section a little later in this chapter.

The Different Kinds of Portable Players

Portable audio players generally fall into two categories: those with flash memory and those with hard drives. The latter, like the Apple iPod and Dell DJ (see Figure 11-2), are popular because they can hold mountains of music—usually upwards of 20 gigabytes (GB) or more. So-called flash players (which get their name from the kind of memory they use) usually have 128–512 megabytes (MB) of storage space, and tend to be smaller and less expensive than hard-drive players. They also have no moving internal parts, which makes them ideal for running, walking, and other athletic endeavors.

What about portable CD players? Different animal. As you learned in Chapter 10, you can use Musicmatch to burn audio CDs—and even MP3 CDs for those players that support them—but that's not the same thing as connecting a portable audio player to your PC and using Musicmatch to transfer songs to it.

In fact, let's get our terminology straight. What we're really talking about here are MP3 players, though we've elected to refer to them as portable audio players, which is technically more accurate. First-generation devices did, in fact, play only MP3 files, but most of the latest models play WMA files as well. Some, like Apple's iPod, play MP3s and the proprietary AAC format. We'll talk more about all this later in the chapter—for now, we just want you to understand why we're not

FIGURE 11-1 In order for Musicmatch to communicate with your portable player, you may need to download a plug-in.

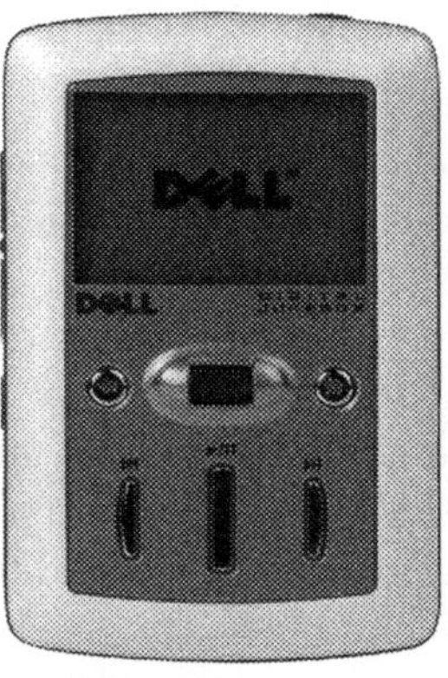

FIGURE 11-2 The Dell DJ is one of our favorite portable players, in part because it has tons of storage space, and in part because it's affordable.

Our Favorite Players

In our previous lives as editors of *Handheld Computing Magazine*, we wrote countless reviews of portable audio devices, so we feel reasonably qualified in sharing our recommendations. And believe us, we have some fairly strong opinions when it comes to this stuff.

Rick: Unless you're specifically looking for a player that's good for exercise, I highly recommend a hard drive player. At press time, the 15GB Dell DJ was selling for just $199—the same price as the 256MB Creative MuVo Slim. (In case you're not familiar with megabyte/gigabyte math, the Dell DJ has roughly 60 times more storage space than the MuVo.) Admittedly, these are two very different players in terms of size, style, and features, but when you look solely at the economics of storage, the DJ is obviously the way to go. It's compact enough to fit in your pocket (or even to hold in your hand while exercising), has great battery life, plays both MP3 and WMA files (the beloved Apple iPod doesn't support WMAs), and did I mention its 15GB of storage space? You might think I'm crowing about the DJ because I'm the co-author of *How to Do Everything with Your Dell DJ*, but you're wrong. If money were no object, I'd definitely grab an iPod—they're just that cool. But the 20GB fourth-generation iPod costs $299, a full $100 more than the 15GB DJ, and its battery life isn't nearly as good.

By the way, if you *are* looking for a player that's good for exercise, it's hard to beat the Creative MuVo TX FM. It's tiny, it includes an FM tuner and recorder, it doubles as a USB flash key (meaning you can use it to store and transport data as well as music), and, at $149.99 for the 256MB model, it's reasonably priced.

Denny: For once, Rick's recommendation is right on. The Dell DJ is one of the best values out there in the portable music player arena, it has great support for songs downloaded from Musicmatch Downloads, and its battery life and capacity are top-notch. If you're a spendthrift like good old Rick—or if you use Musicmatch Downloads—you can't beat the Dell DJ.

But if you're the discerning type who's willing to spend a little extra cash for a product with style, a great interface, top-notch sound, and one of the best consumer electronics designs currently available, may I suggest Apple's iPod. There's just one caveat: The iPod doesn't support Musicmatch Downloads' WMA format, so if you buy songs from the Musicmatch site, you'll need to burn them to CD and re-rip them to MP3 format (as we described in Chapter 6) before you can download them to the iPod. Still, it's such a fantastic little player that it may be worth the hassle.

As for flash players, forget about them. If size is a real issue, go for a Rio mini-hard-drive player such as the Nitrus (or an iPod Mini, taking into account the preceding caveats). Their capacities are generally under 5GB, but for many the small size outweighs the relatively limited capacity.

calling these gadgets MP3 players. But you can feel free to, as long as it's in the privacy of your own home. (Don't let Denny catch you—he's been known to fly into a murderous rage over silly things like that.)

Musicmatch and PDAs

As you may know, most modern PDAs (personal digital assistants—a.k.a., handheld PCs) are capable of playing MP3s. Some can also play WMAs, though not the DRM-protected kind you get from Musicmatch Downloads. Wouldn't it be great if you could use Musicmatch to copy songs and playlists directly to your PDA?

You can! (You don't think we'd do a big buildup like that and then say no, do you?) Pocket PC handhelds are among the portable devices supported by Musicmatch. Alas, the software can't connect with Palm OS PDAs, even those that can play MP3s. You can, however, export your Musicmatch playlists and then manually install them on your Palm OS PDA, provided you're using a software player that supports playlists. Read on to learn more about using a PDA with Musicmatch.

TIP *If you do have a Palm OS PDA that can play music, all is not lost. Musicmatch's Portable Device Manager supports Secure Digital (SD) cards and other removable media—the kind often used to store music on those Palm PDAs. All you need is a card reader for your PC, which will give the card a drive letter when it's inserted. Plug the card in, fire up Portable Device Manager, and copy songs to it like you would any other device. This also works for Pocket PCs and flash players that have memory-card slots.*

Configuring Musicmatch to Work with Your Player

Many portable audio players—and all Pocket PC PDAs—are directly compatible with Musicmatch, meaning you just plug 'em into your PC, turn 'em on, and start copying songs. Other players (most notably the Apple iPod and Dell DJ) require something called a *plug-in*—a tiny file you download to enable Musicmatch to communicate with the player.

Why is it that Musicmatch can automatically communicate with some players but requires plug-ins for others? Without getting overly technical about it, Musicmatch includes a built-in plug-in for Windows Media Device Manager, or WMDM, a standard technology incorporated into many of the latest players. To look at it a different way, if your player is compatible with Windows Media Player, it should also be compatible with Musicmatch.

Here's a list (current as of press time) of the players that require Musicmatch plug-ins:

- Apple iPod
- Archos 6000 Jukebox
- Creative Nomad Jukebox, Jukebox 3, Zen, and Zen NX
- Dell DJ
- Gateway DMP-200/DMP-300
- Intel Pocket Concert
- Irock! 500/700 Series
- Just about every RCA/Thomson-made player

So how do you access and install these plug-ins? We're happy to report it's very easy and a one-time process. Here's how:

1. Start Musicmatch, and then click Portable Device. This will load the Portable Device Manager.
2. Click Tools | Add A Device Plugin. This will start your web browser and take you to the Musicmatch plug-in site (see Figure 11-1). Needless to say, you must have an active Internet connection for this to work.
3. Find your player in the list, then click the link that appears below it. This will download and install the plug-in.
4. Close Portable Device Manager by clicking the X in the upper-right corner. That's it! Your player is now installed, and will be available the next time you start Portable Device Manager.

A Note to iPod Users

Got an iPod? Lucky you. We jest loves dem iPods. However, there's one important limitation to consider when using one with Musicmatch: the iPod doesn't support WMA files. If you have songs in that format or you've purchased songs from Musicmatch Downloads, you won't be able to play them on your iPod. Naturally there's always the option of converting your WMAs (by burning them to CD, then ripping them back to the PC in MP3 format), but that may be more of a hassle than you want to endure—especially if you buy a lot of music. No, the better choice for iPod users may be to stick with iTunes, which offers a lot of the same functionality as Musicmatch—including music downloads that can, of course, be played on the iPod.

Copying Songs to Your Portable Player

Copying songs from your PC to your portable audio player via Musicmatch is a relatively simple process. Here's one way (abbreviated for your convenience) to go about it:

1. Start Musicmatch. Plug in your portable player and make sure it's on.
2. Open or create a playlist containing songs you want to copy. If it's a new playlist, save it before proceeding.
3. In the Playlist Window, click Send To | Portable Device. This will open the Portable Device Manager, which is where all the action happens.
4. All the songs in the playlist will start copying to your player.
5. When the copy process is complete, click Tools | Safely Remove Device. Now you can unplug your player and start listening!

As you might expect, there are plenty of variables along the way. For instance, you can choose to copy your entire Musicmatch Library to your player, instead of just a single playlist. You can drag and drop files from your hard drive, effectively bypassing your Musicmatch Library. There's also that whole synchronization thing, which is pretty cool. So let's get a little more specific, using the Dell DJ as our example.

Hey, Why Won't My Songs Play on My Portable Player?

Here's a common scenario: you copy a bunch of songs to your portable player, only to discover that some of them just plain won't play. There are a few possible reasons for this:

- **No WMA support** If you copy WMA files to your player, but it doesn't support that format, naturally those files won't play. Check your player's documentation or packaging to see if WMA support is mentioned. If not, you'll have to limit yourself to MP3s.
- **No DRM support** There are some players that support the WMA format, but not DRM. In other words, you can copy WMA files ripped from your own CDs (just make sure the Protect Content button is not checked in Tools | Options | Copy Music), but not songs purchased from Musicmatch Downloads. Although they're WMA files, they're also protected by Digital Rights Management (see Chapter 6 for a refresher), and not all players support those kinds of files. The good news is that aside from the iPod, most of the latest and greatest players can handle DRM-protected WMAs. The bad news is that few older players can.

TIP *Check with the device manufacturer to see if a firmware upgrade is available. It's possible that by installing new software on the player, you can add support for WMAs—perhaps even DRM WMAs.*

- **No VBR support** If you ripped your CDs using variable bit-rate (VBR) encoding, the resulting MP3s may not play in your player. Why? Because not all players support VBR files. Hey, don't look at us—we warned you back in Chapter 4 that VBR might pose problems with portable players.
- **Corrupted file(s)** Part of the problem with file-sharing services is that the songs you download are often corrupted (meaning the files themselves are damaged in some way). Even if they play okay on your PC, they can refuse to work on portable players. There's no remedy for this other than to replace the files with ones you rip or purchase yourself.

Case Study: The Dell DJ (or Any Other Hard-Drive Player)

Using Musicmatch with a flash player or PDA is relatively easy—because they have limited storage space, you're usually copying just a couple dozen songs (at most). Toss 'em in a playlist, copy them over using the method described in the previous section, and you're ready to rock 'n' roll (you knew we were going to use that phrase eventually, right?).

Working with a hard-drive player like the Dell DJ is a bit more involved. Because you have enough space (theoretically) to store your entire song library, you'll probably want to copy the whole thing. At the same time, you'll probably want to add or create some playlists to make for easier song navigation on your portable player. Finally, there's the option to synchronize your library or playlists.

Working with the Portable Device Manager

Ready to copy some songs to your player? The Musicmatch module that makes this possible is Portable Device Manager (PDM), which you can load any of the following ways:

- Click the Portable Device button on the left side of the Musicmatch window.
- In Musicmatch's pull-down menus, click View | Portable Device Manager.
- In the Playlist window, click Send To | Portable Device. This option assumes you have an open playlist you want to copy, but it's not mandatory that you do.

NOTE *Before you launch PDM, you should plug your player into your PC and power it on.*

The first time you start PDM, a window will pop up asking you if you want to enable synchronization with your player:

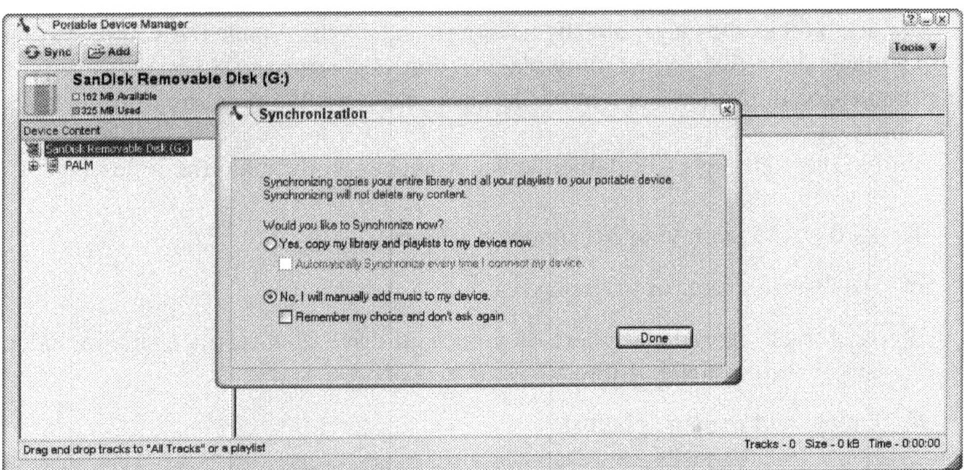

For now, choose no—we'll get to that option later. It's better to get familiar with PDM first, which you can do by checking out this screenshot:

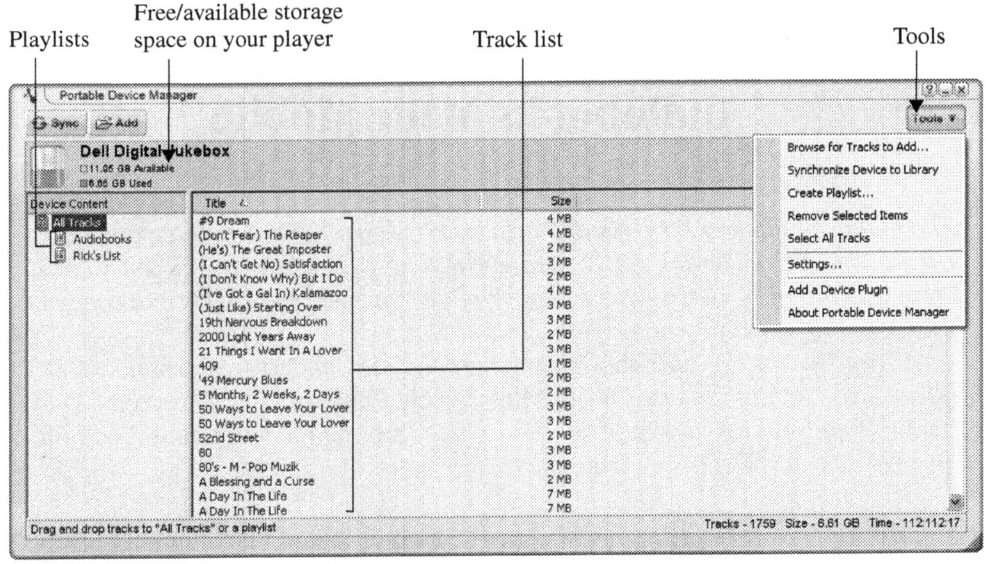

TIP *By default, Musicmatch displays only the title and size of each song on your device. But if you right-click the column bar (where it says "title" and "size"), you'll see a list of other items you can display: artist, album, bit rate, and so on. Click any one of them to add it to the column bar, then resize the columns as needed.*

In our example, the player already has songs and playlists loaded. If you're starting with a blank slate (that is, an empty player), don't be surprised if you don't see anything listed in Device Content or the tracks window. We're going to fill them up shortly.

Within the confines of Portable Device Manager, you can do the following:

- Add tracks from your Musicmatch Library
- Add tracks from (or to) a playlist
- Add tracks stored elsewhere on your hard drive (that is, tracks not included in your Musicmatch Library)
- Create and manage playlists
- Synchronize your player with your Musicmatch Library
- Delete tracks from your player

Let's delve into the nitty-gritty of working with PDM.

Audiobooks Made Mobile

The author of numerous books and articles about personal computers, Sheldon Leemon has been working with, playing with, and writing about PCs since 1980. Here he lends his expertise to the subject of turning audiobook CDs into compact files for your portable player.

I love listening to audiobooks, but hate the idea of carrying around a CD player and eight or ten discs. With Musicmatch, I can rip a spoken-word CD to about 25 megabytes' worth of files, and carry around an entire audiobook on an MP3 player the size of a matchbox. Here's how:

1. *Dial down recording quality.* Spoken words sound fine at quality levels that are too low for music. To pack in more minutes per megabyte, I go to Options | Recorder | Settings and change the format to Windows Media Audio (WMA) at Near CD Quality (48 kbps). You may even be able to get by at FM Radio Quality (32 kbps). (Note that this assumes your MP3 player supports the WMA format—if not, choose MP3 instead.)

2. *Set a tracks directory.* While you're on the Recorder Settings tab, hit the Tracks Directory button, and choose a directory in which to store the files from the CD. I check Make Sub Path Using Artist, so all the files from the book end up in the same directory. I also set Name Track Files From Album And Track Number, using the arrows to move Album to the top, and Track number second.
3. *Turn off CD lookup.* Tracks on audiobook CDs have no names, only numbers, so an Internet search is a waste of time. Uncheck the Enable CD Lookup checkbox from the CD Lookup/Connectivity tab of Options | Settings.
4. *Create short names for artist, album.* Once you've inserted your CD and opened the Recorder window (from View | Recorder), you're ready to rip. When you press the Record button, you'll be prompted for the name of the artist and the album. As these are used for ID3 tags as well as filenames, I make them as short as possible. For CD 1 of J.K. Rowling's *Harry Potter and the Order of the Phoenix,* I'd use JK for the artist name and Order01 for the album. That way, filenames for the first CD will start with Order01-1, Order01-2, and so on. Subsequent CDs will follow the same numbering scheme so that sorting the tracks alphabetically also puts them in the correct playing order.
5. *Rip while doing something else.* Since Musicmatch automates the work for you, it's foolish to sit and watch it do its thing. Rip your audiobook CDs while you're doing something else, like reading e-mail or playing a game. As each disc is done, the CD drive tray will eject. At that point, you can switch CDs, go back to Musicmatch for a minute and enter the artist and album, and then continue what you were doing.
6. *Transfer the files to your player.* If there's a Musicmatch plug-in for your MP3 player (or Musicmatch supports it directly), all you have to do is add the files you've just ripped to the player window, and you're ready to read…er, listen.

Loading Tracks from the Library

This method works best if you want to pick select songs or albums from the Musicmatch Jukebox Library and copy them to the Dell DJ. Here's what you should do:

1. Click the All Tracks entry on the left side of the display to select it.
2. Click the Add button. Alternatively, you can right-click All Tracks and choose Add Track(s) To Dell Digital Jukebox from the menu. Either way, you'll see the Open Music dialog box.

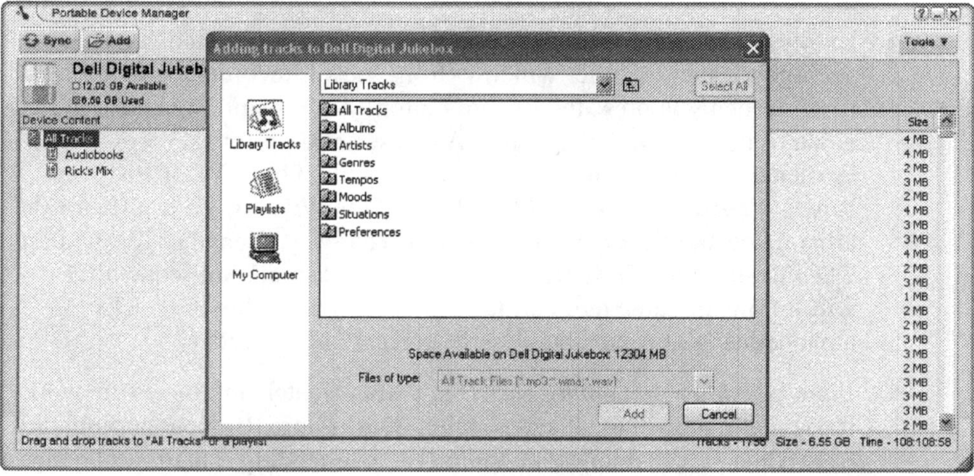

3. Now it's up to you to find your music. You can select tunes by drilling into the dialog box through Albums, Artists, Genres, All Tracks, or other categories. Take Albums, for instance—if you double-click it, you'll see a list of all the albums in your Musicmatch Library. Double-click the album you want and then select the songs you want to add. You can click the Select All button to add all the tracks on an album. When you're done, click Add and the tracks will be immediately added to the DJ.

We should point out that if you want to add a lot of songs, you might want to use a broader category, like All Tracks, since you can't pick songs from two or more albums at once using the Album category—you'll have to keep opening the Add Music dialog box and selecting songs over and over again. Nonetheless, once your songs are copied, you can disconnect the DJ and listen to your music.

Loading Tracks from Elsewhere on the Hard Drive

What if you have songs (or, say, audiobooks—see this chapter's Voices from the Community sidebar) on your hard drive that aren't loaded into your Musicmatch Library? Are you out of luck? Absolutely not. Musicmatch offers an easy way to fetch tracks from your hard drive, and it's pretty similar to the method we just used:

1. Just as before, click the All Tracks entry on the left side of the window.
2. Click the Add button or right-click All Tracks and choose Add Track(s) to Dell Digital Jukebox from the menu. You'll see the Add Music dialog box.
3. Instead of choosing music using the default Library Tracks option on the left side of the dialog box, click My Computer. You now have access to all your computer's drives. Just zero in on the audio files you want to copy to the player. If you're looking for your My Music folder, you'll have to drill down into the C: drive, then Documents and Settings, then All Users, then Documents. Musicmatch still doesn't offer direct access to the My Documents folder (and all the folders therein), a shortcoming that's long overdue to be corrected. *Hellooooo,* Musicmatch!

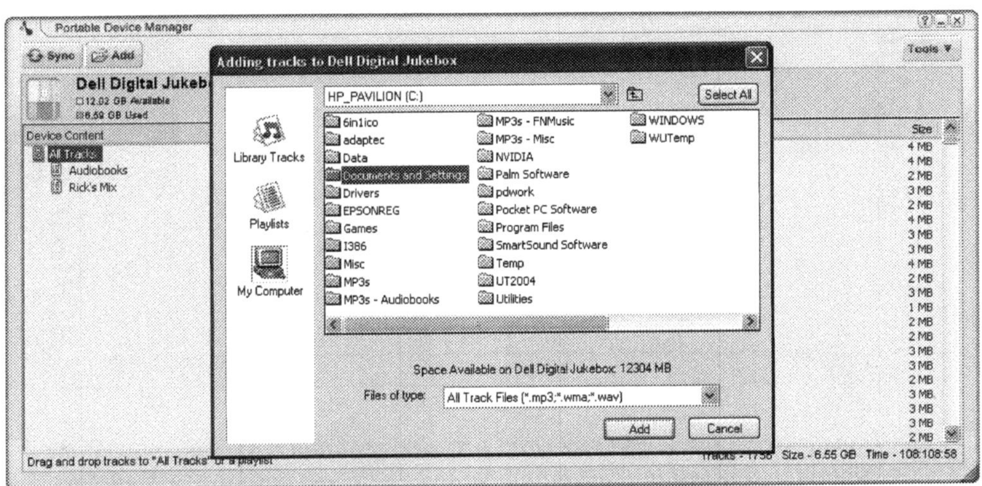

4. When you find the file(s) you want, click Add.

Loading a Playlist

The preceding methods are fine, but they're cumbersome (some would say downright annoying) for copying large quantities of music. Imagine trying to install 10GB of music from 200 different albums using one of those methods! There's a better way:

1. Create a playlist in Musicmatch that includes all of the music you want to transfer to your player. That's pretty easy because you can use any of the techniques we discussed in Chapter 9.
2. In the Portable Device Manager, click Add, and then click the Playlists icon on the left side of the window. This will reveal all the playlists you've created in Musicmatch.
3. Click the desired playlist, and then click Add. The tracks—and playlist—will immediately copy to the Dell DJ.

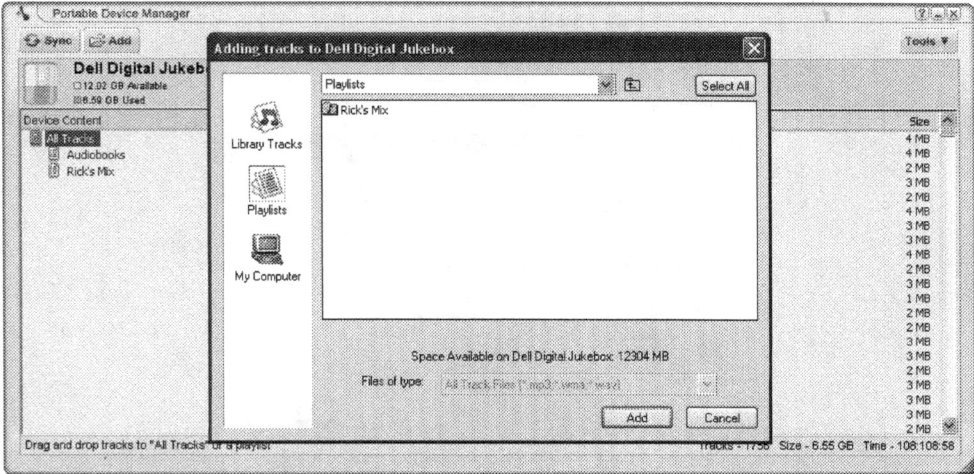

NOTE *If the playlist includes songs that are already loaded on your player, this method will result in them being copied again—meaning you'll end up with duplicates taking up your DJ's disk space. Horrors! You might be better off using PDM to create a playlist right on the player, then dragging and dropping songs to it "on the fly." We'll discuss how in the next section.*

Making a Playlist Let's say you've ripped a bunch of audiobooks to your hard drive (see this chapter's Voices from the Community sidebar) and want to listen to them on your Dell DJ. Ideally, those files should be in their own playlist, which will make them easy to find and keep them separate from your music.

Or, let's say you've just copied a few albums' worth of new music to the DJ and want to listen to them exclusive of everything else, without having to hunt for each and every album or track. Again, a separate playlist is the solution.

Portable Device Manager enables you to create playlists right on your player, and then add tracks to them via simple dragging and dropping. Here's how:

1. With PDM open, click Tools | Create Playlist.
2. Give the new playlist a name (something simple is usually best), then click OK.
3. After a moment, the new playlist should appear in the Device Content section under All Tracks. From here you have several choices. You can right-click the new playlist, click Add Tracks To Playlist, and proceed like you did in the previous sections. If, on the other hand, the tracks are already loaded on your player, click All Tracks, find the one(s) you want, and then drag them to the new playlist and drop them there. Or, you can even drag and drop tracks from an open Windows Explorer window, which will perform the dual task of copying the tracks to the player and adding them to the playlist.

Deleting a Playlist Done with that new playlist? Want to clear out an old one? PDM makes it so easy to delete playlists, we almost didn't bother explaining how. Right-click the playlist, and then click Remove Playlist. Tough, huh? Do be aware that when you remove a playlist, you're deleting only the playlist, not the tracks it contains. Hey, in case you're wondering how many times we can squeeze the word "playlist" into a single paragraph, the count is up to seven.

TIP *If you want to delete actual tracks from your player as opposed to removing them from a playlist, the process is more or less the same. Right-click the track in question, then click Remove (or just press the* DELETE *key on your keyboard).*

Syncing Your Entire Library

We saved the best for last. Want to copy your entire Musicmatch Library to your portable player? You can—as long as you have enough memory available. It's very easy to do. When you start Portable Device Manager, you'll see a window asking if you want to synchronize. Click Yes, and then click Done. Keep in mind, though, that if you don't have enough room on your player, you'll see this:

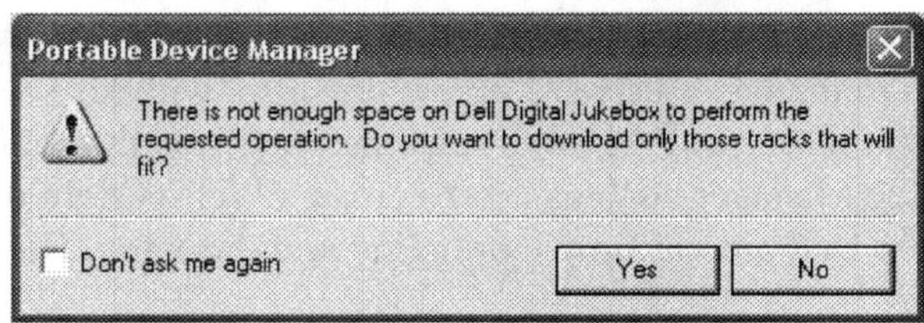

If this happens, you can opt to either copy as much as you have room for, or abort the operation and try a different method, like copying specific tracks into a playlist and copying that to your player. Or, check out the upcoming sidebar, "Downsample Songs," for a really cool way to shoehorn your music into the available space.

Copying gigabytes of music to a portable player takes time, even if you have a fast USB 2.0 connector on your PC. Don't disturb the player while it's receiving music.

After you synchronize your library the first time, Musicmatch will keep track of what's on your player and what's in your Musicmatch Library. If you rip a few new CDs, buy some new music online, or create some new playlists, all you have to do is fire up PDM and click Sync—Musicmatch will automatically copy the new stuff to the player.

You can save a step and make Musicmatch perform this synchronization automatically. The next time you start PDM and it asks if you want to synchronize, click Yes, then check the checkbox marked Automatically Synchronize Every Time I Connect My Device. And to keep this box from appearing every time you start PDM, check Remember My Choice And Don't Ask Again. Click Done and you're done. You'll still have to launch PDM, but the synchronization process will happen automatically, first thing.

What if you want to change these options later on? Start PDM, click Tools | Settings, and then click the Synchronization tab. Here you can enable or disable those very same settings from that pop-up synchronization box. This window also lets you choose whether to sync your entire library or just selected playlists.

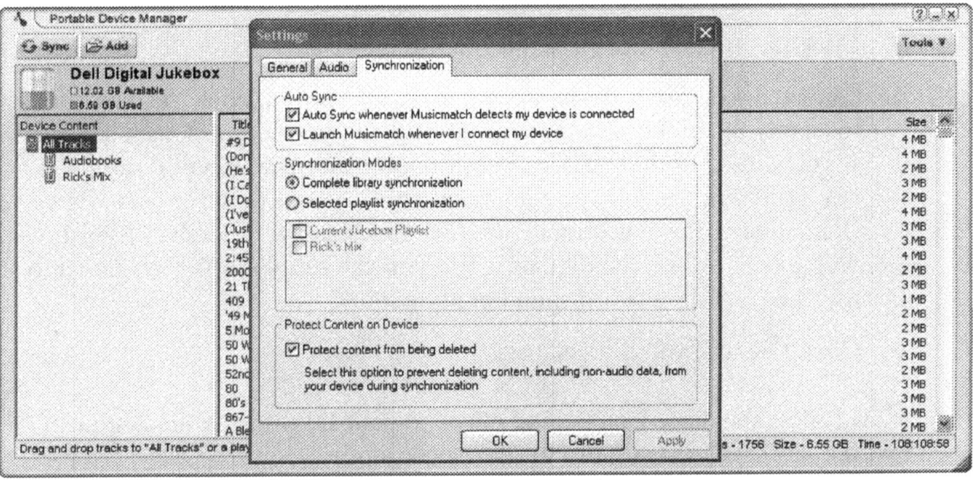

Downsample Songs

Suppose you've ripped your entire music collection to your PC using very high bit rates. It sounds great, but it takes up a ton of space. You'd like to copy the library to your portable player, but it just won't fit—especially if you're using your flash player. There's an easy solution: downsample the songs as they're transferred.

In other words, tell Musicmatch to covert your high-bit-rate songs to lower bit-rate files as they're copied to the player. The original tracks on your PC stay the same high quality, and you don't have to do any manual work. It's really convenient. (It also slows down the transfer process considerably, so plan accordingly.)

Here's what you need to do:

1. Connect your player to your PC and make sure it's on.
2. Open the Portable Device Manager by choosing View | Portable Device Manager from the menu.

3. Click the Tools button, and then choose Settings.
4. Click the Audio tab. In the Resample Rates section, click the checkbox to enable this mode and then set the slider to your desired resample rate. If you slide it to the 128 Kbps position, for instance, it will resample any song that has a bit rate *higher* than 128 Kbps down to 128 Kbps. (Remember: if you're working with MP3 files, going lower than 128 Kbps will take a toll on sound quality. But you can resample WMAs down to 64 Kbps and they'll still sound pretty good.)
5. Click OK to save your changes.

Now follow the directions to load music to your DJ using any technique you prefer, and large songs will "shrink" accordingly.

Chapter 12 Playing Your Music

How to...

- Optimize audio quality with the Jukebox Equalizer
- Get psychedelic with visualizations
- Watch a slideshow while the music plays
- Use volume leveling
- Download sound enhancements
- Convert files to different formats
- Get software updates
- Find help online

"Do I listen to pop music because I'm miserable, or am I miserable because I listen to pop music?" —John Cusack (actor) as Rob Gordon, in the film *High Fidelity*

"I don't like country music, but I don't mean to denigrate those who do. And for the people who like country music, denigrate means 'put down.'" —Bob Newhart, comedian

Okay, we'll freely admit that neither one of those quotes really has anything to do with what's covered in this chapter. But hey, we've reached Chapter 12, the last section of the book, and those quotes were too good not to use. At least we didn't get totally silly and point out that we go to 12, unlike Spinal Tap, who only go to 11. Oops. Guess we did.

Okay, we'll make up for once again proving why we're technology book authors and not standup comics by wrapping this book up with a chapter that's chock full of the coolest things you can do with Musicmatch. From fine-tuning your sound to getting all psychedelic with visualizations, Musicmatch is packed with cool extras that enhance your music experience. Even if you're not into flash and dazzle, stick around, because we're going to wrap up with important information on keeping Musicmatch up-to-date and on where to find technical support.

Tweaking Your Tunes with the Equalizer

Like all impressive stereo component systems, Musicmatch includes a graphic equalizer that lets you fine-tune the sound of your music to match your listening tastes. Equalization modifies the frequency envelope of a sound. Musicmatch features a ten-band equalizer, which lets you modify ten different frequency ranges between 60Hz and 18KHz. If all of that sounds a bit like techie audiophile engineering jargon, fear not. We only kind of understand it ourselves. You don't need to understand what sounds fall in the 300Hz band, you just have to, as Denny claims Rick once put it, "move the pretty sliders around until the music sounds good." (For a general look at where various kinds of sounds fall on the frequency range, check out Table 12-1.) Looking at the equalizer shown in Figure 12-1, the sliders on the left control bass, the sliders in the middle adjust the mid-range, and the sliders on the right adjust the treble level.

To open the Equalizer window, left-click the Options menu, click Player to open the submenu, and choose Equalizer. The Equalizer window shown in Figure 12-1 will appear above the Musicmatch window. By default, the equalizer is turned off, so the first thing you'll want to do is check the Enable EQ checkbox to turn it on.

If the Equalizer window is obstructing the play controls, move it down so you can see them, and then start a song playing by double-clicking a tune from in your Library (see Chapter 8) or by loading a playlist (see Chapter 9). That way we'll be able to listen to how your adjustments affect the music. If you typically listen to a particular kind of music—classical, rock, reggae, etc.—consider building a playlist of your favorite songs that you can listen to while optimizing the equalizer's sound.

Now, just start tweaking! Moving a slider up amplifies the selected frequency, moving it down deemphasizes it. By its very nature, an equalizer distorts sound, so there's no "right" or "wrong" when it comes to equalization settings. Just move the sliders up or down until you achieve a sound that's pleasing to your ear. As you move

EQ Range	Q Range
Lowest sound you can hear	10 to 30HZ
Bass drum	3KHz and down
Female voice	150Hz to 1KHz
Male voice	60 to 600Hz
Cymbals	4 to 18KHz
Highest sound you can hear	16 to 20KHz
Entire frequency range of an MP3	20Hz to 20,000KHz

TABLE 12-1 Where Various Sounds Fall on the Frequency Range

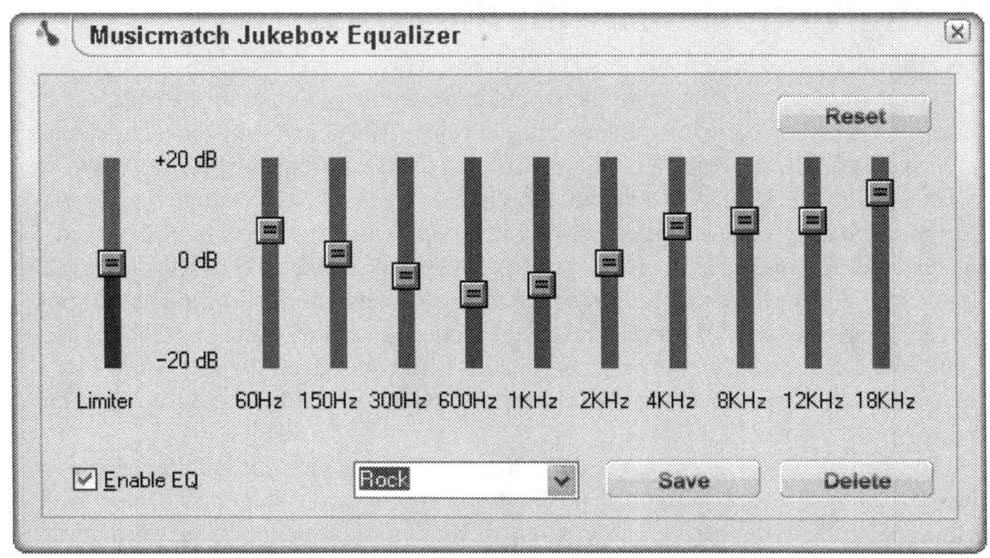

FIGURE 12-1 Musicmatch's equalizer works just like the one on your stereo.

sliders up, their background color will shift to a more reddish tone; move them down and they turn more bluish. That's not really that useful of a feature, but it's a pretty effect. As you fine-tune your settings, try a couple of different songs to ensure that your settings, which may sound great for the Allman Brothers' "Stormy Monday," don't make a total mess of songs like Sarah McLachlan's "Vox." The equalizer settings will remain in place until you change them; the next time you start Musicmatch, they'll still be in effect.

Changes to equalizer settings don't affect the audio immediately; they take a second or two to kick in. So stop adjusting for a moment, listen for a sound change, and then continue fine-tuning the sliders.

No one equalizer setting is going to sound great for all music, so Musicmatch Jukebox Plus supports presets that let you make instant adjustments for the type of music you're listening to. (The Preset selector is present if you're using Musicmatch Basic, but if you make any changes to it, you'll get yet another nagging window asking you to buy Plus.) The Preset selector is at the bottom center of the window; click the down-arrow to view the preset choices, as seen in Figure 12-2.

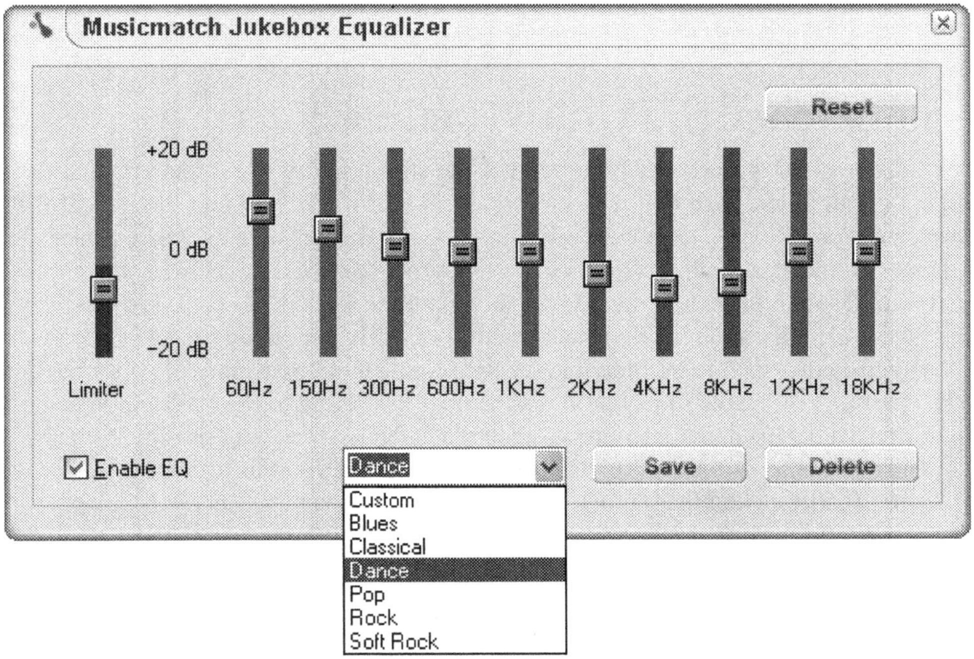

FIGURE 12-2 Musicmatch ships with six equalizer presets; you can also define a custom preset.

Don't choose a preset just yet, though. Click the Save button to save your current preset to the Custom setting, so you can access it later. Now you can try any of the built-in presets by selecting one from the drop-down Preset selector menu. The sliders will change to match the preset selection. You can also adjust the built-in presets to your own liking. Just choose a built-in, adjust it, and then click the Save button. If you mess up a built-in preset and want to revert to the default, click the Delete button and it will revert to the default. (The Reset button, which you'd expect to do this, just sets all of the frequencies to their center setting.)

To create a new preset, click in the text box at the top of the Preset selector and enter a new name for your preset, such as "Den's Dance" or "Rickabilly." Adjust the sliders to your liking and then click Save. The new setting will be entered permanently in your Preset list.

To delete a saved preset, select it using the Preset selector and click the Equalizer's Delete button. Custom presets will be deleted; built-in presets, such as Rock, will revert to their original settings. (The first releases of Musicmatch 9.0 had a bug where custom presets would sometimes not delete; hopefully this will be fixed by the time you read this.)

Getting Psychedelic with Visualizations

If you're over 30, you probably remember the strobe lights you could buy and hook to your stereo that would flash to music. (And if you're under 30, get off the lawn, you darn kids!) There were variations on the theme, such as Radio Shack kits that would flash colored lights in patterns that followed the beat of the record you were playing. As kids in the 70s, we thought these were really cool. In retrospect, they were actually about as high-tech (and as visually appealing) as a Lite Brite.

If you really want to be blown away by a light show to accompany your music, Musicmatch's Visualizations feature is the next best thing to the Pink Floyd laser light show at the local planetarium. You can select from a variety of pulsing, dazzling predesigned patterns, or even use the Visualization Editor to customize your own special effects to accompany your music.

Choosing a Visualization

Before we start playing around with visualizations, let's get some music playing so we can watch the effects change as we experiment. Load a playlist by clicking the Playlists button; it should start playing automatically. (If you haven't created a playlist yet, what the heck are you doing reading Chapter 12? Back to Chapter 9 for you!) Now left-click the View menu, move the mouse pointer down to the Visualizations entry, and choose Show from the submenu that pops up. The media window on the upper-left side of the Musicmatch screen will start displaying an animated Spirograph-like light show, as seen in Figure 12-3.

FIGURE 12-3 By default, visualizations appear in a small window next to the volume control.

Now, a one-square-inch light show isn't very impressive, so let's blow that baby up. You can open the large display window, called the Visualization Editor, by choosing Media Window from the View pull-down menu. There's an easier way to blow it up, though: just double-click the small media window and the large display will open. You can double-click the large Visualization Editor window and your light show will shrink back into the small window at the top left of the main Musicmatch window.

NOTE *Visualizations require a fair amount of processor horsepower. If you're using a slower PC—say, less than about 1GHz—you may not want to enable visualizations if you're doing other work on your computer while the music plays.*

The large Visualization Editor window, seen in Figure 12-4, is a fully resizable window. You can shrink it so that it fits into a corner while you're using your word processor, or stretch it to full screen for display during a party.

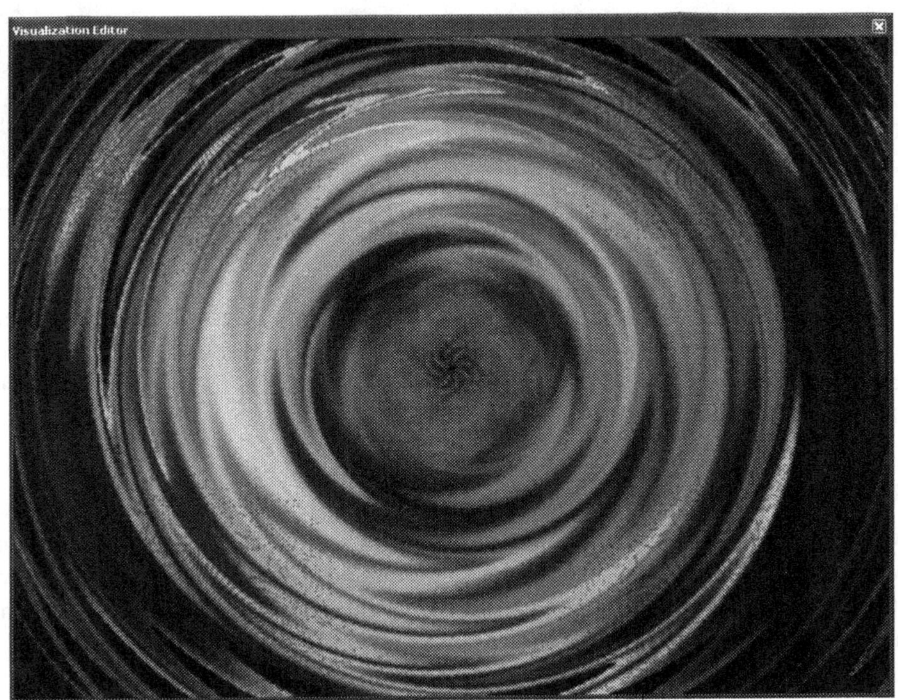

FIGURE 12-4 The Visualization Editor window gives you the big picture view of your virtual light show.

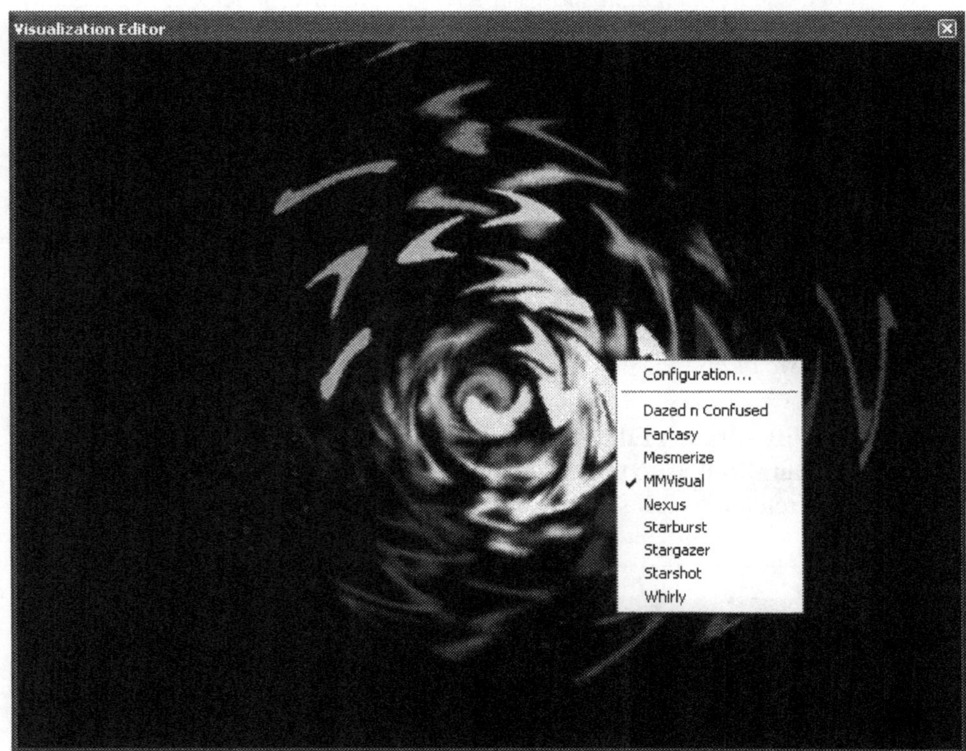

FIGURE 12-5 The pop-up menu accessed with the right mouse button lets you quickly change visualizations.

Musicmatch includes a number of predefined visual effects. To change effects, just click on the Visualization Editor window with the right mouse button to bring up the menu shown in Figure 12-5. Select any effect from the menu and the display will immediately change to reflect your new choice.

Customizing Visualizations

Now let's indulge in a little artistic expression. You can take existing effects, add new patterns of flashing light and color to them, and then save them as your own custom creations. As an example, we'll beef up the Fantasy visualization, which is a bit of a yawner—dancing two-colored lines haven't been impressive since the Commodore 64 days, folks.

First, right-click the Visualization Editor window and choose Fantasy from the pop-up menu. Now, let's get to editing!

1. Right-click the Visualization Editor again and choose the first entry, Configuration. This will bring up the Visualization Editor's customization window, shown in Figure 12-6.
2. Now you can add additional visuals (moving elements) and effects (changes performed on those elements) by clicking the Add Visual and Add Effect buttons. Let's start by adding some effects. Click the Add Effect button and choose Water. The display will immediately change, with the boring lines replaced by cool wet-looking splashes of color.
3. Now let's add a customizable effect. Click Add Effect again and choose Swirl, then click Effect:Swirl in the Editor window. You'll see an adjustment panel on the right side of the screen, as illustrated in Figure 12-7. You can use the sliders to adjust the frequency and direction of the swirl effect, or click the Do Random Change option to let Musicmatch vary the effect with time. You'll usually want to select the Change Sync. W/Beat option as well. This will make the movements react to the beat of the music, creating a much more impressive effect.

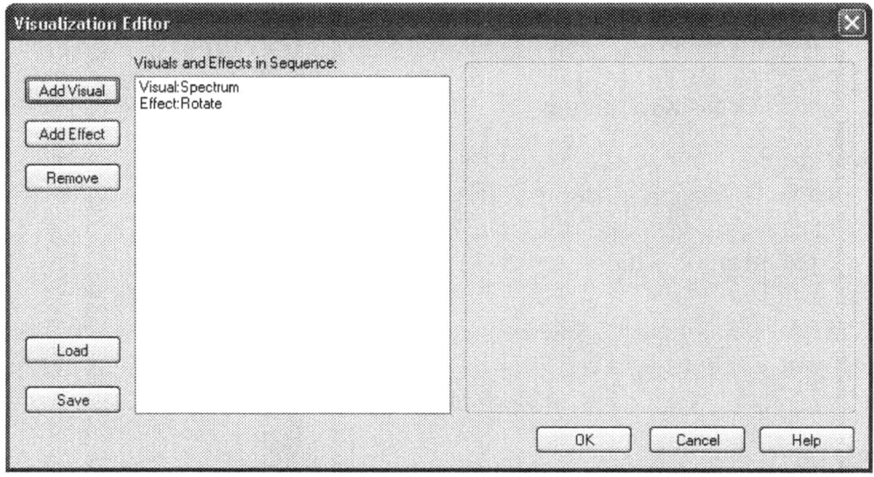

FIGURE 12-6 The Visualization Editor's configuration window lets you add new effects sequences to existing visualizations.

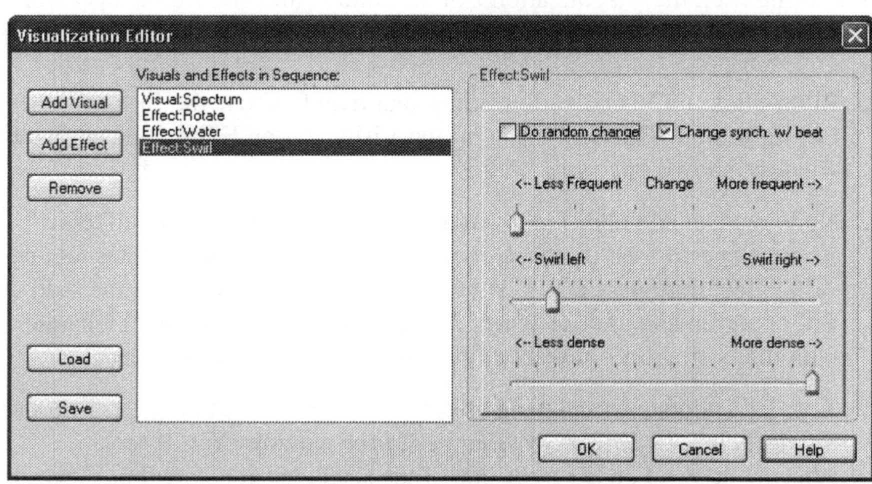

FIGURE 12-7 You can fine-tune the visual parameters of some effects.

4. Now let's add an additional visual to further spruce up our enhanced spectrum lines. Click Add Visual and select Polygon. Now click Visual:Polygon and select Green as the line color. You'll get a cool green oscilloscope line running through the center of your visualization.
5. Finally, click Save. You probably don't want to overwrite the original effect, so type a new name in the File Name text box (such as "SuperFantasy") and click the Save button.
6. Note that your custom visualization won't be added to the right-click menu. To access it later, you'll need to choose Customize from the right-click menu, then click the Load button on the Visualization Editor's customization window to access saved visualizations.

Take a look at Figure 12-8 to see a comparison of the original visualization (on the left) with our enhanced version (shown on the right). Not a bad improvement considering it only took a few mouse clicks!

TIP *While there's no command to create a new visualization completely from scratch, you can do so by choosing an existing visualization, using the Remove button to remove all of the existing Visuals and Effects, and then creating a new sequence. Click Save and choose a new name when you're done!*

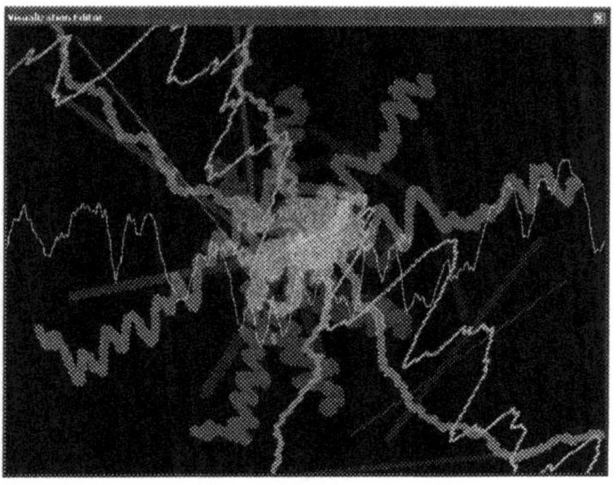

FIGURE 12-8 The original visualization is on the left, while our improved version is on the right.

How to ... Download New Visualizations

You can download new visualizations for Musicmatch from the Web. As this book was written, Musicmatch offered just two additional visualizations for the program, but you can find more from third-party sites such as visualizations.deviantart.com/mmjb/. Use your web browser to search Google.com for "musicmatch visualizations" to find even more. To download the official Musicmatch bonus visualizations, follow this procedure.

1. Left-click the View pull-down menu, and move the mouse pointer down to the Visualizations menu entry.
2. From the Visualizations submenu, click Download.
3. Your web browser will open, displaying the available add-on visualizations.

4. Now click the Download entry for the visualization you want to add. For instance, to download the visualization called G-Force, you simply click—you guessed it—Download G-Force.
5. The visualization will download and install automatically. When the download has completed, a confirmation window will appear telling you the plug-in has been installed.
6. Click Exit to close the confirmation window, and then close the web browser window.

Note that add-on visualizations don't show up on the usual right-click menu. To access a downloaded visualization, click the View menu, mouse down to Visualizations, and you'll see the additional visualizations listed on the submenu that appears. Click an add-on visualization to activate it, or click Visualization Editor to return to the standard Musicmatch visualizations.

Watching a Slideshow While the Music Plays

If flashy lights aren't your cup of tea, how about a nice relaxing slideshow? As an alternative to the standard visualizations, you can have Musicmatch play a sideshow while you listen. By default, it presents a sedate slideshow through the images in your My Pictures directory, but you can change the directory and add a variety of wipe and pan effects to make the images move a bit more to the music—perfect if you want to use Musicmatch to add a soundtrack to make your vacation pictures slideshow a little more dynamic,

To enable the sideshow, left-click the View menu, mouse down to Visualizations, and choose Musicmatch Slideshow Visualization from the pull-down menu. The slideshow will start immediately in its own window, as seen in Figure 12-9. (Music doesn't have to be playing.)

You can change the size of the window, or even stretch it to full screen. Click the (inappropriately named) File menu on the Slideshow window and you'll see three different window sizes, as well as a full screen option, to choose from.

The real customization fun comes when you adjust the settings in the Configuration window, which lets you point to a different directory for photos, as well as add transitions and animations. To open the configuration window, left-click the View menu, select Visualizations, and then click Configure on the submenu. You'll see the settings window shown in Figure 12-10.

FIGURE 12-9 Musicmatch's Slideshow Visualization window presents a little Who in Paris.

At the top of the window, you can click the "…" button to select a different picture folder. Drag the Picture Interval slider to the left to make slides change faster, or to the right if you want slides to stay on the screen longer. The Picture Transitions drop-down menu lets you add wipes and other transitions between slides. If you choose Random, you'll get to see the whole suite of choices. The Picture Animations menu configures Musicmatch to zoom and pan around pictures as they're displayed to give still images a "motion picture" appearance. The last drop-down menu, Full Screen Resolution, lets you choose the screen resolution for full-screen slideshows.

The remaining options are fairly self-explanatory. Cover Entire Screen eliminates any black bars around an image, but may crop portions of the shot to do so. Window Always On Top keeps other programs from obscuring your slideshow. The three Layer checkboxes let you superimpose the filename, date, and song information on the image as your music plays.

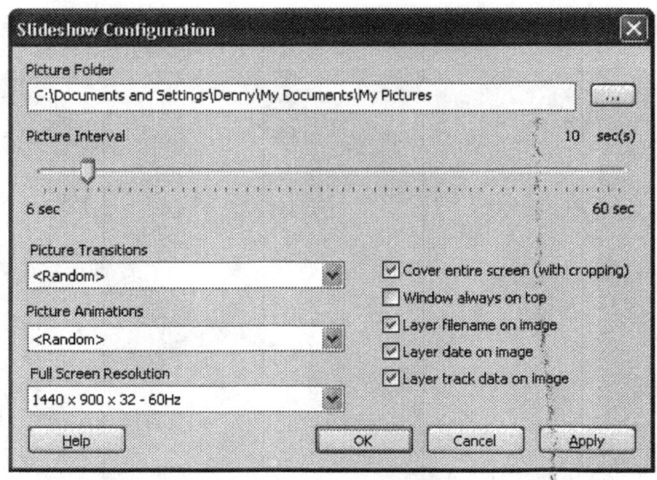

FIGURE 12-10 The Slideshow Configuration window lets you select the directory where your pictures are and adjust transitions and effects.

Volume Leveling: Your Ears Will Thank You

Denny was sitting back in his chair, casually mulling over some numbers in Excel while listening to a playlist composed of a mix of his favorite '80s tunes. Suddenly, Wang Chung blasted from his speakers at double the volume of the previous song, causing him to nearly jump out of his chair. That wasn't the bad part. The bad part was the cat scurrying from the monitor, across Denny's head, and out of the office—with claws fully extended. Don't let this happen to you.

No, we don't mean declaw the cat. That's just mean. We're talking about Musicmatch's Volume Leveling feature, which compensates for the fact that many tracks aren't recorded at the same volume by automatically adjusting their playback level, boosting the volume of quiet tracks and turning down the dial on the really loud ones.

Volume Leveling adjusts the volume of songs when they're being played back with Musicmatch, as well as when they're burned to a CD or sent to a portable player. However, other MP3 playback programs on your PC, such as Winamp and iTunes, will ignore the volume leveling.

To use Volume Leveling with a group of tracks, you must first prepare them. Highlight a group of tracks in the Library using the mouse, then left-click the Options menu and choose Volume Leveling… from the Player submenu, as illustrated in Figure 12-11.

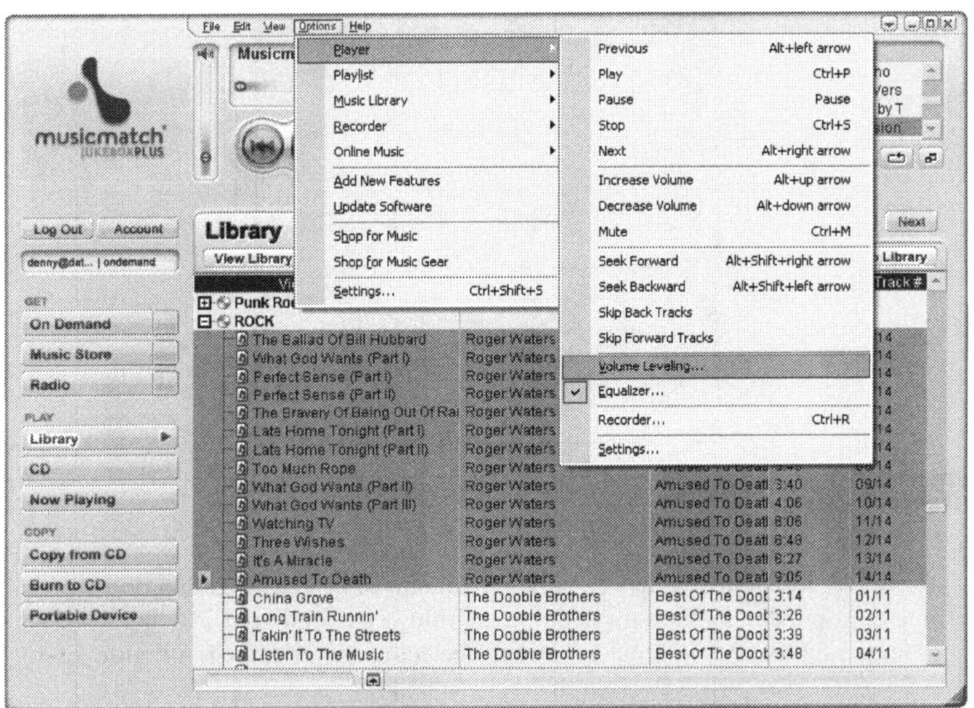

FIGURE 12-11 Selecting a group of files for Volume Leveling

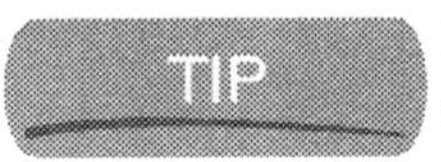

To select multiple tracks, hold down CTRL *and click each track to select multiple tracks; to select a sequence of tracks in a row, hold down* SHIFT*, click the first track, and then click the last track.*

The window shown in Figure 12-12 will then appear, allowing you to prepare your entire library for Volume Leveling, the selected tracks, or the tracks in your playlist. Typically, you'll choose the Selected Tracks options. You can also enable Volume Leveling without preparing any tracks. This last option merely turns on Volume Leveling during playback, during transfer to a portable player, or when burning a CD. (Preparing tracks automatically turns Volume Leveling on as well.)

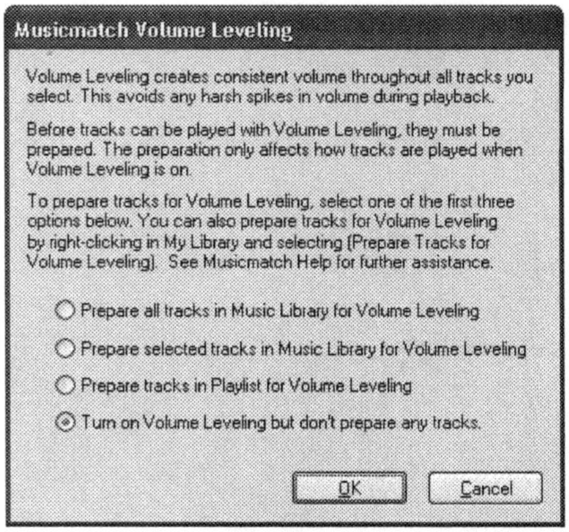

Musicmatch Volume Leveling

Volume Leveling creates consistent volume throughout all tracks you select. This avoids any harsh spikes in volume during playback.

Before tracks can be played with Volume Leveling, they must be prepared. The preparation only affects how tracks are played when Volume Leveling is on.

To prepare tracks for Volume Leveling, select one of the first three options below. You can also prepare tracks for Volume Leveling by right-clicking in My Library and selecting [Prepare Tracks for Volume Leveling]. See Musicmatch Help for further assistance.

- Prepare all tracks in Music Library for Volume Leveling
- Prepare selected tracks in Music Library for Volume Leveling
- Prepare tracks in Playlist for Volume Leveling
- Turn on Volume Leveling but don't prepare any tracks.

OK Cancel

FIGURE 12-12 Musicmatch's Volume Leveling options

Note that Musicmatch takes a variable amount of time (depending on your computer's speed, whether you're doing anything else with your PC, and so on) to process each file for Volume Leveling. The status meter shown in Figure 12-13

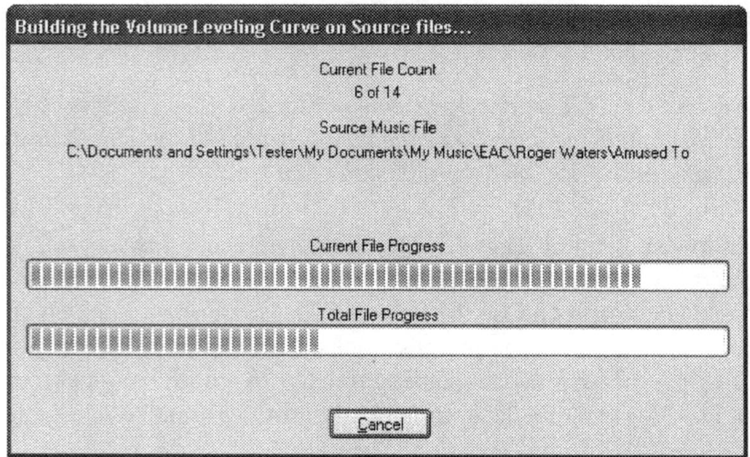

FIGURE 12-13 This progress meter gives you an idea how the volume leveling process is progressing.

will keep you apprised of the program's progress. Keep in mind that preparing a large library of files can take an hour or more on some PCs.

You can have Musicmatch automatically prepare songs for Volume Leveling as you rip them from CD. Just select Prepare Tracks For Volume Leveling from the Recorder submenu on the Options pull-down menu before you rip your tunes.

To see if Volume Leveling is active, left-click the Options menu, select the Player submenu, and look at the Volume Leveling menu item. If there's a checkmark next to it, the feature is turned on. To turn it off, just select the item again, and the checkmark will turn off, as will Volume Leveling.

Volume Leveling doesn't actually adjust the volume of the original file; rather, it adds a chunk of information to the music file that Musicmatch can use to determine the volume during playback, burning, or transfer to an MP3 device. However, we've encountered a few devices that have problems with files that have been processed with Musicmatch's Volume Leveling feature, such as D-Link's DMS-320 wireless media player. Test a couple of volume-leveled files with your favorite player before you process your entire library.

If you encounter problems with volume-leveled tracks, you can remove the Volume Leveling information from them. Just highlight them as mentioned earlier, click the right mouse button, and choose Edit Track Info from the menu that pops up. Now left-click the More tab, click the checkbox under Volume Leveling near the lower-left corner of the window, and click Not Prepared.

Enhancing Your Audio

Musicmatch supports downloadable Sound Enhancements, plug-in modules that let you add special effects and processing to your sounds. Currently there's only a single sound enhancement module, DFX, available from Musicmatch, and we were unable to find any third-party add-ons. Still, DFX is worth a look, particularly if you have more than two speakers.

To download DFX (and any other Sound Enhancement modules, should Musicmatch expand its library), left-click the View menu, select Sound Enhancement, and choose Download from the submenu. A web page will open listing the available sound enhancements. As this book was written, you'd find a feature-limited free version of DFX, as well as the $19.99 full-powered version. Click Try DFX Now to try the free version, or Buy DFX Now to get the full-blown edition. The module will automatically download and launch the installer. Follow the onscreen prompts

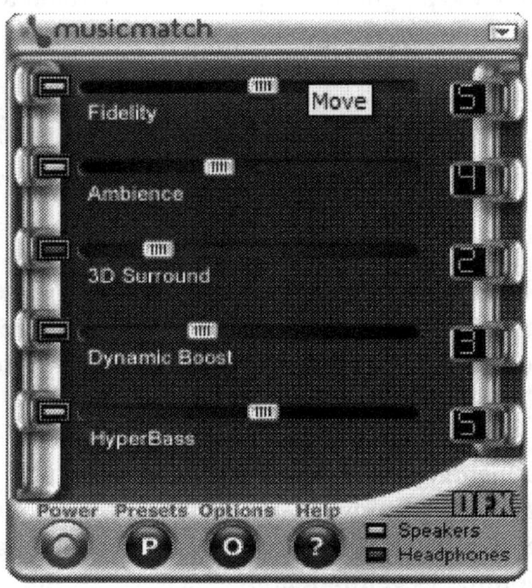

FIGURE 12-14 The $20 version of DFX can make digital music sound really good, but the free version is extremely limited.

to install the program. When it's finished installing, a window will pop up asking you if you want to activate DFX now. If you choose No, you can activate it later by selecting Sound Enhancement from the View menu and choosing Enable. Choose Show from that menu to bring up DFX's adjustment window, shown in Figure 12-14.

The free version of DFX gives you a small taste of the capabilities of the program, but we wouldn't use it day-to-day. Its "buy me!" nags are so in-your-face that it makes Musicmatch's pleas to upgrade to the plus version look subtle. If you adjust any of the sliders much in any one direction, a window pops up asking you if you'd like ordering information. If you try to choose the built-in presets designed to enhance the sound of various types of music—'80s rock, SHOUTcast Internet-streamed files, etc.—a window pops up asking you if you'd like ordering information. Notice a trend here?

If you're willing to shell out the additional money to get rid of the nags, DFX is actually a pretty slick enhancement. It can compensate for high-frequency data lost during the compression of MP3s and other music files, enhance stereo separation, add 3D audio effects, and boost loudness and bass. It offers a headphone mode that adjusts the tonality of sounds to make them sound better when you're listening with a headset, and there are dozens of presets designed for various types of music

Songs of Two Misspent Youths

Remember the terrible music you liked when you were a little kid? The cheesy tunes that somehow foment fond feelings of familiarity (say that three times fast) despite the fact that you'd never admit in public that you liked them? Well, Denny and Rick are about to bare all. (Stop averting your eyes. We mean that figuratively.) Yes, these are the songs we were singing along with before we got to high school and learned about cool music, like Pink Floyd, ELO, and Blue Öyster Cult.

Denny: At least the ancient Super 8 film of a young me dancing to the first entry on this list—in public, yet—is safely locked away in a closet at my Dad's house.

- "Bad, Bad Leroy Brown" —Jim Croce
- "The Night Chicago Died" —Paper Lace
- "Rock the Boat" —Hues Corporation
- "In the Year 2525" —Zager and Evans
- "Convoy" —C.W. McCall
- "Star Wars Theme/Cantina Band" —Meco

Rick: Your dad was kind enough to send me the film, which you can now find on the Internet at www.cruelandunusualpunishment.com. Why, oh why, must you torture me with a list like this? Just yesterday I unearthed a box of my old LP records, which my wife took great delight rifling through. "Cyndi Lauper?!" she'd laugh. "Huey Lewis?!" And now I'm supposed to share my embarrassing early taste in music with the *world?* A pox upon your house.

- "Shaddup You Face" —Joe Dolce
- "Rockit" —Herbie Hancock
- "Love is a Battlefield" —Pat Benetar
- "Venus" —Bananarama

Okay, that's it, I'm done. The other details of my "misspent youth" are going with me to the grave (or the second edition of this book, hopefully).

styles and music files. All in all it's a nice add-on, but FXSound, the producer of the program, would probably sell more copies with a time-limited demo.

If you have a 3D audio-enhanced sound card such as Creative Labs' SoundBlaster Audigy 2, the driver software that comes with your card should allow you to apply many of the same effects, such as 3D Surround and bass boost. So check out your sound card's control panel before plunking down the dollars on DFX—you may not need it.

Converting Files Between Formats

Musicmatch's File Format Conversion module does just what you'd expect from the name—it converts music files between formats. Alas, it's missing Windows Media Audio (WMA) support, so it's not as useful as it could be. The module can read MP3, mp3PRO, and WAV files, and write WAV files, as well as constant- and variable-bit rate versions of MP3 and mp3PRO songs.

Though you probably won't have much occasion to, say, convert mp3PRO files to MP3, the module actually does come in handy for converting files from one format to… the same format! Why would you do that, you ask? Because the module can also change the bit rate of the file as it does the conversion. Say you ripped your music in MP3 format at 90-percent VBR to maintain excellent sound quality. Mission accomplished, but you also ended up with some big files. Now say you want to listen to a couple of hours of those tunes on a 128MB portable MP3 player that's not directly supported by Musicmatch's device manager. Converting those files to 128-Kbps MP3 files will shrink them significantly, allowing you to fit more songs on the player. If you choose a new directory for the files you convert, the original, higher-quality files will remain untouched.

To bring up the conversion module, choose Convert Files from the File pull-down menu. You'll see the window shown in Figure 12-15. Now select the source and destination directories at the top of the conversion window. At the bottom, you'll see a drop-down menu labeled Source Data type. Select the type of song you'd like to convert and they'll appear in the center window; highlight the songs you'd like to convert using the mouse. Finally, select the Destination Data Type from the drop-down menu at the lower-right corner of the window, and adjust the slider below the menu to the desired compression level. Finally, click Start to begin the conversion process.

You can also apply effects from the currently selected audio enhancement module to the converted tunes. Just click the box next to Apply Active Signal Enhancement During Conversion.

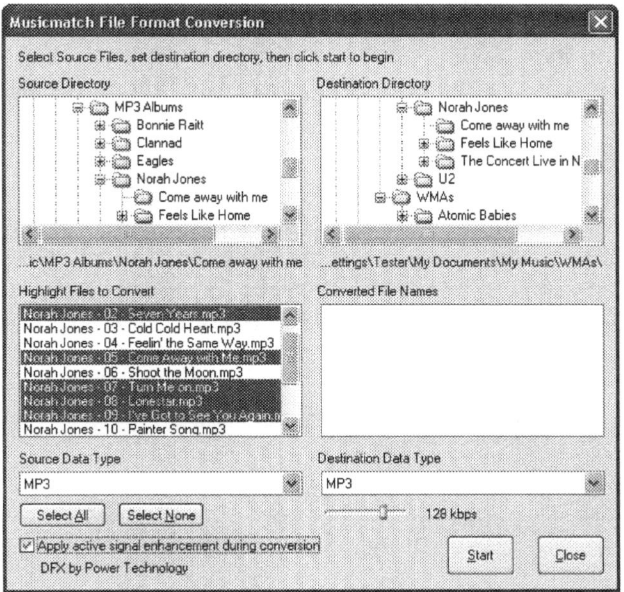

FIGURE 12-15 Musicmatch's File Format Conversion module is handy for recompressing files to make them smaller.

Keeping Musicmatch Up-to-Date

Musicmatch periodically updates its software to fix bugs, enhance its online capabilities, and occasionally even to add new features. While "major version" upgrades, such as from version 8.2 to 9.0, cost $19.99, smaller upgrades are free. At times, the program will notify you when a new version is available, but you can also manually check for new versions.

To see if there's an update available, choose Update Software from the Options pull-down menu. A window will open asking you to confirm your choice; click Update to check for a new version. (Of course, you'll need to be connected to the Internet to check for the update.) If an update is available, it will be downloaded automatically. If you have the latest version, Musicmatch will display a window notifying you that there's no update available.

NOTE *The update process causes Musicmatch to exit so that the new version can be installed, so be sure you're not doing critical operations such as burning or ripping a CD when you try the update command, as they'll be stopped when Musicmatch exits to install and reload the new version.*

Finding Help Online

We did our best to try to address all the possible glitches and snags you could run into with Musicmatch over the past 12 chapters. But PCs can be as unpredictable as Seattle weather, so as much as it pains us to think this, you may just run into a problem that isn't addressed in this book. If that happens, there are a few possible sources of help. (Denny originally listed Rick's home phone number in this paragraph, but Rick insisted he delete it. And here Denny thought Rick had a good sense of humor…)

The first place to go for help is Musicmatch's Frequently Asked Questions page, which you'll see in Figure 12-16. It lists dozens of common problems and step-by-step

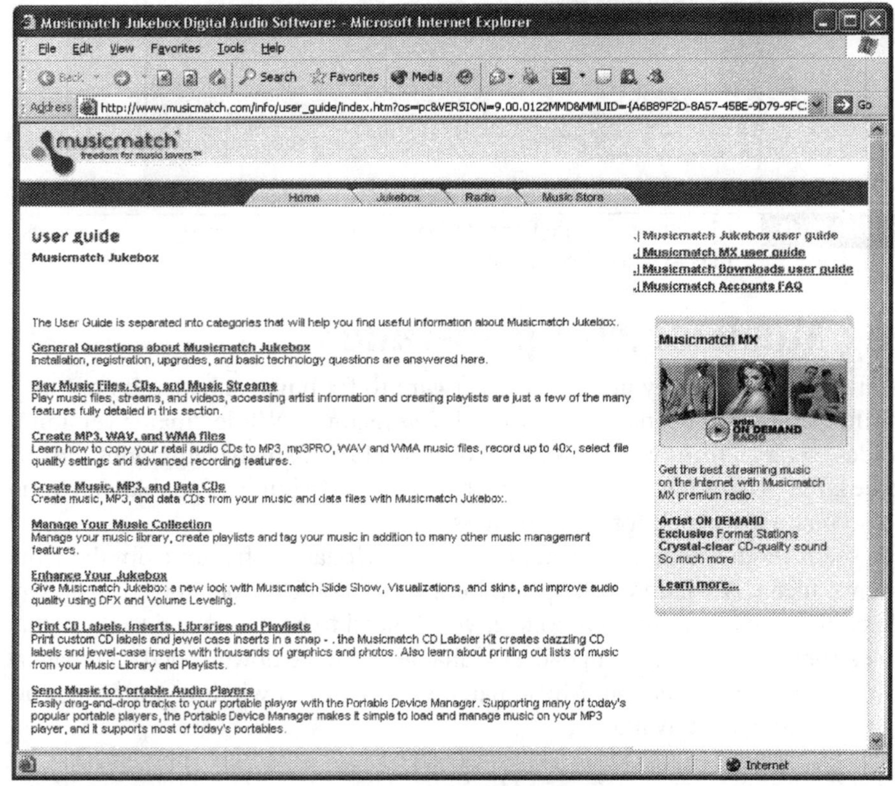

FIGURE 12-16 Musicmatch's online FAQ page

solutions for them. To reach the page, left-click the Help menu, choose the Additional Help Online submenu, and click Frequently Asked Questions.

If you can't find help in the FAQ, you can get assistance from a real live human tech support specialist. Musicmatch includes a built-in module for requesting help that also sends lots of information about your current PC and Musicmatch configuration, which can help the company's support specialist determine what's going wrong. To access the module, left-click the Help menu and choose Request Technical Support. You'll see a window like the one in Figure 12-17.

At the bottom of the screen, you'll see a number of checkboxes allowing you to select which files you'll allow Musicmatch to send to the support techs in order to help diagnose your problem. Note that these are all Musicmatch-related data files and don't contain information about the other applications or data files on your system, so we can't see any privacy concerns. We'd suggest sending them all since the more information you include, the better the chances that the support folks can figure out what's going wrong.

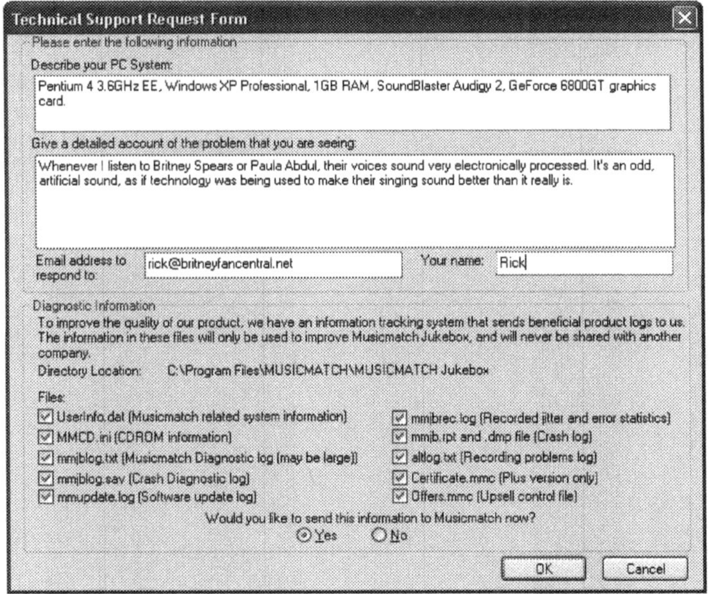

FIGURE 12-17 Musicmatch's technical support module sends information on your system configuration to help the company's techs figure out what's going wrong.

Once you've filled in the form, click OK to send the support request to Musicmatch. You'll receive a response in your e-mail box. We used tech support a couple of times while writing this book (without identifying ourselves as book authors) and received prompt and accurate responses—something you can't always count on with today's tech support organizations.

Index

Numbers

2.1 speaker systems, 29
4.1 speaker systems, 29
5.1 speaker systems, 29

A

AAC (Advanced Audio Coding) file format, 56, 71, 72
accessing music in Library view, 179
Adaptive TRansform Acoustic Coding (ATRAC), 72
Add Track(s) To Dell Digital Jukebox dialog box, 260, 261, 262
Add Tracks to Music Library dialog box, 57
Add Tracks To Saved Playlists command, 205–206
Adobe Audition
  editing analog music, 105–108
  overview, 104
  where to find, 115
Advanced Recording Options dialog box
  Auto Song Detect options, 99, 100–101
  illustrated, 100
album art
  creating front cover collage for, 245–246
  using Musicmatch, 242
albums. *See also* analog devices
  adding ID3 tags to tracks from, 110–113
  adjusting input and speaker volume for turntables, 96–97
  Auto Song Detect options, 100–101
  consolidating double albums, 163
  editing music, 105–108
  ID3 tags added to ripped tracks, 110–113
  isolating songs from, 103–105
  preparing to rip, 97–101
  recording analog, 95–99, 101–103
  recording both sides of, 102
  ripping songs from, 84–85
  searching for, 123–128
Alexander, Cherish, 158
Also Add Tracks from Subfolders checkbox (Add Tracks to Music Library dialog box), 56, 57
Always Check WatchFolders At Startup checkbox (WatchFolders dialog box), 58
analog devices
  adjusting turntable input and speaker volume, 96–97
  cabling to computer, 90–94
  computer too far away from, 94
  jacks for computer connections, 89–90
  plugging into sound cards, 85, 87–89
  pre-amplifying, 89, 90
  recording audio from, 95–99, 101–103
  ripping songs from analog media, 84–85
Apple iPod
  about, 27–28, 251
  downloading music to, 136
  WMA unsupported by, 28, 251–252, 254
Apple iTunes
  about, 143
  download price for, 141
Archos Jukebox Recorder, 94
artists
  effect of pirated music on, 238
  on file-sharing services, 157–158
  finding album art on Web sites, 242
  searching by, 123–128
ATRAC (Adaptive TRansform Acoustic Coding), 72
audio. *See* digital audio
audio CDs, 219. *See also* CDs
  Audio Cleaning Lab
    overview, 109
    where to find, 115
audio formats, 68–73
  AAC, 56, 71, 72
  ATRAC, 72
  choosing, 81
  configuring, 48
  converting unsupported, 136, 137, 146, 148
  FLAC, 149
  MP3, 3–4, 69, 71
  MP3Pro, 70–71, 72
  OGG, 56, 72
  setting in Recorder Settings window, 98, 99
  SHN, 149
  WAV, 73
  WMA, 70, 71, 72
Audio Home Recording Act, 150–151, 153
Audio tab (MUSICMATCH Burner Options dialog box), 232–233
audiobooks
  bit rate settings for, 68
  converting to portable player files, 258–259
  ripping from CDs, 76–77
  ripping from tape, 86
Audiotools
  overview, 104–105
  where to find, 115
Auto Song Detect options
  gap level settings, 101
  setting gap length, 100, 233
  turning off, 99
AutoDJ
  creating random mix tape CD, 217
  creating random playlists, 186, 188
AVOne All to MP3 Converter, 222

B

backing up purchased songs, 132
Berkley, Joni, 39–40

bit rates
- CBR vs. VBR, 67–68
- choosing, 66–67
- defined, 5
- suggested settings, 68
- WMA's lower, 4

broadband Internet connections, 24, 166–167, 190
Browse for Folder dialog box, 74
building external hard drives, 25–26
Burn tab (MUSICMATCH Burner Options dialog box), 232
Burner Plus window
- configuring Settings window, 230–235
- enlarging, 227
- options in, 227–230
- SmartSplit options, 236
- Tools button options, 228–230

burning CDs, 216–246. *See also* Burner Plus window; CD drives; CD labels; CD media; CDs; jewel cases
- blank media for, 224–226
- default label for blank CDs, 228
- DRM limitations for downloaded songs, 237–238
- hardware for, 223–224
- kinds of CDs burned, 219
- making labels, 238–244
- preventing playlists being split between CDs, 236
- reasons for, 218–219
- specifying default speeds for, 232
- steps for, 216–218, 226–227, 235, 237
- WMA CDs, 221–222

Buskirk, Eliot Van, 237
Buy.com, 31
Buy Track buttons, 130
buying music, 118–137, 140–174. *See also* file-sharing services; Musicmatch Downloads
- buying and downloading songs, 129–132
- cancelling music purchases, 130, 131
- converting audio formats to MP3, 136, 137, 146, 148
- delivery methods of download services, 142–143
- downloading to unsupported devices, 136, 137
- editing ID3 tags, 160–163
- fixing filenames, 163–165
- live-concert downloads, 148–149
- moving music to new computers, 135, 136
- Musicmatch DRM restrictions, 133–134
- Musicmatch Radio, 133
- other online services for, 141–142
- overview, 118–119
- setting default music players, 143–144
- setting up Musicmatch Downloads account, 119–122, 123

BuyMusic, 141

C

cabling
- accessories for, 92
- analog sources to computers, 90–94
- ensuring high-quality sound, 93–94
- Monster Cable, 93
- RCA-to-mini-phone jack Y-cable, 91
- stereo-to-RCA cable, 32

cancelling music purchases, 130, 131
cassettes. *See also* analog devices
- audiobooks ripped from, 86
- Auto Song Detect options, 100–101
- cabling analog sources to computer, 90–94
- cleaning up noisy audio, 108–110
- editing music, 105–108
- ID3 tags added to ripped tracks, 110–113
- internal tape decks for PC, 103
- isolating songs from, 103–105
- portable tape players for preamplifying, 89, 102, 103
- recording analog audio, 95–99, 101–103
- ripping songs from, 84–85

CBR (Constant Bit Rate), 67
Cd3o c300 digital audio receiver, 35
CD Baby, 15–16
CD drives
- CD-ROM, 11
- CD-RW, 223–224
- specifying default speeds for, 232
- speed ratings for, 224
- upgrading, 23

CD Label Settings section (Print CD Insert dialog box), 243–244
CD labels, 238–244
- brands supported by Musicmatch, 239
- default, 228
- effect of adhesive on CDs, 241
- labeling kits, 239–240
- previewing, 244
- printing, 11, 241–244
- recommendations for, 238

CD Lookup service, 77–78
CD media
- CD-R vs. CD-RW, 217, 224
- converting audio formats using CD-RW, 146
- setting burning options for, 229
- testing compatibility of, 225
- Verbatim Digital Vinyl, 226, 246

CDs. *See also* burning CDs; CD drives; ripping songs
- audio and MP3, 219
- burning, 216–218, 235, 237
- converting music to MP3 from, 136, 137, 146, 148
- creating random "mix tape", 217
- mute while recording, 80
- playing, 54–56, 188–189
- playing in DVD players, 223
- purchasing blank, 224–226
- ripping speeds, 11
- selecting analog or digital recording mode, 81
- setting Musicmatch as default player, 64
- unbalancing with adhesive labels, 241
- WMA, 221–222

clipping, 110
CNET.com, 35
color-coded jacks, 88–89
compressing music
- bit rates and compression, 67
- disadvantages of, 62
- importance of, 4–5
- MP3 standards for, 3–4
- sources of compressed files, 5
- WMA standards for, 4

Computer Geeks Discount Outlet, 224

computers. *See also* notebook computers
adjusting volume in Windows, 38–39
broadband connections for, 24
cabling analog sources to, 90–94
headphones for, 29, 196, 199
internal tape decks for, 103
locating components for, 41
memory, 21, 22
moving downloaded music to new, 135, 136
requirements for Musicmatch, 20–21
sound card upgrades, 36–38
speakers for, 21, 24, 26, 28–36
too far away from analog sources, 94
upgrading your, 21–24
USB ports, 24, 26
using Musicmatch Downloads for multiple, 123, 135, 137
Configure Replay Radio Settings dialog box (Replay Radio), 167
configuring Musicmatch Jukebox, 49, 51–53, 54
confirming music purchases, 130, 131
connectors
cabling analog devices to computer, 90–94
line in, 88
output, 88, 89–90
RCA-to-mini-phone jack Y-cable, 91
consolidating double albums, 163
copying songs to portable audio players, 254
copyrights. *See also* DRM
artists on file-sharing services and, 157–158
Audio Home Recording Act and, 150–151, 153
ethical issues of music, 154–155
illegal activities for file-sharing services, 156
legal activities for file-sharing, 155–156
Napster and copyright infringement, 153–155
peer-to-peer file sharing, 156–157
corrupted portable audio files, 255
coupler for cabling, 92
Create Account button (Musicmatch window), 120
Create Filename from Tags dialog box, 164
Create Front Cover With A Collage checkbox (Print CD Insert dialog box), 244, 245–246
Creative MuVo Slim, 251
Crucial.com Web site, 22
Custom installs, 47
custom streaming radio stations, 192
customizing
Equalizer presets, 271
Musicmatch windows, 54
visualizations, 274–277

D

DAR (digital audio receivers), 33–36
Darby, Diana, 158
data CDs, 219
default options
default drive speeds, 232
label for blank CDs, 228
setting default music player, 143–144
delayed recording, 79
deleting
Equalizer presets, 271
playlists on hard-drive players, 263
Dell DJ, 256–265
about, 27–28, 251
adding playlists on, 262–263
disabling synchronization, 256–257
duplicate copies of songs added to, 262
illustrated, 250
loading songs from Musicmatch Library, 260
locating tracks not in Library, 261
overview, 256
working with Portable Device Manager, 256–258
DFX (digital effects), 233
DFX sound enhancement module, 283–284, 286
downloading, 283–284
illustrated, 284
sound cards providing same effects, 286
digital audio
advantages of digital music, 49
compressing music, 4–5
history of, 3
MP3, 3–4
WMA, 4
digital audio receivers (DAR), 33–36
digital effects (DFX), 233
digital rights management system. *See* DRM system
Directly Download The Installation File (Download Confirmation screen), 46
directories
designating for newly ripped songs, 73–75
exporting songs in playlists to new, 210–211
locating Musicmatch playlists, 209
downloading
CD sales and download sites, 15
delivery methods of download services, 142–143
ethical issues of, 154–155
legal and illegal file-sharing activities, 155–156
live concerts, 148–149
Musicmatch Jukebox, 44–46
peer-to-peer file sharing, 156–157
plug-ins for portable audio players, 250, 253
prices for music downloads, 9, 141–142
Replay Radio, 167–168, 174
status window for music, 132
to unsupported devices, 136, 137
visualizations, 277–278
downsampling songs, 265–266
DRM (digital rights management) system
defined, 119
limitations for downloaded songs, 237–238
Musicmatch restrictions, 6.17-6.18
unable to play songs protected with, 255
WMA's, 4
DVD drives
burning CDs on, 23
playing CDs on, 223
specifying default speeds for, 232
speed ratings for, 224
upgrading from CD to, 224

E

Edit Track Info feature, 188
Edit Track Tag(s) dialog box, 111, 112, 162
editing
    analog music, 105–108
    ID3 tags, 160–163
    playlists, 207–208
editing programs, 104–105, 115
Eiger Labs F-10, 150
electronic formats, 4
e-mailing playlists, 212–214
eMusic
    about, 143
    download price for, 141
Enable CD Lookup checkbox, 259
Enter Show To Record With Replay Radio dialog box (Replay Radio), 170
Equalizer, 269–272
    delay in effect of, 270
    illustrated, 270
    opening, 269
    presets for, 270–272
Era tab (Music Downloads), 128
Etree.org, 174
Export Playlist Tracks window, 210, 211
exporting songs in playlists, 210–211
Express installs, 47
external hard drives, 25–26
external sound cards, 37

F

Featured Music tab (Music Downloads), 128
File Format Conversion dialog box, 286–287
file formats. *See* audio formats
filenames
    customizing, 75–77
    fixing, 163–165
    ID3 tags vs., 160
files. *See also* audio formats; filenames; file-sharing services
    burning MP3 CDs from WMA, 221–222
    converting formats, 286–287
    corrupted portable audio, 255
    customizing names of, 75–77
    M3U file format, 209
    naming ripped audiobook CD, 77
    navigating to existing music libraries, 56–58
    saving Musicmatch installer program, 45–46
    transferring audiobook files to player, 259
file-sharing services, 149–159
    artists' opinion of, 157–158
    ethical issues of music, 154–155
    history of, 149–151
    illegal activities with, 156
    legal activities with, 155–156
    MP3.com, 151–152
    Musicmatch as alternative to, 159
    Napster and copyright infringement, 153–155
    peer-to-peer file sharing, 156–157
finding
    album art on Web sites, 242
    music by album and artist, 123–128
    new bands and singers, 125, 173
5.1 speaker systems, 29
FLAC format, 149
flash players, 249
folders
    creating, 72, 73
    selecting, 74
    storing ripped songs in subfolders, 73–75
Forman, Dr. Seth, 193–194
4.1 speaker systems, 29
free MP3 encoding, 237
Frequently Asked Questions page, 288–289
Fresh Air, 169–170

G

gap length, 100, 233
Gap Length option (Advanced Recording Options dialog box), 100
Gap Level option (Advanced Recording Options dialog box), 101
gap level settings, 101
GarageBand, 145
General tab (MUSICMATCH Burner Options dialog box), 231
General tab (Settings dialog box), 144
Genres tab (Music Downloads), 128
Goldwave, 105, 115

H

hard drives
    building external, 25–26
    space requirements for, 21
    upgrading, 23
hard-drive players, 256–265. *See also* Portable Device Manager
    disabling synchronization with PDM, 256–257
    duplicating songs on, 262
    loading playlists, 262–263
    loading songs from Library, 260
    loading tracks not in Library, 261
    overview, 256
    working with Portable Device Manager, 256–258
hardware requirements. *See also* CD drives; sound cards
    CD drives, 23, 223–224
    hard drives, 21, 23
    overview, 20–21
    sound cards, 21
    speakers, 21, 24, 26, 28–36
    USB ports, 21
headphones, 29, 196, 199
Help online, 288–290
Hersh, Kristin, 157
High Fidelity, 218
Himmelman, Peter, 158
history of digital audio, 3

I

ID3 tags
    about, 79
    adding to ripped analog tracks, 110–113
    editing, 160–163
    fixing multiple, 162
    manually editing, 163
    organizing songs on MP3 CDs by, 235
    playlists and, 203
    sorting tracks by, 183
Ignore System Folders checkbox (Add Tracks to Music Library dialog box), 56, 57
installer
    launching, 47–48
    saving, 45–46
installing Musicmatch, 47–48
Internet. *See also* Internet radio
    broadband connections, 24, 166–167, 190
    CD Lookup service, 77–78
    CD sales and download sites, 15
    connection requirements for, 21

influence on music purchases, 16
resources for new music on, 63
sources for compressed files, 5
Internet Archive, 174
Internet Explorer 5.0, 21
Internet radio, 165–173
about, 165
broadband connections and, 166–167, 190
Musicmatch, 133
Musicmatch Radio, 191–192, 194–195
Replay Radio, 167–173
SHOUTcast, 189–190
sources for, 166
iTunes Music Store, 140

J

jacks
RCA, 32, 91
selecting for analog devices, 89–90
sound card color-coding for, 88–89
jewel cases
buying in bulk, 225
printing inserts for, 228, 244–246
Johnson, Dave, 63

K

Kazaa, 174
keyboard shortcuts, 197–198
keyboards
adjusting speaker volume from, 39
selecting multiple songs with mouse and, 181

L

labeling kits, 239–240
launching Musicmatch Jukebox, 49–51
leaders, 110
Leckness, Chris, 49
Leemon, Sheldon, 258–259
Library
accessing music in Library view, 179
Edit Track Info feature, 188
loading songs to hard-drive player, 260
navigating to existing music libraries, 56–58
saving multiple music libraries, 57
sorting CD collection, 182–185
synchronizing with Portable Device Manager, 263–265
Library view, 179
lifetime key option, 12
line in connectors
selecting as recording source, 98
sound-card connections for, 88
Linn, Mark, 158
live-concert downloads, 148–149
loading playlists on hard-drive players, 262–263
login name for Musicmatch Downloads, 121
Lola, 34
LPs. *See* albums

M

M3U file format, 209
Magix Audio Cleaning Lab 2004, 96
Mase, Dana, 158
Master Volume dialog box, 38, 97
maximizing Playlist window, 207
media. *See* CD-R media; CD-RW media
memory
requirements for, 21
upgrading, 22
microphone connections, 88
Microsoft Internet Explorer 5.0, 21
Microsoft Windows
adjusting Master Volume settings, 38, 97
launching playlists from, 209
required for Musicmatch, 21
Sound Recorder, 105
volume settings in, 38–39
mini-phone jacks, 90
mix tapes
about, 218
authors' favorite, 220–221
creating random CD, 217
Modify Folder Structure dialog box, 235
MP3
about, 3–4, 69, 71
bit rates for, 68
converting music from CDs to, 136, 137
copyright controversy over, 150–151
dragging file icons to Playlist window, 205
file format supported, 56
history of, 149–151
ID3 tags embedded in songs, 79
Musicmatch encoding capabilities for, 237
ripping songs from CDs to, 64, 65
sources for compressed files, 5
transferring cassette audiobooks to, 86
MP3 CDs
burner options for, 234
defined, 219
organizing by ID3 tags, 235
MP3.com, 145, 147, 151–152
MP3 players. *See* portable audio players
MP3 tab (MUSICMATCH Burner Options dialog box), 234–235
MP3Pro file format
about, 70–71, 72
dragging file icons to Playlist window, 205
suggested bit rates for, 68
supported by Musicmatch, 56
MPEG (Motion Picture Experts Group), 3
Music Center, 51, 55
music.download.com, 145–146
music formats. *See* audio formats
music libraries. *See* Library
MUSICMATCH Burner Options dialog box, 231, 232, 233, 234
Musicmatch download screen, 45, 46
Musicmatch Downloads
burning MP3 CDs from WMA files, 221–222
buying and downloading songs, 129–132
DRM restrictions, 133–134
features of, 119
searching for music by album and artist, 123–128
setting up account for, 119–122, 123
ways to use, 122–123, 128–129
Musicmatch File Format Conversion dialog box, 286–287

Musicmatch Jukebox 8.2
about, 6–7
adding existing music libraries to, 56–58
adding ID3 tags to tracks from albums, 110–113
alternative to file-sharing services, 159
Basic version, 9–10
brands of CD labels supported, 239
burning CDs, 216–218, 226–227, 235, 237
changing look of, 52–53, 54
computer requirements for, 20–21
configuring, 49, 51–53, 54
configuring for portable audio players, 252–253
customizing windows, 54
downloading, 44–46
downsampling songs, 265–266
DRM restrictions, 133–134
features of, 7–147
file formats supported by, 56
installing, 47–48
keyboard shortcuts for playing music, 197–198
launching, 49–51
lifetime key option for Plus, 12
MP3 encoding capabilities in, 237
playing CDs, 54–56
Plus version, 10–12, 45
portable audio players supported by, 249, 250
recording analog audio, 95–99
setting as default CD player, 64
Small Player view, 196–197
updating software, 287
upgrading to Plus version, 14, 50–51
user interface, 6, 51
using album art in, 242
version 9.0 features, 12–13, 249
versions of, 9–13
wireless PC-to-stereo connections and, 33
Musicmatch Jukebox 9.0, 12–13, 249
Musicmatch Jukebox Plus
downloading, 45
upgrading to, 14, 50–51
Musicmatch On Demand
about, 12, 192
creating playlists of streaming songs, 206
e-mailing playlists, 212–214
illustrated, 195
Musicmatch Radio. *See also* Musicmatch On Demand
buying music from, 133
illustrated, 194
Musicmatch On Demand, 192
Musicmatch Radio Gold, 191
Musicmatch Radio Platinum, 191
playing, 62–63, 192, 194–195
recording, 171
Musicmatch Setup Wizard, 47
muting sound while recording
Replay Radio, 170, 171
setting in Recorder Settings window, 80
My Matches tab (Music Downloads), 126

N

Napster
about, 143
copyright infringement and, 153–155
download price for, 141
Neato CD Labler Kit, 239, 240, 246
Nero, 174
new bands and singers, 125, 173
New Releases tab (Music Downloads), 127
New Tracks Directory Options dialog box, 74
Newegg.com Web site, 25, 31
Nitrus, 252
noise
cleaning up analog audio, 96
power cords and, 94
reducing, 108–110
sampling leaders for, 110
notebook computers
external sound cards for, 37
ripping analog sound with, 54
USB cards for, 26, 27
NPR.org
about, 166
Fresh Air, 169–170
This American Life, 171–173

O

O'Connell, Billy, 157
OGG (Ogg Vorbis) file format, 56, 72
Online Music Service Cache feature, 47
online services. *See also* copyrights; file-sharing services
delivery methods of, 142–143
Internet radio shows, 165–173
Napster and copyright infringement, 153–155
peer-to-peer file sharing, 156–157
price of songs, 141
output connectors
for analog devices, 89–90
sound-card connections for, 88

P

password protection, 120–121, 123
PDAs (personal digital assistants) as audio players, 252
peer-to-peer file sharing, 156–157
Personalize button, 126, 127
Pettigrew, Tom, 128–129
Pick a Show dialog box (Replay Radio), 169
pirating music, 238
playback controls
CD, 55–56
illustrated, 51
song position marker on, 52
playing music, 178–199, 268–292
accessing music in Library view, 179
adding songs to playlist, 179–181, 204
audio CDs, 54–56, 188–189
AutoDJ, 186, 188
choosing visualizations, 272–274
converting files between formats, 286–287
customizing visualizations, 274–277
double-clicking file icon, 181–182
enhancing speakers and headsets, 196
fine-tuning music with Equalizer, 269–272
Internet radio, 189–192, 194–195
keyboard shortcuts for, 197–198
Musicmatch Small Player view, 196–197
overview, 178
slideshows while, 278–280
sorting CD collection, 182–185

sound enhancement modules, 283–284, 286
volume leveling, 280–283
Playlist window
about, 52, 203
illustrated, 51
maximizing, 207
playlists, 202–214
about, 202–203
adding songs to, 79, 179–181, 204
creating for AutoDJ, 186, 188
creating for On Demand streaming songs, 206
editing, 207–208
e-mailing, 212–214
exporting songs in, 210–211
loading for hard-drive players, 262–263
making and deleting for hard-drive players, 263
preventing splitting between CDs, 236
saving changes, 208
shuffling, 186, 203
unable to save CD, 55
using, 204–206
worst, 211–212
plug-ins
defined, 253
downloading for portable audio players, 250, 253
players requiring, 253
portable audio players, 248–266. *See also* hard-drive players
configuring Musicmatch for, 252–253
converting audiobooks for, 258–259
copying songs to, 254
downloading plug-ins, 250, 253
downsampling songs for, 265–266
loading duplicate songs on hard-drive players, 262
MP3 players vs., 249, 252
overview, 248
PDAs as, 252
recommended, 27–28, 251–252
supported by Musicmatch, 249, 250
synchronizing Musicmatch Library to, 263–265
troubleshooting tips for, 255
types of, 249–250, 252
Portable Device Manager
before launching, 256
creating playlists on player, 263
disabling synchronization, 256–257
improvements to, 249
support for Secure Digital cards, 252
synchronizing Musicmatch Library to, 263–265
using hard-drive players with, 256–258
post-production tasks for analog sources, 103–113
adding ID3 tags to tracks, 110–113
isolating analog songs in files, 103–105
noise reduction techniques, 108–110
using audio editors, 105–108
power cord noise, 94
pre-amplifying analog devices, 89, 90
Prepare Tracks For Volume Leveling option (Recorder submenu), 283
presets for Equalizer, 270–272
price comparison Web sites, 31
PriceGrabber.com, 31
Print CD Insert dialog box, 11, 240, 241, 243
printing
on blank CDs, 225
CD labels, 241–244
jewel-case inserts, 228, 244–246
processor requirements, 20

Q

Quick Record dialog box (Replay Radio), 172

R

radio. *See* Internet radio; Musicmatch Radio; Replay Radio
RAM (random access memory), 21, 22
random feature, 186, 203
Ray Gun
overview, 109
where to find, 115
RCA line-in jacks, 32, 91
RCA-to-mini-phone jack Y-cable, 91
RealPlayer Music Store
about, 143
download price for, 141
downloading RealPlayer, 167
Reclaim Media Files Without Asking checkbox (Settings dialog box), 144
Recorder Settings window
illustrated, 65, 69, 70
options on, 79–81
preparing to record LPs, 97–101
recording
analog audio, 95–99, 101–103
cassettes, 102
Musicmatch Radio, 171
Replay Radio, 168–173
source options for, 81
Recording Industry Association of America (RIAA), 150–151, 153
Recording Source pop-up menu (Recorder Settings window), 98
records. *See* albums
remote speakers, 29
Replay Radio, 167–173
about, 165
automatically recording, 168–171
configuring, 167–168
downloading, 167–168, 174
manually, 171–173
muting sound while recording, 170, 171
window for, 168
Rhapsody, 146
RIAA (Recording Industry Association of America), 150–151, 153
Rick and Denny's music picks
best films about music, 95
best songs of 80s, 152–153
favorite players, 251–252
favorites from childhood, 285
music for moods, 187
ultimate mix tapes, 220–221
worst playlists, 211–212
Rio PMP300, 150
ripping songs, 62–81
analog media, 84–85
audio formats available for, 71
audiobook CDs, 76–77, 258–259
bit rates, 66–68
CD Lookup service, 77–78
choosing audio formats for, 68–73
customizing filenames, 75–77
defined, 66
designating directories for new songs, 73–75

ripping songs *(cont.)*
MP3 format, 64, 65
options on Recorder Settings window, 79–81
Roxio Easy Media Creator 7, 96

S

satellite speakers, 29
saving
multiple music libraries, 57
Musicmatch installer program, 45–46
playlist changes, 208
SBR (Spectral Band Replication), 70–71
Screenblast Sound Forge, 104, 115
searching. *See* finding
Secure Digital (SD) cards, 252
Settings window, 230–235
Audio tab, 232–233
Burn tab, 232
General tab, 231
MP3 tab, 234–235
Recorder tab, 69
SHN format, 149
SHOUTcast, 189–190
shuffle mode, 186, 203
skins
changing, 52–53
designing new, 54
Skip Tracks Smaller Than checkbox (Add Tracks to Music Library dialog box), 56, 57
Slideshow Configuration dialog box, 280
slideshows, 278–280
Small Player view, 196–197
SmartSplit tab (MUSICMATCH Burner Option dialog box), 236
software
editing programs, 104–105, 115
noise reduction, 108–110
song position marker, 51
songs
adding to music library, 57
adding to playlist, 179–181, 204
backing up purchased, 132
buying and downloading, 129–132
consolidating with ID3 tags, 163
copying to portable players, 254
customizing filenames for, 75–77
downsampling, 265–266
dragging and dropping multiple, 181
DRM limitations for downloaded, 237–238
editing analog, 105–108
exporting playlists to new directories, 210–211
finding by album and artist, 123–128
finding new bands and singers, 125, 173
ID3 tags, 75, 79, 235
isolating in individual files, 103–105
locating tracks not in Musicmatch Library, 261
moving to new computers, 135, 136
playing by double-clicking file icon, 181–182
preparing for volume leveling, 80, 283
price of online, 9, 141
sorting in Library, 182–185
storing in subfolders, 73–75
watching directories for new, 57–58
won't play on portable players, 255
Sony Walkman, 89, 102, 103
sorting
by track information, 182, 184
ordering with View Library By button, 183–185
songs in Library, 182–185
tracks by ID3 tags, 183
Sound Blaster devices, 36, 37, 286
sound cards
color-coded jacks for, 88–89
external, 37
plugging analog devices into, 85, 87–89
providing same effects as DFX, 286
requirements for, 21
reviews about, 38
types of connectors on, 88
upgrading, 36–38
Sound Forge, 104
sound quality
cabling for high, 93–94
effect of converting audio formats to MP3, 148
selecting for Replay Radio recordings, 170
Sound Recorder (Windows), 105
speakers
adjusting volume for analog devices, 96–97
enhancing, 196
recommended, 30–32
requirements for, 21
surround-sound, 37
upgrading, 26, 28–32
using stereo, 28, 32–36
Web sites for good, 199
speed ratings
for CD and DVD drives, 224
for CD media, 225
default speeds for burning CDs, 232
Squeezebox, 35–36
stereo speakers. *See* speakers
stereo-to-RCA cable, 32
Steup, John, 15–16
Stewart, Jimmy, 113–115
streaming audio
creating playlists for On Demand songs, 206
custom streaming radio stations, 192
defined, 165
subwoofers, 28, 29
Super Tagging, 162, 183
surround-sound speaker systems, 37
synchronization
disabling, 256–257
enabling, 263–265
Synchronization window, 257

T

tags. *See* ID3 tags
tape cassettes. *See* cassettes
tape players
internal computer, 103
rescuing cassettes with, 89, 102, 103
Technical Support
getting assistance from, 289–290
Jukebox Plus, 12
Technical Support Request Form, 289
testing compatibility of CD-R media, 225
This American Life, 171–173
throwingmusic.com, 63

Tools button, options on, 228–230
Top Music tab (Music Downloads), 127
track clips for Web sites, 80
tracks. *See also* ID3 tags
- adding to saved playlists, 205–206
- allowing duplicate, 233
- fixing filenames of, 163–165
- fixing multiple ID3 tags, 162
- ID3 tags for sorting, 183
- searching for, 123–128
- selecting for random play by criteria, 188
- sorting by criteria, 182, 184

troubleshooting
- portable audio players, 255
- update processes, 287

turntables, 96–97
2.1 speaker systems, 29

U

updating Musicmatch, 287
upgrading
- broadband connections, 24
- CD drives, 23
- hard drives, 23
- memory, 22
- Musicmatch Jukebox 9.0, 249
- Musicmatch Jukebox Plus, 14, 50–51
- sound cards, 36–38
- speakers, 26, 28–32
- USB ports, 24, 26, 27

USB (Universal Serial Bus) ports
- requirements for, 21
- upgrading, 24, 26, 27

user interface
- changing Musicmatch skins, 52–53, 54
- customizing windows, 54
- features of, 51–52
- illustrated, 6, 51
- look on startup, 50
- Replay Radio, 168
- Small Player view, 196–197

V

VBR (Variable Bit Rate), 67–68, 255
Verbatim Digital Vinyl, 226, 246
versions
- advantages of downloading, 45
- Musicmatch Jukebox Basic, 9–10
- Musicmatch Jukebox Plus, 10–12, 14
- new features of 9.0, 12–13

View Library By button, 183–185, 205
View menu, 54
Visualization Editor
- about, 273–274
- customizing visualizations in, 274–277
- illustrated, 275, 276, 277

visualizations, 272–280
- choosing, 272–274
- customizing, 274–277
- downloading, 277–278
- slideshow, 278–280

volume
- adjusting for turntables, 96–97
- preparing tracks for volume leveling, 80

Volume icon, placing on System Tray, 38
volume leveling, 280–283
- applying, 233
- options for, 282
- preparing tracks for, 80
- progress meter for, 282–283
- selecting files for, 280–281

W

Walmart, 141, 142
WatchFolders, 57–58
WAV file format
- dragging file icons to Playlist window, 205
- ripping CDs to, 73
- support for, 56

Web sites
- computer components and accessories, 41
- finding artist art on, 242
- Frequently Asked Questions page, 288–289
- labeler kits, 246
- making track clips for, 80
- price comparison, 31
- Verbatim Digital Vinyl, 246

webcasts, 166
Wi-Fi networks, 33–35
Winamp audio player, 174
Windows. *See* Microsoft Windows
windows
- configuring Settings, 230–235
- customizing Musicmatch, 54
- enlarging Burner Plus, 227
- Playlist, 51, 52, 203, 207

Windows Media Audio. *See* WMA
wireless PC-to-stereo connections, 33
WMA (Windows Media Audio)
- about, 70, 71, 72
- burning MP3 CDs from WMA files, 221–222
- Dell DJ support for, 27
- dragging file icons to Playlist window, 205
- DRM restrictions for Musicmatch tunes, 134–135
- Musicmatch support for, 4, 56
- sources for compressed files, 5
- suggested bit rates for, 68
- unable to play, 255
- unsupported by iPod, 28, 251–252, 254

www.ingramcontent.com/pod-product-compliance
Lightning Source LLC
Chambersburg PA
CBHW080352060326
40689CB00019B/3977